WESTERN CA[PE]
WALKS

70 graded hikes and trails in the Western Cape

DAVID BRISTOW

STRUIK

Struik Publishers (a member of the Struik Group (Pty) Ltd)
Struik House
Oswald Pirow Street
Foreshore
Cape Town
8001

Reg. no.: 63/00203/07

First published 1991

Text © David Bristow

Photographs © David Bristow

Illustrations © David Kuijers

Designer: Petal Palmer
Cover design: Abdul Amien
DTP conversion by BellSet, Cape Town
Reproduction by Fotoplate (Pty) Ltd, Cape Town
Printed and bound in Goodwood by National Book Printers

ISBN 1 86825 173 X

PUBLISHER'S NOTE
While every effort has been made by the publisher to ensure the accuracy of both the hike descriptions and maps, it is the hiker's personal responsibility to use the best maps available.

FOREWORD

*'When we reach the mountain summits we leave behind us all those
things that weigh heavily on our body and our spirit. We leave behind
all sense of weakness and depression; we feel a new freedom, and a great
exhilaration, an exaltation of the body no less than the spirit'.*
Jan Christian Smuts

What Smuts said many years ago holds true even today, and every person who has ever set his foot on a mountain, be it on a hiking way, on a faint footpath, on a virgin slope or on a precipitous crag will have had some of that experience. And we in the western Cape are particularly blessed with beautiful mountains within easy reach of the major metropolitan areas.

This guide leads us into these mountains and whichever route may be followed, from the easiest to the most strenuous, will unfold for the mountaineer an experience of beauty and splendour which I have found to be without parallel. *Western Cape Walks* will help the general public to easily get to those areas of our mountains which are accessible to them. And this is right – all people, not only a select few from recognized mountain clubs, should be able to enjoy the beauty of our mountains. But as you enter these mountains, I urge you to heed all the good advice given in the guide so that you may enjoy them in safety and leave them with as few scars as possible. We owe that to those that will come after us.

Piet van Zyl
Chairman
Mountain Club of South Africa
Cape Town Chapter

CONTENTS

ACKNOWLEDGEMENTS

Although this book bears my name, in fact for much of the hiking and information collecting I was assisted by a team of Environmental and Geographical Science graduates from UCT. Without their help I would not have finished the task. My gratitude and thanks are therefore extended to:

Gavin Heath – mountaineer extraordinaire who knows these hills like no-one else I know;
Laura Kuginis – who seemed to hike happily without ever eating;
Rushdien Ibrahim – the only person I know who hikes in summer, dressed for winter;
Debby Brown – superwoman, no peak too high, no task too great.

The CPA Nature Conservation Department helped me plan and execute this project. Extremely helpful were Terry Newby and Rudie Andrag. Also, all the foresters in the western Cape who help to keep the mountains here in shape.

For getting me into the air to take aerial photographs, my thanks to all those of 101 Squadron, Southern Air Command, especially David Ogilvy and Keith Davidson.

Fred Roux, collections manager of the Compton Herbarium, helped me to identify many of my flower slides, with the occasional help of Dr John Rourke and Dee Paterson-Jones. Botanists are nice people.

To Piet van Zyl, chairman of the Mountain Club of South Africa, Cape Town Section, for contributing a Foreword to the book.

To my wife Tracey, who kept the home fires burning in winter and the beers cold in summer. While I was out walking, she laboured to produce something far finer, of greater and more lasting beauty. This book I dedicate to Daniel Julian Bristow, the orchid of my eye, prospective mountaineer and first generation of the new South Africans – born 26 April, 1990.

The author particularly wishes to thank Dave Barry of Backpacker who gave a kind sponsorship of his company's top-quality mountaineering products for the duration of this project. Backpacker has long been an active sponsor and promotor of individual climbers and expeditions, both local and overseas. Their products have thus been tested from the Antarctic to Mount Everest.

INTRODUCTION

The western Cape's folded mountains are perhaps not as lofty as the Natal Drakensberg, but they are geologically far older, more rugged and more complex. The predominating fynbos vegetation is one of the world's natural wonders – the Cape Floral Kingdom, smallest of the world's six floral kingdoms.

The geographical area covered in this book stretches from Clanwilliam in the north to Swellendam in the east, the towns being equidistant from the central location of Cape Town. It creates a homogeneous and manageable region that includes all the western Cape's main mountaineering areas bar one. That exception is the Hex River Mountains. I originally planned to include this range in the book, but finally decided that it did not fit here. My main motivation for this was that this range is not easily accessible to the general hiking public – at whom this book is aimed.

The Hex River Mountains are the last mountaineering wilderness left in the western Cape, and are, I feel, best left to the more serious mountaineers who have no need of my route descriptions. For those who want the challenge of true adventure, this is your destination. But there was a second, more practical reason for omitting the most rugged range in southern Africa. Even though much of the upper catchment areas of the range falls under state control, most access routes are across public land and open only to members of the Mountain Club of South Africa (MCSA) and affiliated clubs. The MCSA has, over the last century, spent much time, money and diplomacy securing its access rights to these areas, and it doesn't appreciate non-members jeopardizing all that hard work.

Jan du Toit's Kloof may be visited with the permission of the landowner, as can one other kloof which shall remain nameless at the request of the landowner, who does not want to publicize that very special place. Other than that, permits to certain areas are available from the Kluitjieskraal Forest Station outside Wolseley. From there you are on your own.

This book is an attempt to give people access not only to enjoyment in the mountains, but also some knowledge of nature and mountaineering traditions, so that they may venture forth in the true spirit of the mountains. The publication of this guide coincides with the Mountain Club of South Africa's centenary celebrations, a club of which I am extremely proud to be a member.

The foreword by Piet van Zyl, chairman of the MCSA's Cape Town section, is timeous and appropriate as it was in the western Cape that this mountain madness began. Although this book is in no way connected to the MCSA's centenary celebrations, it is in that spirit that I offer this contribution to the enjoyment and protection of our mountains by all South Africans.

How to use this book

I have divided the western Cape into eight hiking regions, each fitting a basic geographical area. Each of these regions is prefaced by a general introduction, which is followed by the hike descriptions, arranged more or less geographically.

To get the most out of any hike, you should first familiarize yourself with the chapter *A Short Natural History of the Western Cape*, and then read the introductory section for the relative region. Before you start a hike, read the route description through to get a feel for the area. The more you know about the hike and its environment, the more you will enjoy the outing.

Each hike in this book is prefaced by an easy-to-read key of vital information. All the information you need to complete and enjoy the hike is to be found there, but not so much that I actually do the hikes for you. Carefully consider this information, check details on accommodation, weather conditions, water availability and gradients, and calculate your likely walking time. Finally, plan transport, and make sure you have all the necessary permits.

The seven categories of the information keys are:

Name of the hike;
Route;
Distance;
Duration;
Grade;
Booking authority;
General information.

The *name of the hike* will have an alpha-numerical prefix, using the first letter of the area name and a sequential numbering system, so that a hike in the Cederberg might be titled Kliphuis to Dwarsrivier: Hike C3;

Route will be a very basic description, such as 'from Kliphuis campsite to Krakadoupoort pass';

Distance is always given for the complete hike (i.e. if the hike entails hiking seven kilometres from point A to point B and back, the distance is given as 14 kilometres);

Duration is always given for the entire route. If the route is linear rather than circular, separate times are given for the journey there and back, as the gradients will be reversed on the return trip. It has been assumed that the average hiker with a moderately heavy pack on a not-too-steep gradient walks three kilometres per hour. If necessary, this can be adjusted according to weight of pack, weather conditions, and your physical condition. The duration given does not include the time taken for tea and photographic stops, swimming or general lazing

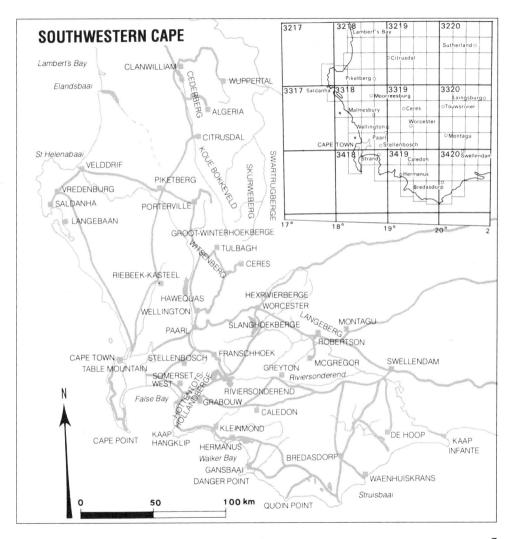

about – which should be an integral part of any hike;

Grade is according to my own system, and denotes only the strenuousness of the route. From the three-kilometre-per-hour average, you should add or subtract time accordingly where backpack, fitness or steepness of path varies. I stop frequently (for tea, for a swim, to take a photograph, or to take a breather), and consequently enjoy my hikes far more than the masochists who steam off in pursuit of the next overnight stop. The weather will affect not only your personal perceptions of a trail, but your performance as well, as will the company you choose and the speed at which you walk.

A very important factor to consider when grading a route is the availability of water. Since ours is a winter rainfall area, the long hot summers become very dry. A hike that in spring is a flower garden with wonderful mountain pools may, by late summer, have become an endurance test for the French Foreign Legion. I have not considered this factor in my gradings – but you must when planning your hike.

My five point grading system is as follows:
easy – a short walk, of between one and three hours (10 kilometres), along a reasonably flat route;
fair – this walk may be short but on a relatively steep path, or of longer duration but on an easy gradient;
moderate – usually a day's outing, but with no sustained ups or downs. The distance should be between 12 and 16 kilometres;

severe – this will be a relatively steep but not very long walk, or a long but not very steep one. Some sustained ascents and descents are almost certain to be encountered;
extreme – this will be a long walk along steep gradients, possibly involving a climb over and down a high point. Not all extreme hikes are equal, so the 'general' section will detail the finer conditions.

Not everyone will agree with this system, but it does offer a consistent standard by which all the hikes may be judged.

Booking Authority is a useful category in a region controlled by numerous authorities. The category refers to the body through which bookings and access permits are granted, which may not necessarily be the same as the landowner;

General information is a short (well, usually short) paragraph used to give background information about the area of a hike, and to clarify, where necessary, any of the categories above.

Abbreviations I have used few abbreviations in this book; those that I have used are:
NHW – National Hiking Way
NHWB – National Hiking Way Board
MCSA – Mountain Club of South Africa
CPA – Cape Provincial Administration, conservation division.

Permits and land control
With a few exceptions, for instance the non-restricted areas in the Table Mountain reserve, you will need a permit to enter the areas covered in this book. They are all conservation areas and therefore in need of control; don't spoil your children's chances of going there by not obeying the rules.

Permits vary in cost (some can be obtained for free), with National Hiking Way (NHW) trails being among the more expensive because of the facilities provided. A one-day's permit, however, seldom costs more than the price of a movie ticket.

Permits for the NHW trails must be obtained from a National Hiking Way Board (NHWB) office, in Cape Town, Pretoria or Pietermaritzburg, telephonically, in writing or in person. For other forestry areas, permits (usually free) are obtainable from the local forestry station concerned. Provincial and regional services council reserves will have their own controls, as will private reserves and trails. Municipal reserves may be controlled at the gates or from the local municipal offices. The key at the beginning of each hike description gives the relevant booking authority, with all the information on people to contact in connection with a region contained in Appendix 1 at the back of this book.

Some confusion over control still exists in mountain catchment areas since, in the interests of privatization, the Directorate of Forestry was stripped of its conservation authority. Conservation and recreation control is now vested in the provincial conservation department, with 'forestry' now being confined to timber production. But these two functions are not always easily separated, especially where plantations fall within catchment and conservation areas. Local forestry stations usually combine both functions, under the auspices of the provincial Nature Conservation Department.

Maps and interpretation

Unlike the Drakensberg, which has been comprehensively mapped in 1:50 000 hiking maps, only the Cederberg and two NHW trails (Swellendam and Hottentots-Holland) have been afforded such luxuries in the western Cape. Hiking shops should have a selection of maps of varying scale, covering different areas though concentrating on the Peninsula. Camp and Climb has its own 1:50 000 map of the Cederberg, and some lucky people will still have the excellent Slingsby map of Table Mountain.

Interpreting maps comes with practice, and often the help of a compass. Just remember that compasses point to magnetic north (currently about a 23° 5′ deviation west of true north), while maps are drawn along true north longitudinal lines. Of course these are abstract projections, since the earth is a geoid (more or less spherical with bulging middle and flattened poles), while maps are flat; for such a small area, though, this fact is irrelevant. Another problem with using a compass is that, being a magnet, it will be affected by any sympathetic material in its vicinity.

My sketch maps are taken from standard 1:50 000 topographical base maps, but I have interpreted the landscapes, highlighting the main features for easy recognition.

The 1:50 000 maps are obtainable from Map World, Dumbarton House, Church Street, Cape Town 8001 (Tel. (021) 22 1767) or Surveys and Mapping, Rhodes Avenue, Mowbray 7700 (Tel. (021) 685 4070). The western Cape area map on page 7 gives the reference number of each 1:50 000 map of the area. The map is divided into large squares, each represented by a four digit number. The large squares are divided into four smaller squares labelled A to D, starting at the top left. Each block of four squares is once again quartered on the same lettering pattern. Under this system Cape Town centre is found in the map 3318CD.

Hiking preparation

Just about every year at least one person dies in the mountains through carelessness, mostly due to hypothermia caused by not having warm and waterproof clothing. The most important thing to remember is that you can freeze in the Cederberg in midsummer, just as you can fry there in winter – and this applies to all the ranges in the western Cape. If you are planning to set out on anything longer than a half-day's outing, be prepared for the best and the worst. If you are going away from home, check the weather forecasts for the period you will be away. Watch the clouds and the wind direction, and learn to do your own forecasting in that way; you can always keep 12 hours ahead of the weather by being vigilant (see the 'Climate' section on page 16).

If you are an inexperienced hiker then don't rush off into the heart of the mountains on your first outing. You can learn by going with someone more experienced, or you can teach yourself by starting small – battle out storms first in the valleys and then in the foothills, and venture higher only once you feel you can handle those conditions. Mountains can be extremely dangerous and unpredictable places: the weather can vary in a day between boiling hot and freezing.

An important consideration when planning a hike is the availability of water. You can survive for at least a few, rather uncomfortable, days without food, but you can't hike even for a day without water. Check on maps, and with locals, what the water conditions are in the area, and carry at least one litre per person for emergencies.

A further point: you must give thought to transport to and from the beginning and end points, as, at the end of a long hike, you will hardly want to walk another step, let alone all the way home.

I firmly believe that hiking and mountaineering should be a learning process: you should learn by experience how to cater for your personal needs and which foods are best; how to misread a map, get lost and then read it more accurately next time; where to find water in a seemingly waterless landscape; and, most important, how to look after yourself under conditions of stress. Hiking demands some physical effort, and mountaineering even more. You have to learn what your physical limit is and how to break through various pain thresholds before you can venture forth with confidence and eagerness. These are things I cannot tell you, though I can give you basic guidelines.

Equipment

The cardinal rule of hiking is to travel light; a heavy pack can turn the most sublime dreamscape into a nightmare – and you into a grumbling ghoul. The principle of using a layered clothing system is the first step to eliminate unnecessary items. If there is something which must be taken – for instance a tent, if you are going where there is no other shelter – remember when buying the item that its weight is going to be a determining factor in the enjoyment of your hike. Sometimes, instead of taking a tent, I hike with only an outer flysheet to keep weight down, plus my foam sleeping mat and a space blanket. Most of your weight will be in the food department, so that is where you can reduce most weight.

Packing a backpack takes some skill, especially when you want to take more than the bag says it is willing to carry. Start by keeping all the plastic jam, herb and other containers in the kitchen to use for decanting into. Never carry glass (bottles, jars etc.) in your pack, as it taints the pleasure of good wine when broken, cuts your innards and ends up littering the landscape.

The recommended way to pack is to fit all your clothes into the bottom of the pack, then put perishable and breakable foods into pots, pans and other containers. Pack those tightly on top of the clothes, and then squash the smaller stuff in between to make a tight fit. The side and top pockets should be used for things that you want easy access to: toilet bag, field guides, maps and permits, etc. You may also want to put binoculars and a gas stove with limited tea-making paraphernalia – for easy access – in these pockets.

A large camera can go into its own holster bag, which can then be looped onto your pack's waistband with its strap fastened to the top of the pack's harness. A smaller camera can fit into a nylon bicycle tool-kit bag, and then onto the pack where it is easy to reach. You must decant all fluids – drinking and cooking – into plastic or, preferably, aluminium bottles. Get rid of heavy packaging and repack your food into your containers; it saves space, reduces weight and eliminates garbage. I stuff my sleeping bag right on top (under the lid), sometimes with my raincoat, a warm top, and soft shoes for easy access. If there isn't enough space, these last can go into the bottom pouch. What doesn't fit now, doesn't go.

Backpacks There is a wide range of backpacks available in all hiking shops. The best are locally made ones, and most packs today have internal frames. I believe that, when choosing a pack, you must try it on with a weight inside. The pack should sit comfortably and high, so that, when you walk, it does not bounce against your backside – after several hours of that you will want to return it, but then it will be too late. The ideal pack should have a 70-80-litre capacity, two internal compartments that can join to one, two or four outside pockets, a lid that can expand to fully cover the biggest load the pack can take, quick release buckles, and a very well-padded waist strap. The waist strap is crucial since that is where you should carry all the weight; the shoulder straps are for balancing. A smaller day pack is useful for short walks – if you can afford one. I have never used a pack cover but have often thought of getting one.

Clothing The weight of my pack does not differ much from summer to winter, but for the clothes I am wearing. When packing clothes, I use a system of layers that can go on or come off: underwear, shorts and T-shirts, long shirt and trousers, fibre-pile top and long-johns or warm track suit (in winter, add gloves and a balaclava). One change of underwear will do for any hike, for while you are wearing one, you wash the other. One T-shirt and pair of shorts should also be sufficient, so long as you keep fresh clothes in your vehicle or at base camp. Keep your spare clothes dry by packing them into heavy-duty rubbish bags before putting them in your backpack.

A rain suit is essential if you wish to go hiking in the mountains. The best is a full gortex suit, which I always carry. Luckily I bought an imported one when they were still quite cheap, but a local version is now available at a good price. This type of material 'breathes', so it really keeps you warm and dry. The traditional waterproof is a kagul pullover, while some people use large ponchos that fit over body and pack, and double as a one-person tent of the uncomfortable type. The cheapest solution is strong garbage bags: you should be carrying one or two to keep your pack's contents dry anyway. Cut small holes for your head and arms, and your torso will remain dry in the fiercest storm. Any raincoat is better than none.

To my mind, the scarf and the hat are, for size and weight, the best value on a hike. Think about it... A floppy hat with a brim keeps the sun off your head and out of your eyes, as it does with rain; it can be turned up or down on any side to provide protection or to ventilate; it can be used to wipe off sweat, dipped in streams for cooling or tied down to keep your ears warm. In summer, a cap will do as a poor replacement. To complete your colour scheme, either a matching or clashing scarf (depending on your fashion taste) is essential – only designer accessories please! Really, a scarf complements the hat in keeping you either cool or warm, dry or damp to suit the weather. These items can be used to fine-tune your body's thermoregulation. Just wash them well when you get home.

Footwear For day walks with a light pack, running shoes or lightweight boots, even velskoens, are suitable. With a heavy pack, however, you need to protect your feet and ankles from the extra strain. When wearing any kind of boot, always wear two pairs of socks – thin inners and thick outers, to prevent blisters and increase comfort. Always hike with at least two pairs of each. Depending on the weather and type of hike, I choose between running shoes, a pair of 'Wuppertal' car-tyre boots, and my faithful Austrian leather boots for heavy going. I also carry a spare pair of light shoes or sandals for the end of the day. Good leather boots are so expensive these days, that for serious hiking I would recommend a pair of the new generation lightweight, synthetic-fibre boots. Finally, gaiters are light accessories that are more than worth their weight in the wet or scratchy fynbos.

Sleeping bags If you are planning to go near the top of any mountain, don't buy your sleeping bag from a supermarket. The very best sleeping bags are expedition bags, but we don't need to go quite that far. A superdown bag, or one that is part superdown part ordinary down is sufficient, but check that the stitching does not go right through to the inside of the bag, as this will allow in cold air. Also check for a padded strip around the inner zip, which denotes quality design. Some local manufacturers are making bags out of synthetic fibre, and these are quite good. But in very cold weather they don't stand up to a good down bag. I'm a married man so I have a synthetic bag for the bottom and a down one for the top, zipped together. The biggest advantage with a synthetic bag is that it will keep you warm even when wet, which a down bag won't. If you have a suspect tent, then buy a holofill-type bag, and sleep in warm clothes and socks in cold weather. Remember, though, that down bags are lightest and pack smallest.

Sleeping mats Most people think that closed-cell roll-up mats are meant for comfortable sleeping on hard ground; sorry, not so. They are to keep you warm and dry, preventing the moisture which rises from the ground at night from dampening your sleeping bag. Closed-cell pads were first used for ice conditions. In Africa, they also help to protect your sleeping bag on harsh ground. At very high prices, you can buy air-filled sleeping mats for warmth and comfort, but there is a much cheaper solution, and this is one time that you should visit a supermarket. Buy a plastic-covered, foam deck-chair cover that folds double. This can be carried on the outside of your pack underneath the lid straps. Wrap a space blanket around it to keep it dry. The blanket can also be used most effectively to keep off light rain, and to keep you warm on cold nights.

Tents Once again, if you are serious about hiking and hope to do it for some time, don't buy a tent in a supermarket. These tents are made from inferior fabrics and with poor stitching. The designs, too, are inferior. The most efficient design is a dome, but a good mountain dome is very expensive. If you can afford it, then buy one (again, I was lucky to have bought an imported one when still inexpensive). Honest local manufacturers accept that they can't make ones to last. But they do make excellent A-shape tents. The best have inner and outer sheets; bells at one or both ends on the outer; and a guide rope to pull the sides of the tent – inner and flysheet – out to form a semi-dome shape. This last feature shows the difference between good and not-so-good designs. Again, a specialist hiking shop will be able to advise you about the best compromise between quality and price.

Food If I am going on a hard hike, I may reduce my rations to dehydrated basics: Chinese noodles and soup, some dehydrated meat substitute; small sachets of herbs, garlic and chillies; chocolate and wholewheat biscuits; small packets of dried fruit and nuts; tea bags, coffee and powdered milk (you have to experiment with this one); some muesli; cheese; a small salami; a few small tins of fish; and finally whisky and chocolate for spiritual comfort. If the hike is more than three days long, then I take some noodles and some rice or packets of instant mashed potato. On this, man, and even woman, can live most happily. I do tend to get bored with muesli, so I may take (English) cheese in a tube and a loaf of high fibre bread to eat with my morning coffee instead.

If you can afford to carry more weight, you can add any of the following items: extra whisky and chocolate; dried and fresh fruit; some lightweight foods like mushrooms, cucumber, onions, tomatoes and maybe even an avocado in a plastic box; pâtés and cheeses for sundowners with a (plastic or alloy) bottle of wine.

I have seen people haul crates of beer, bottles of hard tack and wine, tins of meat, and radios and cassette tapes with detachable speakers from their packs. I also have a friend who doesn't eat while hiking. I like the middle ground.

Cameras Since photography occupies much of my time while hiking, I reduce the food quota for camera gear. I carry a large 35 mm SLR (Nikon 801 AF) with a 28-80-millimetre lens with macro-focus – since my 50-millimetre macro lens was stolen. I do have a monopod, but most often use a walking stick as a tripod. If the hike is a short one, I take along a 300-millimetre lens, pocket binoculars, botanical field guide and *Roberts* for birds. I have standardized film with Fujichrome slides, which I believe to be the best. I use 100 ASA, which can be rated at 200 for low light or action shots, without losing quality. This is the best compromise between film speed (available light) and grain (the faster the film, the grainier it is).

If you are interested in general landscapes and people shots, then I recommend any one of the compact 'instamatic' type cameras, which are today very sophisticated boxes. Prints are fine for personal records, but only slides are of high enough quality for reproduction: if you harbour intentions of having your photographs published, then start taking slides – the best can be made into prints at little cost. The total cost of slide film is cheaper than that for prints (developing costs under R10-00 for a 36-frame film, and the film itself costs less than R25-00).

Medical supplies For years I carried only a bandage in my hiking kit, and never used it. No sooner had I discarded it, than I developed shin splints and ended that hike with my long socks wrapped around my knees. Now I limit my medical supplies to what fits into my toilet bag. So, along with my toothbrush, toothpaste, small cake of soap and miniature shampoo bottle, go the following: a roll of plaster; methyalate, small scissors, painkilling tablets, a bandage and suntan lotion. You may also like to carry antihistamine cream, if you are susceptible to inflammation and rashes.

Hiking ethics and helpful hints
The major reason for retaining the mountains as pristine natural regions is that they are important as water catchment areas in an essentially arid country. Where this function can accommodate other uses, such as recreation, then those too are permitted. But if hikers abuse their access privilege, then it will be taken away and everyone will suffer for the bad manners of a few. It is, therefore, every hiker's responsibility to ensure that correct hiking ethics are adhered to.

If you see anyone causing unnecessary damage to the environment, and are unable to reason with them (for often it takes no more than a suggestion to correct improper behaviour), then report it to the local conservation officer or NHWB office. If you don't, then you too are indirectly responsible for the damage caused. The Cape Parliament Library Act No. 33 of 1893 states that only 'quiet and considerate persons' have the right of access to public libraries – so it should be with mountains.

I am frequently shocked at the lack of ethical awareness among hikers, though I have come to the conclusion that it is due more to ignorance than to malevolence. No matter how many notices and forms plead with us not to litter, not to take short cuts and so on, many people believe that their own behaviour is somehow exempt from these controls. The rule is simple – never let anyone get away with bad mountain behaviour without questioning that behaviour. It is only through example, persuasion and finally pressure that bad ecological habits change. It is a long education process; not everyone was as fortunate as myself to have learnt their mountaineering ways through the purist school.

I often wonder just what it is that drives some people to creating nasty little monuments to themselves: names carved in trees and bunks, or scratched on cave walls to deface irreplaceable rock art. It probably has something to do with an inner doubt about our own worth in an industrialized society, resulting in people leaving little reminders to themselves that they really do exist. What a pity that some bring this small-mindedness with them into the wilds. Rather, we must learn to practise the National Hiking Way motto of 'take only photographs, leave only footprints'.

In research conducted on hiking trails in the western Cape, it was found that the awareness among hikers as regards accepted codes of behaviour in the natural environment was very low. Unexpectedly, this applied just as much to MCSA members as it did to non-member hikers. As far as ethics go, there are some simple rules you should follow:

1. Leave no litter, anywhere, for any reason. No exceptions.
2. Never take short cuts, anywhere, for any reason. They cause erosion and unsightly scars and, anyway, are harder on your legs than the longer zigzag route.
3. Don't make unnecessary noise in the wilds. Neither fellow hikers nor the animals appreciate it.
4. No radios – this is what we are trying to get away from, after all.
5. Never use detergents in or near water bodies – they kill the small organisms that keep the water clean and drinkable. Carry water away from a stream or pond, to soap and rinse yourself or your dishes.
6. Where no toilets are provided, carry a gardening trowel, and make use of it as

far away from paths and campsites as you can – see 'Mountain ablutions' below.
7. Enjoy yourself, and let everyone else enjoy themselves too; don't cause anyone else to find fault with your behaviour, and let them know if they offend you (this does not apply to anyone's personal appearance of course).

Mountain ablutions Consider for a moment how many people hike along a popular path in a month; then consider the amount of human and other waste that they leave behind. It is important that every hiker does his or her bit to keep pollution minimized – not only for aesthetics, but for good ecology too. Some basic pointers are:

- For washing yourself, utensils and clothes, always carry water away from the tap or stream and let it soak into the ground;
- Be kind to the environment by using biodegradable soap – if you don't, why bother mountaineering?;
- Do not leave any food scraps. This may seem extreme, but it invites invader Argentine ants (these displace the indigenous species, which play a role in germinating fynbos seeds). It also makes baboons aggressive and troublesome, and just looks bad;
- If toilets are not provided, always use your garden trowel to dig a small hole for your defecations, then cover it up with sand and rocks. Choose a spot well away from paths, with a good view and backrest for comfort if available.

Knees, ankles, feet and blisters Having started off with as light a pack as you can, the next cardinal rule is that prevention of sores and ills is better than cure. The ecological law, that a change to one component of a system results in a change throughout, should be considered: if you develop sore feet, you will most likely end up with sore ankles, knees and heart from walking awkwardly. Prevent blisters by hiking with thin inner and thick outer socks. The second you feel a hot point developing on your feet, whip off your boots and whip on a thick strip of padded plaster. If you wait even a minute, you will already be too late to save the situation. Carry methyalate for popped blisters, treat, cover with a good plaster and you'll be able to walk again the next day.

Unless you know that you have strong ankles, wear boots that hold them. Well-bound ankles, however, are no good when your soles collapse inward and you end up walking on the inside of your ankles. If your feet do tend to collapse inwards, buy inner soles that push your instep up, and resole your boots before they wear down. If your knees hurt, it may be a sports injury, or possibly shin splints just below the knee from carrying too heavy a pack. As soon as you feel the pinch, bind your knees with an elastic knee guard, elastic bandage, or a long hiking sock bound just below and above the kneecap. To prevent the soles of your feet getting sore, you can pad your boots with a rubber insole.

Hypothermia and hyperthermia These are both potentially fatal afflictions, but ones you should be able to handle in all cases. Hypothermia is the abnormally low body temperature that occurs when the body loses an excessive amount of heat and succumbs to a slow but painless 'eternal sleep'. Fatigue, coldness and dampness all contribute to this, and if the coldness reaches the brain, death will occur in a few hours. To avoid hypothermia, wear warm (wool is best) and dry clothing – a balaclava to keep your head warm is a vital piece of equipment in cold and wet conditions. Eat regularly and drink sweet, hot drinks – but avoid coffee and alcohol. The symptoms are dizziness, disorientation and vagueness, then drowsiness. The afflicted person will not realize that he or she is in danger, so the rest of the party must act swiftly to warm and stabilize them. Try to get the person out of the wind and wet, and get him or her dry. Also, make sure that the afflicted person eats and drinks energy foods and gets some rest (but don't, under any circumstances, let them sleep). If someone suffering from hypothermia sits down in the cold and wet to rest, however, they will surely die.

Heat exhaustion or sunstroke are names for greater or lesser degrees of hyperthermia: our bodies are bio-chemical engines and need to be cooled by fluids and sweating. If you exert yourself in warm to hot conditions, there is a danger of you dehydrating and your body overheating. When hiking in hot conditions, be sure to rest frequently and drink regularly – even if you don't feel particularly thirsty. The symptoms of hyperthermia are, progressively, headache, dizziness, accelerated pulse, nausea and vomiting, cramps, disorientation and possibly unconsciousness. If not treated, death can occur. The first thing to do is to find or make shade; then strip the person down, sprinkle him or her with water and fan to aid cooling. Water must be administered slowly, or it will just be vomited up. If vomiting persists, concentrate on cooling down and resting, and later administer liquids in small amounts.

Snakes I really don't know why people panic so much at the sight of a snake, when I think of how terrified a snake must be when confronted by a galumphing human giant. There are only three types of snake in the western Cape of which you should be wary: the Cape cobra, puff-adder and berg adder. In 20 years of hiking, preceded by five collecting snakes, I have never been bitten. Under normal conditions your reflexes should be faster than a snake's. I always walk with a stick, to help me up and down steep slopes and across rivers, and to prod the ground for snakes. Most often, however, it does service as a camera tripod.

Regarding snakebite, forget all about cutting and spitting, tourniquets and serum. If you know or suspect the bite is poisonous, you must stabilize the victim: keep him or her warm and calm, then go for help. Doctors today prefer to treat snakebite cases symptomatically. Pumping a victim full of serum usually increases shock and possibly allergic reaction; it should be given with great discretion. Keep your ankles covered and your wits uncovered and you will be better able to enjoy these attractive creatures of the wild.

KEY TO THE SKETCH MAPS

– – ...	Possible detour/other hike
→	Hiking route
▬	(Major) road
- - - - -	Jeep track
•	Mountain peak
△	Trig beacon
⌾	Cave
⊞	Chain ladder
⤞	Bridge
♧	Forestry station
─╫─	Waterfall
⬤	Dam
▲	Camp site
⌂	Caravan park
⌂	Hut

NATURAL HISTORY OF THE WESTERN CAPE

Historical Geology and Topography

More than half of South Africa is underlain by rocks that are between 450 and 160 million years old, dating from the late Ordovician to the early Jurassic periods. During this time, the mineral deposits of the Cape Supergroup of rocks were laid down – *see Diagram 1*. The Karoo rocks, dealt with in depth in this book's companion volume, *Drakensberg Walks*, are the youngest and uppermost of the major stratigraphic (geological) groups in South Africa – and therefore the highest. On the whole, they lie conformably (without interruption) on the Cape Supergroup, in the great horizontal layers that give us the typical Karoo landscapes.

The Cape Supergroup however (with which we are more concerned here), shows evidence of a far more traumatic past. Twisting and folding of gigantic proportions can be seen in many places in the contorted layers of sandstone and shale. The mountains of the southwestern to southeastern Cape are known as the Cape Folded Mountain ranges, and the process which caused these great crustal contortions is called tectonic folding. Most of the world's highest, and youngest, mountain ranges have been caused in this manner: the earth's continental plates push up against each other, and one or the other buckles along its leading edge. The Himalayas, for instance, are still being pushed ever higher, as the plate on which India lies has been pushing northwards under the Asian plate ever since it broke away from the southern supercontinent of Gondwanaland.

It was, in fact, during the period of Gondwanaland's breaking up – starting about 200 million years ago – that the Cape Supergroup was so twisted and buckled (Africa formed the central part of the supercontinent). So great were the tectonic forces involved, it has been calculated, that in places

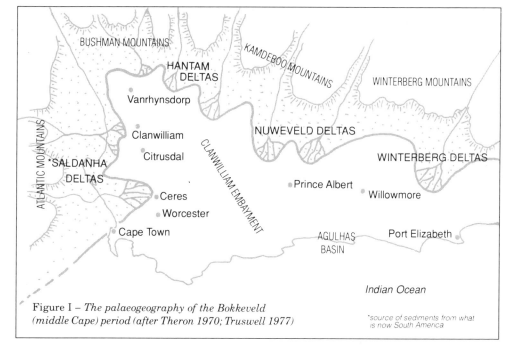

Figure I – *The palaeogeography of the Bokkeveld (middle Cape) period (after Theron 1970; Truswell 1977)*

*source of sediments from what is now South America

the folds arched six kilometres vertically into the sky. What we see today as impressive mountain peaks, is merely the eroded base of the bottommost of the three major groups of rock that constitute the Cape Supergroup, the Table Mountain Sandstone (TMS) Group (the other two are the Bokkeveld Shale Group and the Witteberg Group).

The 350-million-year-old Cape deposits were laid down both conformably and unconformably (on an eroded base) on rocks ranging from about 1 billion to 500 million years old: the Nama, Malmesbury, Cape Granite, Klipheuwel and Cango groups. As you will probably have noticed, the groups are named after the place where the 'type' or typical formation was identified in the field (as with the Dwyka, Ecca, Beaufort and Stormberg groups of Karoo rocks). A view along Chapman's Peak Drive, Cape Town, clearly shows where the Cape rocks rest on top of the lower Cape Granite suite, the obvious line chosen by the road engineers on which to lay their road.

The TMS rocks can be seen as mountains from northern Namaqualand to Grahamstown, with small island outcrops occurring in Natal and Zululand. The TMS deposits were laid down as shallow marine sands, which compressed into a very hard quartzitic sandstone. As sea level and climatic conditions changed over exceedingly long periods, this area became a great delta system, fed by several major rivers flowing southward and eastward. The resulting Bokkeveld rocks were thus derived from finer grained silts, with more organic matter

than the TMS beach sands. These rocks weather to very fertile clayey soils, compared to the barren sands derived from the marine-originated TMS. Trilobite and brachiopod fossils are common in the Bokkeveld rocks, but very few remains have been found in the older TMS layers.

Finally, the sea level rose once more, and the last of the major rock groups in the Cape supergroup, the Witteberg Group, was deposited in much the same way as the TMS rocks. Very little of the Witteberg group remains in the area covered in this book, as it comprises relatively soft rocks and, being the uppermost of the supergroup, has been mostly eroded away. It is most conspicuous as a belt of hills – the Witteberg hills lying parallel to, and south of, the N1 between Touwsrivier and Laingsburg.

From *Diagram 2* it can be seen how the various groups were laid down, subsequently folded and then eroded. At the high points of the folds, the TMS, being the most resistant group, now forms the uppermost mountain ridges and peaks, despite being the first of the three Cape groups laid down. The Bokkeveld shales form the valley floors where their rich soils are suited to cultivation and stock farming. Due to extensive cultivation of the lowlands, the various nutritious types of lowland fynbos vegetation are today all but extinct. Most of what remains of the region's natural vegetation is the montane fynbos, growing on nutrient-depleted, beach-like TMS soils. It is not only the marine origin that has caused this infertile soil, but the leaching of nutrients by heavy rainfall on the mountains

Climate
Climate is the average weather pattern over a long period (a few decades), whereas weather is the actual atmospheric conditions at a particular time and place. So, while the western Cape has a hot and dry summer climate, you could well find yourself standing in the mountains in cold and blustery weather in mid-December – as I have.

The pattern of hot, dry summers and temperate, wet winters that we experience in the western Cape is known as a Mediterranean climate. Other places that have a similar climate are, naturally enough, the Mediterranean coastal areas, as well as southwestern Australia, northwestern Chile and southwestern California. These places also share the same macchia-type vegetation that here we call 'fynbos'. (An interesting point about the vegetation in these areas is that, while the plants of these regions all look very much the same, they share very few common species, genera or even families; they have evolved such similar forms and functions due to corresponding environmental conditions.)

An important factor in determining the climate, and indeed in learning how to 'read' the weather of the western Cape, is the wind: once you tune into the changing wind patterns and what they mean in terms of oncoming conditions, you will be well prepared. The prevailing wind in summer is south-southeast, while that in winter is northwest, and brings rain. Occasionally in winter, one may also get what is known as a 'black southeaster', which also brings rain. Most people presume the cold fronts that pummel the Cape throughout winter originate in the Antarctic, but the real picture is somewhat more complicated...

It starts with a high energy build up over the Pacific Ocean off the coast of Peru and Ecuador. The resultant warm air rises and is blown eastwards until it is forced up against the Andes, and then pushed right into the upper atmosphere. Here it is chilled and descends due to increased density, becoming a low pressure cell. It is then deflected southwards by the earth's rotation, touches down in the region of the Falkland Islands, and is again deflected, this time up to the northwest.

The cell passes Gough and Marion islands before reaching the Cape. As it passes we can detect it in a barometer, which rises for a high pressure cell, and drops for a low pressure one (Which, in everyday parlance, is called a 'cold front').

After passing the Cape, the cell turns off the east coast of Africa and sweeps up past the west coast of Australia, eventually moving past northern Australia towards Japan.

In winter, the cold fronts tend to hit us at an average rate of one every six days, causing the weather of the western Cape to approximately follow this pattern:
Day 1 – Southeast winds prevail with accompanying high pressure;
Day 2 – Low pressure cell moves in, and wind backs up to the northeast bringing dry warm berg winds;
Day 3 – Wind backs up anti-clockwise to the northwest with cirrus clouds heralding the cold front;
Day 4 – Wind backs up again, this time to the southwest, bringing colder air and possibility of snow;
Day 5 – High pressure cell approaches and weather begins to clear;
Day 6 – Southwest winds prevail.

It is the backing up of the wind direction, and the cloud formations, that you should be aware of, in order to predict the weather.

In summer, the prevailing southeaster comes off the South Atlantic High Pressure System, which builds to its maximum strength around November and then slacks off towards February. But, year by year, the

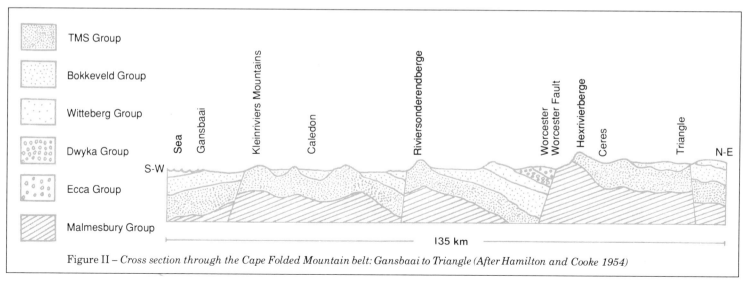

Figure II – *Cross section through the Cape Folded Mountain belt: Gansbaai to Triangle (After Hamilton and Cooke 1954)*

relative strengths of these two major systems can vary greatly, and it is not unknown to have black southeasters bringing squalls to the Peninsula and snowfalls on the Boland mountains around Christmas time. Likewise, between the swathes of cold fronts in winter, the weather can clear for a few days at a time, giving beautifully clear and warm weather.

Spring and autumn are the best times for hiking, for the weather is mostly even and kind. I say mostly, for again I have hiked in the Langeberg in spring, once in soaking conditions and once in snow, and yet again in the most glorious conditions that I have known anywhere. There is certainly an element of luck when planning a hiking trip but my advice is this: the best months are March to May and September to November. Not only is the weather at its best, but so is the vegetation. If the weather turns bad over your planned period, just take warm and rainproof clothes and go, as poor weather usually alternates with good conditions, possibly more than once in the same day. These conditions can prove most exciting – not to mention the fantastic photographic opportunities provided by the dramatic and changing light conditions.

Vegetation

From the time I first became interested in natural history, I had heard of the wondrous splendours of the Cape fynbos, but even some years after moving to Cape Town from Johannesburg, I remained a doubting 'Vaalie'. I mean, the flowers were certainly pretty and varied, but where were these great floral spectacles that the locals 'oohed' and 'aahed' about. Then I walked the Swellendam Trail one spring, and became a true fynbos nut. It was everything I had dreamed of and more: whole hillsides glazed with bright yellow leucadendron leaves; proteas of many colours and varieties bursting out on the hillsides; gladioli and watsonias,

King Protea

mimetes and ericas painting the valleys in the brightest natural palette I had ever seen.

Some years later – while collecting the material for this book in fact – I walked the same mountains in midsummer, and the orchids were on show. During this time I saw over 10 different species of ground orchid, among them some rare colour varieties and species. I saw painted ladies, fire heaths, king proteas, rocket pincushions, moederkappies and blushing brides. In other words, all those flowering beauties that up till then had been for me mere mythical names of some far floral kingdom.

With the exception of a few patches of Afro-montane forest and dune scrub, the entire area dealt with in this book is covered with fynbos. The three most characteristic families of the fynbos are the erica heaths, the reed-like restio plants, and the many genera of the Proteaceae family. There are many more families represented in the fynbos biome – more than in any other veld type in the world, in fact, but these are the distinguishing ones.

The Afro-montane heathlands from which fynbos is derived originated in the tropics, and skipped down to the Cape along the mountain ranges of East Africa. As the continent's climate has fluctuated over time, forests and heathlands have advanced and retreated up and down the mountain slopes. When the climate became wetter, the forests moved up from the lowlands and the heathlands were excluded from all but the highest mountain peaks and ridges. During the periods when the climate was drier, the forests would be greatly diminished and the heathlands would advance down the mountain slopes, joining up with other expanding patches. When this happened, the genetic composition of the veld type would be greatly invigorated, as the time between these genetic intercourses was sufficient for new species and hybrids to evolve in each separated patch.

But today, the mountain environments all down east and southeast Africa are all much the same, and, truth be told, the montane heathlands did not change that much over all this time. However, when they reached the Cape, they encountered contorted mountain ranges running east-west, with very dry interconnecting valleys, sandy and calcareous coastal plains, extreme weather conditions and quite different soils. The vegetation took to this new territory like exuberant pioneers in a new and promised land, resulting in the huge quantity of extremely diverse species we have come to know as fynbos.

The term 'fynbos' comes from the Dutch word *'fijnbosch'* used to describe the prickly, narrow leaves of so many of the plants found in the Cape flora. However, the word in no way describes the protea bushes, the few endemic tree species, or the many broadleaved Sandveld and coastal-fynbos shrubs. A more correct, general term is 'Mediterranean sclerophyllous shrublands': Mediterranean for the climatic region, sclerophyllous for the ability of the plants' leaves to withstand the harsh summer conditions prevailing, and shrublands for the obvious reason. Alternatively, you could say 'Fynbos Biome', which denotes the entire biotic community of these shrublands. 'Cape Floral Kingdom' could also be used – to describe the region's wider floral status – as today, despite its relatively tiny area, the Cape flora is afforded the status of its own floral kingdom, one of six into which the vegetation of the entire planet is divided. Nowhere else on earth is every square metre of ground occupied by such a variety of flowering plants.

A possible explanation as to why fynbos flowers so profusely, is the region's poor soils. Given that most of the fynbos that has survived plough and bulldozer is found on nutrient-poor, marine-derived soils, this extreme reproductive effort compensates for the vegetation's otherwise anorectic state. Since the biological rule is to survive at all

Marsh Rose

costs, this wild abandon in flowering must overcome the fynbos's poor diet and adverse environmental conditions – snow in winter, fire in summer, waterlogging in autumn and heat in spring.

The floral splendour of fynbos is most visible during the years following a veld fire. Some species, often thought by botanists to be long extinct, have the habit of suddenly bursting forth after a fire – species such as the delicate marsh rose (*Orothamnus zeyheri*) which is now found in a few small communities on the Kogelberg and Hermanus mountains. Recent successive and widespread fires there, might, however, have endangered their survival.

While regular fires are thought to be good for this fire-adapted vegetation, too-frequent burning is doubly harmful, as trees will not survive regular burns, and some plants, including the larger proteas, need up to 20 years to reach full reproductive maturity. Two burns in 20 years will discourage these species from reproducing, while two fires in less than 10 years will almost certainly obliterate their presence. For this reason, no fires are allowed anywhere in the conservation-controlled fynbos areas – the ecological risks are just too great.

The forest patches, like those found at Newlands on the Peninsula, on parts of the Swellendam Trail and in protected river valleys throughout the area, are sad remnants of once widespread Afro-montane forests. Both climate and man have played their parts in decimating these primeval woodlands, through progressive drying, felling and burning. These mature, moist forests, which make a canopy about 30 metres high, are also called podocarpus forests, after the yellowwoods (genus *Podocarpus*) that naturally dominate them. These are the same type of forests as those in Knysna, on the Drakensberg foothills and on the escarpment edge in the Transvaal. Apart from yellowwoods, the forests contain impressive tree species such as mountain hard pear, stinkwood, ironwood, Cape beech, Cape holly, rooiels, wild peach and assegai.

The riverine bush consists of wild almond trees (that may grow into old and very large, spreading trees), lance leaf trees (genus *Metrosideros*), some protea species like *Leucadendrom salicifolium*, the restio *Elegia capensis* (Cape bamboo) and water witels. The list of plants and flowers is so extensive that I am unable to give anything even approaching a complete list in this slim volume. The colour photographs of flora that appear in this book are a further guide to the riches of the Cape Floral Kingdom.

Animals

As I have said in both the preceding geology and flora sections, an important limiting ecological factor in the region is the poor nutrient status of the soils and natural vegetation. For animal life, this means that the plants grow slowly and have limited food value. Consequently, the area has little in the way of fauna. It is true that, at the time when white colonists first landed at the Cape, lions, leopards, elephants, buffalos and hippos were to be found right where the city of Cape Town now rises, but their numbers could never have been significant, as the fynbos food chain cannot, and never could, support a large biomass.

For the novice birdwatcher, however, this situation is ideal. Once you have got to recognize some 20 odd species here, you are well on your way to mastering the identities of the area's avian corps. Like the animals, birds were once more numerous. For instance, the lammergeyer (bearded vulture), an endangered species in southern Africa found only in the Drakensberg/Maluti

Cape Vulture

massif, was once numerous throughout the mountains of the western Cape. Another species that is endangered in the Cape is, ironically, the Cape vulture, with the only breeding colony being at Potberg in the De Hoop Nature Reserve (see Hike O1).

For our purposes, we can distinguish between the forest and montane fynbos species – for these are the two main habitats dealt with in the book – and, to a lesser extent, shore birds of the southern coast. Most conspicuous of the fynbos species is the Cape sugarbird, with its streamer tail feathers and long, curved bill. Similar but smaller species are the sunbirds, most numerous of which is the orange-breasted sunbird. This is a warbler-sized bird with a brilliant orange-and-blue breast and a blue-black head. It is a jittery bird that won't stay long in one place, flitting around and probing

erica, protea and other blooms with its slender curved beak. Other sunbirds are the lesser collared one of similar size, and the malachite sunbird, a larger bird with a narrow elongated tail.

In rocky areas, there are four main types of bird likely to be seen. The first is the Cape rockjumper, whose habits make identification fairly easy. It has a buff-coloured belly, chocolate-brown head with prominent white beard, patchy brown crown and neck, and a buff rump. The rockjumper is a thrush-sized bird that jumps about rocks on long legs.

Next is the ground woodpecker, a starling-sized woodpecker with spotted olive-and-yellow-green plumage and a bright-red rump that is only conspicuous in flight. They are well camouflaged on rocks, which they tend to hide behind if people approach, although their harsh, sawing call easily gives them away.

The Cape and sentinel rock thrushes are hard to tell apart: males have blue-grey heads and orange bodies, while the females' heads are spotted orange-brown. The sentinel rock thrush is slightly the smaller of the two, the males have the blue-grey head-colour extending down the back and wing tops, and the female has a whiter chest than the Cape rock thrush. Their habits and habitats are otherwise much the same.

Raptors are not common in the area, but a few species are conspicuous. Most impressive are the black eagles which, although nowhere numerous, are likely to be seen throughout the higher mountain areas – including the Peninsula. These majestic birds will soar above you, often to beyond your own limit of vision and at great speed, or circle in wider and wider turns until they swoop away to hunt something a little smaller. If you are lucky, a breeding pair will entertain you with a display of fine aerobatics – swooping, turning and tumbling with great agility and obvious enthusiasm.

Jackal buzzards are perhaps the most common medium-sized birds of prey, their elegant black-and-white wings with a black trailing edge, fan-shaped grey tail, buff chest and spotted belly being diagnostic in flight. Rock kestrels are small raptors which are common in the high mountain areas. Their striped dark-brown-and-white tails, speckled brick-red bodies and wide, lightly striped and spotted wings make them easy to identify. On the lower and middle slopes, especially on the southern and eastern ranges, black harriers are likely to be seen. They are unmistakable, with stark black-and-white wings and bold black and white striped tails. They hunt by flying low and lazily over the slopes, often alighting on the ground, in the typical harrier fashion.

Canaries and seedeaters are numerous, and the species include the sparrow-like protea seedeaters, Cape buntings with their distinctive black and white head stripes, the attractive grey-yellow Cape canaries that live in large flocks and often in the company of other seedeaters, and the Cape siskins – small endemic birds that forage in bushes or on the ground, in small groups. They are easily recognized by the white dots on the tips of their tails.

The rank fynbos is the habitat for warblers of various kinds, but all fall under the description of 'lbj' (short for 'little brown jobs'), a term used by birders to describe the many infuriatingly hard-to-identify species of similar-coloured, similar-sized birds. There are grassbirds and neddickys, cisticolas and prinias, warblers and titbabblers… but you'll have to go to some other source to help you further.

In the forests, you should see small Cape battises, robins, sombre bulbuls, doves, and the occasional red-breasted sparrowhawk hunting above the canopy. The shores are home to different species of seagull, terns, oystercatchers and the like.

I have concentrated on birds here, for these are the most likely fauna to be seen. Baboons are, however, also conspicuous – and noisy – but they hardly need to be described. While on the Swellendam Trail I reread Eugene Marais' classic work *The Soul of the Ape* and renewed my awe of the man and my appreciation of these, our primate relatives. Leopards are more frequent than many would think, but the closest I have even come to sighting one is fresh spoor, and hearing one cough very nearby at dusk.

Other common animals are the small antelope such as klipspringer, grysbok, steenbok and duiker as well as the medium-sized grey rhebok. Lynx are common and a problem to stock farmers; brown hyena are less so but nevertheless persecuted wherever they are found. Aardvarks and porcupines (a rodent species) are nocturnal hole diggers, and seldom seen, while, in contrast, the endearing dassies are seen everywhere. Mongooses, genets, striped polecats and hares are also widespread, but seldom common. In the wetter eastern areas, calcified droppings often show the presence of clawless otters, though I have yet to hear of a sighting in these mountains.

Genet

THE CEDERBERG

After the Drakensberg, this range is my favourite mountain wilderness area in South Africa. Deep erosion of the Table Mountain Sandstone formation has left a number of parallel ridges, with towering peaks and incised valleys, while a prominent shale band forms a level platform – known as Die Trap (the step) – around most of the major peaks. This shale 'running board' gives easy hiking access to much of the range.

The Cederberg is perhaps best known for its fantastical rock formations. These have been caused by eons of rain and snow eating into the quartzitic sandstone boulders and cliffs, and pocking and carving them into weird forms: winged goddesses, massed chess pieces, many-headed monsters – the imagination soars. It is not so much mechanical erosion at work here, for water, no matter how hard it falls, cannot erode rock. It is the chemical action of rain water, a weak acid solution, that erodes the rock surfaces.

The Cederberg range was first recorded by a VOC expedition commissioned in 1661 by the then governor of the Cape, Simon van der Stel, to explore the hinterland. The expedition reached the Olifantsrivier at the base of the Cederberg, and by the early 18th century the fertile Olifantsrivier valley had been settled and farmed.

Towards the end of that century, woodcutters began to exploit the hard, sweet-scented wood of the endemic Clanwilliam cedars (*Widdringtonia cedarbergensis*). By 1840, travellers from the Cape complained bitterly to the authorities about the wanton destruction being wrought on the once extensive cedar forests – as much by uncontrolled burning as by the timber industry – but the colony was hungry for good quality wood, having plundered the nearby forests at Hout Bay and Newlands, and scant attention was paid. Only in 1876 was the first forester appointed to the Cederberg, and from then on the area was slowly brought under conservation control.

Today, the Cederberg is one of the country's principal catchment areas and one of its finest wilderness regions. Apart from the Clanwilliam cedars, the mountains are a delight to naturalists and botanists for the many other rare and interesting plants that are to be found here. Most attractive of all, perhaps, is the snow protea (*Protea cryophila*) whose specific name means cold-loving.

The rocket pincushion (*Leucospermum reflexum*) grows only in the northern Cederberg, though it is a common garden plant. Other commercially exploited plants include buchu (*Agathosma* spp.) – found in the kloofs – rooibos and elephant's foot (*Dioscorea elephantipes*), which grow on the lower mountain slopes and from which cortisone was first obtained. For the rest, it is mostly typical fynbos country, with heaths, proteas and flowering bulbs.

The Cederberg's relatively great distance from Cape Town, and its inherent ruggedness, have led to the area being declared a leopard sanctuary. Farmers throughout the western Cape are encouraged to allow conservationists to capture any 'problem' animals, which are then set free in the Cederberg. Research in the Boland mountains indicates that Cape mountain leopards do not stick to defended territories, as is the case with most other predators, but roam across vast areas. Farmers in the greater Cederberg area have shown great foresight in agreeing to this pioneering conservation scheme.

Cape wildcat and caracal, bat-eared fox on the sandy Karoo side, brown hyaena, black-backed jackal, aardvarks and porcupines are all found in the wilderness region. Bird life is abundant – in 1977, 81 bird species were recorded here – most conspicuous of which are the raptors. Most of the birds mentioned in the natural history chapter will be found here.

Reptiles likely to be seen are Cape rock agamas, geckos and skinks. There are 15 species of snake, including berg adders (the most common snake in the area), puffadders and Cape cobras – these last two can both inflict fatally toxic bites. Remember at all times, however, that ignorance and carelessness are your greatest dangers when dealing with poisonous snakes.

Hiking in the Cederberg

One of the advantages of hiking in the Cederberg is that Die Trap shale band makes an easy stroll out of many hikes in this otherwise rugged range. Also, the numerous forestry huts that are maintained essentially for management purposes may be used to give comfort in times of grim weather. Huts are to be found at Heuningvlei, Boontjieskloof, Crystal Pool, Sleepad, Sneeukop, Middelberg and Sneeuberg. These huts are maintained for forestry staff working in the area and may be used by hikers only when not otherwise occupied. They are rudimentary shelters, with not much more than four walls and a roof, usually supported by chunky cedar beams. There are also a number of caves found along popular hiking routes which make for convenient shelters.

Many hiking paths through the Cederberg are of exceptionally high standard, making hiking here an extremely pleasurable experience. They were built by the woodcutters, whose donkeys had to haul heavy logs down from the high-plateau forests around Heuningvlei, Boontjieskloof, Middelberg and Sneeuberg.

The Cederberg wilderness area is divided into three management sections: the northern, central and southern sections. The northern Cederberg is a relatively unfrequented region compared with the rest of this wilderness area; this isolation, and the rugged Krakadou region's natural splendour, gives the area a special charm. Two historic attractions near the Pakhuispas are the graves of C. Louis Leipoldt – whose family name is immortalized at nearby Leipoldtville – and a young officer of the Gordon Highlanders, laid to rest under these southern stones during the South African War. Another great attraction of this area is the ease with which hiker's can appreciate the unsurpassed beauty.

The central section is the most frequented area in the Cederberg, not because it is the easiest hiking area, but because this is where the Algeria Forest Station and the beautifully situated Algeria campsite are found. In fact, the impressive ridges that encircle the area to give it its dramatic scenic appeal, cause every path from Algeria to lead in a decidedly upward direction.

One short and easy walk is Van der Merwe se Wandelpad, from the causeway up either side of the Rondegatrivier to Uitkyk educational camp at the foot of the Uitkykpas. The hardest route goes up the 'far' (west) ridge above Algeria. The path goes up Suurvlak se Kloof, and along the left-hand side of Vensterberg (1 427 m). This is very steep, dangerous in wet weather and not described here, good luck.

The southern area includes the fantastic Wolfberg arch and the range's highest peak, the Sneeuberg. For more languid sojourns, there are the elegant white and lusty red cultivars of the Cederberg, obtainable from Dwarsrivier farm's cellars.

A maximum of 12 hikers is allowed in each section at a time. Permits for the entire wilderness area must be obtained from the local forestry station and it is advisable to book in advance. All visitors to the Cederberg must report to the Algeria Forest Station to collect their permits.

Accommodation facilities in the Cederberg are as follows:

Northern section *Kliphuis forestry campsite* on the Pakhuispas; R6-00 per night per person, a tranquil, grassed site with ablution and braai facilities; permit from the local ranger.

Wuppertal village private campsite with no facilities, or cottages, both arranged through the local church.

Central section *Algeria campsite*, a beautiful, luxury camping and caravan park with full ablution and braai facilities but nothing else; R6-00 per night per person. It is essential to book in advance if you wish to stay over weekends or during holidays.

Southern section *Sanddrif private campsite and bungalows*, owned by the Nieuwoudts of Dwarsrivier farm, where permits, petrol (93 octane) and fine wines can be procured (Address: Nieuwoudt Brothers, Dwarsrivier, P. O. Cederberg 7341).

Kromrivier, run by another Nieuwoudt clan, where you can hire bungalows or camp (Address: A. P. C. Nieuwoudt and Son, Kromrivier, P. O. Citrusdal 7340).

Hikers can camp anywhere in the wilderness area, with the exception of rock shelters that have any rock art on them.

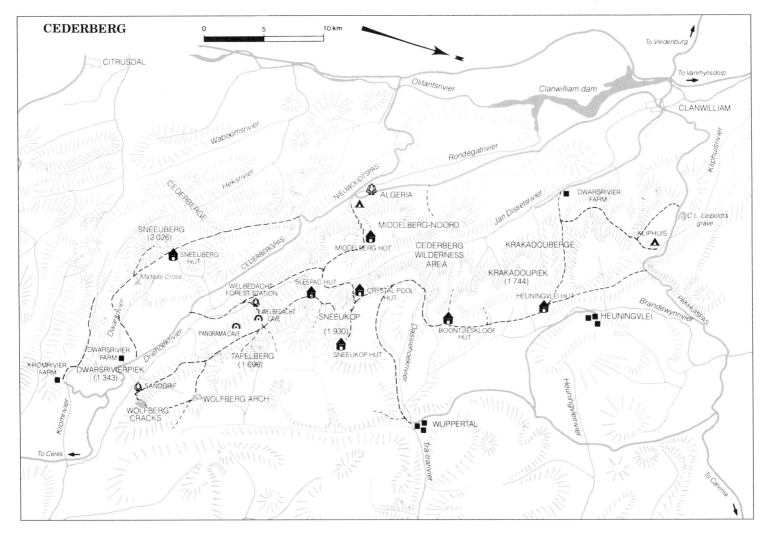

CEDERBERG

0   5   10 km

To Vredenburg

CITRUSDAL

Olifantsrivier

Clanwilliam dam

To Vanrhynsdorp

CLANWILLIAM

Waboomsrivier

Rondegatrivier

Kliphuisrivier

Heksrivier

CEDERBERGE

Jan Disselsrivier

DWARSRIVIER FARM

C.L. Leipoldt's grave

SNEEUBERG
(2 026)

NIEUWOUDTSPAS

ALGERIA

MIDDELBERG-NOORD

CEDERBERG
WILDERNESS
AREA

KRAKADOUBERGE

KLIPHUIS

SNEEUBERG
HUT

CEDERBERGPAS

MIDDELBERG HUT

KRAKADOUPIEK
(1 744)

Maltese Cross

WELBEDACHT
FOREST STATION

SLEEPAD HUT

CRYSTAL POOL
HUT

HEUNINGVLEI HUT

Brandewynrivier

PAKHUISPAS

Dwarsrivier

WELBEDACHT
CAVE

SNEEUKOP
(1 930)

Dassiehoekrivier

BOONTJIESKLOOF
HUT

HEUNINGVLEI

PANORAMA CAVE

DWARSRIVIER
FARM

Driehoekrivier

TAFELBERG
(1 696)

SNEEUKOP HUT

Heuningvleirivier

KROMRIVIER
FARM

DWARSRIVIERPIEK
(1 343)

SANDDRIF

WOLFBERG ARCH

Kromrivier

WOLFBERG
CRACKS

Tra-tra rivier

WUPPERTAL

To Ceres

To Calvinia

Pakhuis Stroll
Hike C1

Route: Circular walk along the jeep track from Kliphuis campsite
Distance: 7 kilometres
Duration: 2 hours
Grade: Easy
Booking Authority: Algeria Forest Station (Tel. (02682) ask for 3440) (permit needed)
General Information: This easy stroll gives a good introduction to the type of scenery and vegetation that one encounters in the western Cape's hiking paradise. From the Pakhuis road, it is worth taking the short detour to the grave of C. Louis Leipoldt, who grew up in the shadow of the Cederberg.

▶ From the Kliphuis campsite, take the path southward, starting behind the forester's quarters. The path climbs gently, over and through exposed rock faces, and then follows a little river valley onto Amon se Vlak. When you reach a junction, take the left-bearing path and follow the edge of a ridge, passing through some typically beautiful and fanciful weathered rock sculptures.
▶ This path meets up with a jeep track; turn right here to follow the track down a slope and over numerous rocky ridges towards the Pakhuispas road. From the point where the jeep track meets the road, the grave of poet C. Louis Leipoldt lies a few hundred metres up the road to your left (towards Clanwilliam). Without doubt, this man was one of South Africa's most brilliant and versatile sons. He was a journalist, war correspondent, medical practitioner, poet, playwright,

writer of short stories and author of books on viticulture, traditional cookery and the supernatural. He was, for a time, medical superintendent for the Cape country districts, bringing to the attention of the authorities the problems of malnutrition among the rural poor. The grave is a modest one, resting underneath a small, naturally eroded canopy.
▶ This is actually a short detour off our route since Kliphuis campsite is reached by turning right here. The campsite is just under two kilometres down the dusty road, which winds between low ridges and typically sculptured sandstone boulders. As you approach Kliphuis, the cliffs and peaks of the Pakhuisberge converge on the road, forcing

it to swing progressively to the south. The main peaks, in order, are: Pakhuispiek (1077 m), Charity (1088 m), Hope and Faith – the last of which stands over a hairpin bend in the road, two kilometres southeast of Kliphuis.

Walking along the sandy flats, you are likely to come across the deep holes dug into the ground by aardvarks, the energetic real-estate developers of the animal world. They dig holes both for food and shelter, being able to work in even the hardest soils.

You are unlikely to see the animals themselves, however, as they are almost exclusively nocturnal. But keep an eye out for and avoid the holes as, once an aardvark abandons its hole, other creatures move in: brown

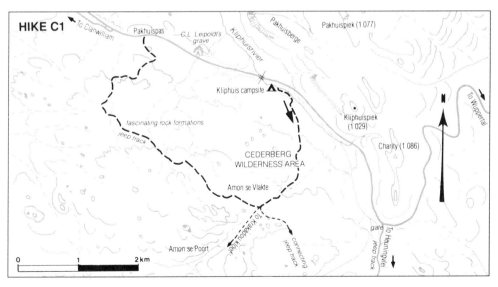

25

hyenas, jackals, porcupines, hares, snakes, lizards – perhaps even leopards.

Krakadoupas
Hike C2

Route: *Dwarsrivier farm to Heuningvlei*
Distance: *12 kilometres*
Duration: *5 hours*
Grade: *Severe*
Booking Authority: *Algeria Forest Station (Tel. (02682) ask for 3440) (permit needed)*
General Information: *The remote Dwarsrivier farm here is not to be confused with one of the same name in the southern area, well known to mountaineers and wine lovers alike. My colleagues thought that no-one in their right mind would want to venture either up or down this steep path. They did concede, however, that this strenuous walk reveals the true character of the Cederberg: its unique-ness, remoteness, and the diversity of its landscapes and plant life. In spite of this trail's proximity to the Dwarsrivier, water is hard to come by, so carry enough with you. The walk is linear, so it would be a good idea to take two cars and park one at either end, unless a five-hour uphill hike doesn't deter you from walking all the way back.*

This hike begins at the Dwarsrivier farm, reached 12 kilometres after taking a gravel road to the right off the Pakhuispas road immediately after passing the Clanwilliam Agricultural School.
❱ Start at the grove of oak trees to the right of the farmhouse, and follow the path across farmland; the level going, over the ploughed

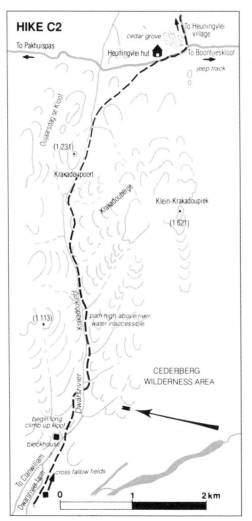

land, is a bit tedious. The natural vegetation is dominated by succulent Karoo plants such as euphorbias and bottertrees (*Cotyledon paniculata*), reminding one that Namaqua-land is not far off.

The trail follows the perennial Dwarsri-vier, but access to the water is not easy as the path keeps mostly well above the river, crossing it only near the beginning (twice) and near the top of the gorge (once). Along the way, you will encounter numerous side paths that lead off to nowhere in particular. Your path, however, is well defined.
❱ After the first river crossing, the path be-gins its steep ascent of Krakadoupas, which becomes ever steeper as you progress. The gutted remains of a blockhouse will be passed just before the path begins its zigzag journey up the pass. The blockhouse dates from the South African War when the Brit-ish built many such fortifications on all the known routes from the north in an attempt to block imminent invasion of the Cape. To reach the top of the pass, you will need to ascend 800 metres over a horizontal dis-tance of six kilometres – a big favour to ask any pair of legs.
❱ Follow the gorge as it rises steadily to your right, cut only by various stream gullies, to the pinnacle that is Klein-Krakadoupiek (1 621 m). To the south you see the land rising up in steps to various lesser peaks and ridges. Continue up through seemingly end-less hairpin bends to a large tree, whose shade provides the ideal rest spot.
❱ From here on, the path, although well defined and easy to follow, is overgrown with bracken and cliffortia bushes, which can be

cruel to uncovered legs. Wabooms (*Protea nitida*) are also plentiful, their large creamy-white flower heads adding variety to the pink splashes of flowering ericas. Near the top of the poort the views are truly magnificent, and one is further rewarded by secret hollows, carpeted with fields of golden brown restios and the soft woolly forms of slangbos plants.

▶ The gentle descent begins through the bizarre rock landscapes for which the Cederberg is famous, and nowhere are they more impressive than here.

▶ Finally, nearing Heuningvlei, you will reach a jeep track coming south from Pakhuispas (see Hike C12, Day 1). Turn right here and follow the level but very sandy path around a magnificent stand of cedar trees, past the Heuningvlei hut, to the gate at the edge of the wilderness area. If you have planned well, there should be a car waiting here to take you back to the land of hot showers, cold beers and hamburgers.

Kliphuis to Dwarsrivier
Hike C3

Route: *From Kliphuis campsite to Krakadoupoort pass*
Distance: *15,5 kilometres*
Duration: *5-6 hours*
Grade: *Severe*
Booking Agent: *Algeria Forest Station (Tel. (02682) ask for 3440) (permit needed)*
General Information: *This path has fallen into general misuse over the years, and has*

become somewhat overgrown; the conservation authorities at Algeria are, however, planning its redevelopment, so you should check its condition with them. It is shown on the Slingsby 1:50 000 Cederberg 'flowerland' map (1980, out of print), but not the more recent (1981) 1:50 000 Directorate of Forestry map. Whatever the condition of the path, this 'contour' route is demanding, as it seldom keeps to the contours. This is a linear hike, so take two cars, one to park at each end.

▶ From Kliphuis campsite (just off the Pakhuispas about 20 kilometres from Clanwilliam), follow the path in a south-southeast direction across the very rocky Amon se Vlak. You head diagonally into a valley, and reach an intermittent stream after two and a half kilometres.

▶ The route follows the stream course to Amon se Poort, and then into Amon se Kloof. Passing through the kloof, you cross the two major tributaries of the Taaiboskraalrivier – spaced one and a half kilometres apart – as well as a few lesser kloof branches.

▶ After leaving Amon se Kloof the path loops around the first of three increasingly long spurs (you will descend a total of 300 metres while rounding these spurs). The loop around the second spur involves a steep

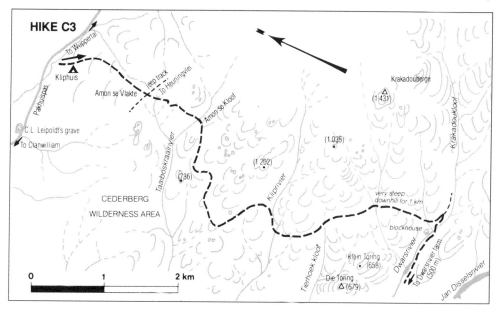

HIKE C3

climb and descent over very rocky terrain. Between the second and third loops, you will near a corner boundary of the wilderness area. From here you head up for about 60 metres, following close to the inside boundary for a little over one kilometre, before finally rounding the last spur and heading down away from the boundary. You will now be walking diagonally down a wide slope between a continuation of the Krakadouberge on your left and Die Toring (679 m) and Klein Toring (657 m) on your right.

❯ After levelling out for one and a half kilometres, the path again heads uphill towards two spurs which jut out from the Krakadou ridge – and yes, this does mean some more sharp ascents and descents. Along this section you can look down to Dwarsrivier farm, which is your destination.

❯ Having rounded the second spur, the path descends, crosses the Dwarsrivier, and obliquely joins the main Krakadoupas path.

❯ Turn right down the Krakadoupas path, and recross the river a little further downstream. The path then moves well above the river until passing the remnants of an old South African War blockhouse. Cross the river once again, and from here to the farm you will have the river on your left.

It is possible from the farmhouse to link up with a south-running route, following a gravel road and then a path up the Jan Disselsrivier valley. At Warmhoekkloof you can turn left (east) up the Erdvarkkloof and then take either Klein Koupoort to Boontjieskloof or Groot Koupoort to Heuningvlei. Otherwise you can turn right (west), over Warmhoekkloof and around to Algeria.

These would all constitute multi-day epic hikes. Since none of these is a circular route, make sure of the necessary transport arrangements to get home.

Algeria to Wuppertal
Hike C4

Route: From Algeria campsite to Wuppertal mission village
Distance: 28 kilometres
Duration: 2 days
Grade: Severe
Booking Authority: Algeria Forest Station (Tel. (02682) ask for 3440) (permit needed)
General Information: Despite a few steep uphill sections, this hike is extremely satisfying and perfect for a weekend. The only problem will be a logistical one – to arrange transport to and from the start and end points. The drive from Algeria to Wuppertal, over the Pakhuispas, is about 100 kilometres – mostly along winding gravel roads – but the journey is spectacular and well worth it, especially in spring.

Day 1: Algeria to Crystal Pool hut – 13 kilometres (6 hours)
❯ From Algeria (take the N7 from Cape Town and turn right onto the Nieuwoudtspas road between Citrusdal and Clanwilliam), climb the very steep, long, path up to Middelberg hut, then bear right up to the Cathedral Rocks and down to Grootlandsvlakte.
❯ At the end of the vlakte you must turn left in the shadow of Sneeukop peak, down the

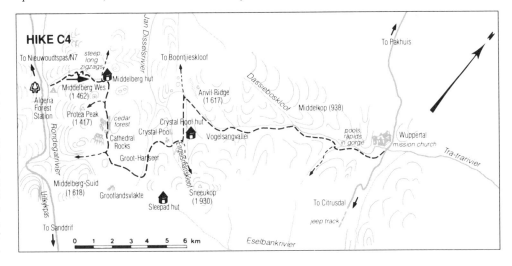

Groot-Hartseer valley to Crystal Pool. The path from the vlakte to Crystal Pool is a fairly strenuous one, but gloriously rugged and scenic. Here you can feel that you have penetrated the heart of the mountains.

A fuller route description for this first-day's 13-kilometre-long walk can be had by retracing the path along the description for Hike C12 – Cederberg Traverse Route, four-day alternative, day four: Crystal Pool to Algeria. The extra hour given for this route description, is to account for the fact that the stretch from Algeria to the Middelberg hut is a climb rather than a descent. Also, once at Crystal Pool, you still have to climb the wickedly steep hill behind to reach the hut.

Day 2: Crystal Pool hut to Wuppertal – 15 kilometres (6 hours)
▶ Continue from the Crystal Pool hut, until the path divides. Take the left-hand option, and head down the Engelsmanskloof stream (don't turn right up Engelsmanskloof) towards Boontjieskloof.
▶ After about two kilometres the path swings off to the left, around a small koppie, and then heads back to the river.
▶ Cross the river at the 'swemgat' where a single tree offers shade. From here turn sharp right, moving diagonally up the opposite (northeastern) side of the river, below Turret Ridge. The 1:50 000 map differs from the actual paths, showing a branch off to the right before the river. Whatever the case, you should now be on the left-hand bank facing upstream.
▶ The well-laid-out path heads obliquely uphill (away from the river) towards the enchanting sounding Vogelsangvallei. It continues generally uphill for nearly one kilometre after the 'swemgat', and then does a 'more-or-less' contour all around the outer right-hand side of the valley, keeping well above the river course (between 60 and 120 metres above).
▶ The route crosses five intermittent streams before coming to a major kloof with a perennial river flowing through it. Here the Vogelsangvallei stream drops down into a deep gorge, where it joins with other streams to become the Sandrivier, a long way down to your left.
▶ The path goes up and down to the top of another side gorge with a flowing river, and then rounds a slope to join another river coming down from the right, two and a half kilometres from the beginning of the Sandrivier. This is the upper reaches of the Dassieboskloofrivier, which flows down and through the impressive Dassieboskloof to Wuppertal.
▶ The path keeps above the river on the right-hand bank for some way before dropping down into the gorge, where it levels out still about 60 metres above the river. Ahead of you, you will soon be able to make out a wide valley where the Dassieboskloofrivier is joined by one of its tributaries coming in from the right.
▶ You now descend an even slope to the valley floor, crossing the Eselbankrivier just before the two rivers meet. The path follows the river across this relatively open valley floor, with a small descent and ascent where another river comes down from Groot Koupoort on your left.
▶ From here the river enters a deeply incised gorge, where the path crosses over to the left-hand bank. It climbs steeply up a ridge, looking down on the snaking river as it races through the gorge below.
▶ The main path then descends the ridge to cross the river. It makes a horseshoe bend within the gorge, crosses over the far eastern ridge and turns left along a valley path into Wuppertal.

Duiwelsgatkloof Bypass
Hike C5

Route: *From Uitkykpas to Eikeboom via Sneeuberg hut*
Distance: *16 kilometres*
Duration: *6 hours*
Grade: *Severe*
Booking Authority: *Algeria Forest Station (Tel (02682) ask for 3440) (permit needed)*
General Information: *Although there are some fairly steep ascents and descents along this route (none too long) the severe grading has been given mainly for the hike's duration. This is a magnificent walk along one of the less-used paths in the vicinity, contouring for most of its length around the eastern side of Duiwelsgat. This cavernous kloof is an awesome topographical feature, dropping over 800 metres, in places, to the Slangvlei and Heks rivers below. A path does descend at one place into the Duiwelsgat, but it peters out after a while – this is reserved for only the most intrepid of explorers. The terrain on this walk is often difficult, so good footwear is*

recommended. The walk is linear, so make the necessary transport arrangements.

To reach the starting point, travel up Uitkykpas from Algeria. Pass the turnoff to Uitkyk itself and follow the pass as it winds steeply up the Uitkykrivier gorge. Where the pass makes a hairpin bend it is possible to pull over onto a flat area on the right, which is where our hike begins. The path continues straight up the river valley, known as Klein Duiwelsgat, while the road swings out around the outside of Uitkyk se Piek.

There is a signboard here declaring 'Cederberg Wilderness Area', behind which the path goes.

▶ The path follows the Duiwelsgatkloof (Devil's hole gorge) between Uitkyk se Piek and Smalberg and it is not without reason that the gorge was named, for this is one devil of a climb – 400 metres from Uitkykpas to the top of Klein Duiwelsgat. Although the stream is crossed several times on this first section, the only pools big enough to cool off in are to be found near the beginning of the hike, though water is plentiful.

▶ About halfway up, the valley opens out to reveal some dramatic views. Here the path crosses from the left to the right-hand bank and zigzags above the river. The crossing is a good watering spot, with an excellent view back toward Algeria. There is plenty of evidence of baboon activity here, as this is an obvious spot for the veld's greatest opportunists to frequent for food, water and shelter.

▶ At the top of the climb the path levels out, and you are rewarded with a soothing scene, where a boggy area creates a soft-green aspect. Once here, the hardest part of the walk

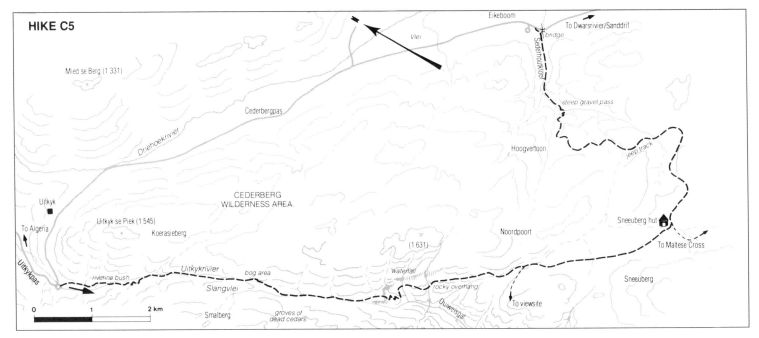

HIKE C5

is over. It is well worth taking the next section of the path slowly, to appreciate the profusion of geophytic (bulbous) plants that liven up the grassy stretches. Unfortunately, the path is badly eroded where it crosses marshy patches, and, in winter, you are likely to get your boots muddied. You will have to keep a sharp eye out to follow the cairns which mark the route through this area.

▶ As you cross the watershed, the path begins a gentle descent, and you will catch your first glimpse of the far-off Duiwelsgat.

▶ The path winds down to the edge of a precipice overlooking the Duiwelsgatkloof, where you can stop under the shade of an old waboom (*Protea nitida*) to enjoy the breath-taking scene, before taking a sharp turn to the right and dropping down the broken line of cliffs.

▶ Follow the path carefully as it zigzags around to the left to pick its way along the rock face, as it is often boggy, especially near waterfalls. A large rock overhang along the line of cliffs provides an idyllic lunch spot. Get your blood sugar up here, for after this the path climbs out of Duiwelsgat and the heat can become intense.

▶ As you near the top of the climb to emerge through a saddle on Die Trap shale band, watch carefully for the path: it crosses the stream and then turns left onto the open plain at the base of the Sneeuberg. Across to the east you will see Tafelberg.

▶ The path hereafter crosses the plain to the hut. From here, head along the jeep track eastwards from the hut, down Sederhout-kloof to Eikeboom (for a fuller description, reverse Hike C7).

Alternatively, you could overnight at Sneeuberg hut. A number of other paths lead off this route, so once you have followed all the detailed hikes in this book, why not set off with the aid of the 1:50 000 hiking map and go exploring. That, after all, is what a wilderness experience is all about. Then again, you could simply return the way you have come.

Tafelberg Ascent   Hike C6

Route: *Welbedacht forestry base to Tafelberg summit*
Distance: *16 kilometres*
Duration: *4-5 hours (there); 2-3 hours (back)*
Grade: *Extreme*
Booking Authority: *Algeria Forest Station (Tel. (02682) ask for 3440) (permit needed)*
General Information: *Anyone with a mountaineering spirit will be hard pressed to ignore this challenge. Perhaps because it was my first hike in the Cederberg, it remains special to me. Perhaps also because it is so much more than just a hike. The route to the summit involves a tricky rock scramble that should be avoided by inexperienced climbers when weather conditions are wet. You can make this strenuous walk a deal easier and more pleasant by turning it into a weekend outing, overnighting at the Welbedacht cave.*

To get to the start, drive from Algeria up the Uitkykpas and into the elevated Driehoekri-vier valley. At Moutonsklip turn left to a car park – the start of the walk.

▶ From here, head left into a pine plantation and cross the causeway to the old farmhouse that is the Welbedacht forest station. The path continues behind the farmhouse, and up a gully. Climb for about 70 metres, crossing the stream four times.

▶ The path then veers up even more steeply to the left, towards a side gully. Ascend this gully for about another 70 metres, again crossing the stream a few times, until a small, intermediate headland is mounted. There are numerous large rock pinnacles on the surrounding ridges here, along with the stark forms of dead cedar trees.

▶ The path curves around to the right, rises and descends across the fairly open head-land, and then climbs up again, heading back into the main gully that was originally followed. A steep 200-metre climb, up a good path with rough steps built by old-time woodcutters, follows the stream. In the wet season, parts of the path may be sodden.

▶ At a high point, a rock wall seems to block your way, and the actual path becomes indis-tinct in a rocky area: go to the left around the wall, keeping to what you judge to be the main gully. From here, the Welbedacht cave is a little way further up. It overlooks the stream on the right, in an area where some mature, cedar trees grow on the left-hand bank. The cave is very comfortable, and straw bedding is usually to be found.

▶ The path continues up the gully and reaches a four-way junction just after breaching Die Trap. Turn right and continue along the path for just under one kilometre, until you reach a small cairn indicating the route up towards Tafelberg.

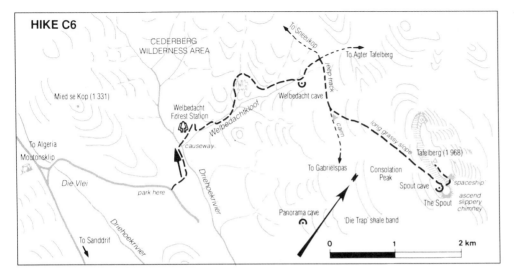

valley and across the Tanqua Karoo are equally impressive. Descend the same way – carefully.

Sneeuberg Hut   Hike C7

Route: *From Eikeboom, up Tierhok, to Sneeuberg hut*
Distance: *14 kilometres*
Duration: *2-3 hours (there); 2 hours (back)*
Grade: *Moderate*
Booking Authority: *Algeria Forest Station (Tel (02682) ask for 3440) (permit needed)*
General Information: *For anyone wishing to spend quality time in this wilderness area, this hike provides the most relaxed way to gain maximum pleasure and adventure. This description takes you to Sneeuberg hut and back in one day. However, if you wish, you can overnight at the hut, from where you can head north to Uitkyk along the exciting Duiwelskloof path (reverse Hike C5), head south past the Maltese Cross and down to Dwarsrivier (reverse Hike C9), or climb the Sneeuberg (see Hike C8), at 2 026,8 metres the highest peak in the Cederberg.*

Eikeboom car park is reached beyond Uitkykpas from Algeria, in the Driehoek valley. About three and a half kilometres south of Moutonsklip, you will see a clump of oak trees on your right where you can park – and from here the hike begins.

▶ It sets off on a gentle ascent of Sederhoutkloof, where a waboom (*Protea nitida*) forest has replaced the cedars along the stream banks. This tree protea is fire resistant –

▶ Follow the paths diagonally across Consolation Peak ridge, and through a saddle from where Tafelberg proper rises. After the saddle, the gradient eases off for a while as the path crosses a watershed with Consolation Peak immediately behind to the right.
▶ The path then heads diagonally up the Tafelberg's scree slope, to the gully between the main peak and The Spout. The Spout cave can be easily seen on the right as one approaches the gap between the two massive rock walls. A low wall has been built around the mouth of the cave. You may not consider this luxury accommodation – until you are caught up here in a blizzard.
▶ Keep moving up towards the top of the gully, until you reach another gully on the left, cutting into the flank of the Tafelberg.

Follow this canyon-like gap until it turns and narrows into a chimney. The chimney's sides have been polished smooth by grit carried down by the wet-weather waterfall that pours over the lip above. It is a fairly slippery but quite manageable scramble for anyone who hasn't a fear of heights.
▶ On reaching the summit, you will be greeted by one of the wonders of the western Cape – a rock formation that looks exactly like a space ship, to the extent of seeming to float above the ground; you can even climb inside the 'ship'. The intricately incised summit rock is fun to explore, and you can reach two summit beacons, the farthest one being the true summit at 1 968,5 metres. Views over to the Sneeuberg and eastwards down a much longer fall-off to the Agter-Tafelberg

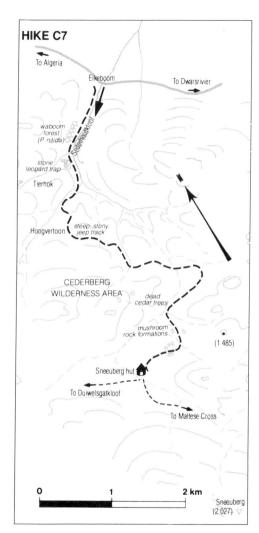

HIKE C7

To Algeria
Eikeboom
To Dwarsrivier
Cederhoutkloof
waboom forest (P. nitida)
stone leopard trap
Tierhok
Hoogvertoon
steep, stony jeep track
CEDERBERG WILDERNESS AREA
dead cedar trees
'mushroom' rock formations
(1 485)
Sneeuberg hut
To Duiwelsgatkloof
To Maltese Cross

0   1   2 km

Sneeuberg (2 027)

which the cedars are not – and this may be one reason for its occurrence here.

▶ The path follows the right-hand bank up the stream and into Tierhok, where an old, stone leopard trap can be seen. I have yet to see a leopard in the Cederberg, but I once saw very fresh spoor right next to this trap.

▶ After nearly one kilometre, the path, which at this stage is a disused jeep track, swings off to the right, up a side gorge, crosses the tributary, and climbs steeply for 160 metres up the Hoogvertoon promontory and away from the stream.

▶ Next it swings southwards, alternately contouring and gently climbing through a rocky area where occasional cedars can be seen growing in rocky recesses

▶ Still following the jeep track, the route crosses two intermittent streams before coming to a permanent river (sometimes more of a bog) four-and-a-half kilometres from the start of the walk. Having crossed the river, the path climbs around the left outside slope of a small spur, before heading up a small (intermittent) stream for a short distance.

▶ The final, two-kilometre stretch to the hut is very easy, crossing a wide sandy plain with numerous sandstone outcrops, some of which have been eroded to resemble mutant fungal growths.

▶ The hut is situated above a small stream, often dry in summer, among a clutch of boulders. An acquaintance once reached this hut in the dark, exhausted after having got lost in a snowstorm. Another party had already 'claimed' the hut and would not grant her and her family entrance, so they had to sleep in the snow without a tent. The moral here is two-fold: firstly, you can never be guaranteed a place in one of the forestry huts, and secondly, the ethic of mountaineering has no place for selfishness. May the party who denied others a place in Sneeuberg hut during a snowstorm have the favour revisited on them.

Sneeuberg Ascent   Hike C8

Route: *From Sneeuberg hut to the top of Sneeuberg*
Distance: *16 kilometres*
Duration: *4 hours (there); 2 hours (back)*
Grade: *Extreme*
Booking Authority: *Algeria Forest Station (Tel. (02682) ask for 3440) (permit needed)*
General Information: *This walk can be done as the second day of either Hike C7 or Hike C9. The route described here is not the shortest, but it is the easiest and safest way to the top of the highest peak in the Cederberg (2 026,8 m). Because Sneeuberg hut is relatively high, the climb here is actually less than the ascent of Tafelberg, a slightly lower peak, described earlier. This route is not for novices, as it requires C-grade rock scrambling with fearful exposure.*

▶ As one walks along the contour path from Sneeuberg hut towards the Maltese Cross, the Sneeuberg towers above you to the right. Looking up at the peak, you will see a prominent gully running up slightly from the left. Where the gully intersects the path, leave the path and ascend the gully.

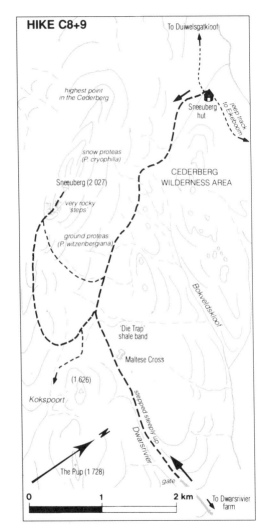

To Duiwelsgatkloof

highest point
in the Cederberg

Sneeuberg
hut

*jeep track
to Eikeboom*

snow proteas
(P. cryophilla)

CEDERBERG
WILDERNESS
AREA

Sneeuberg (2 027)

very rocky
steps

ground proteas
(P. witzenbergiana)

Bokveldskloof

'Die Trap'
shale band

Maltese Cross

(1 626)

Kokspoort

stepped steeply up

Dwarsrivier

The Pup (1 728)

gate

To Dwarsrivier
farm

0   1   2 km

▶ After about 400 metres of steep climbing, you will reach a nek, from where you will be rewarded with fantastic views of the range and lowlands sweeping away to the west.

▶ From the nek you turn right (northwards) to follow the ridge up towards the top of the mountain. As one makes progress towards the summit, the ridge narrows; if you suffer from vertigo this route is not for you. After climbing steadily, you will reach the massive summit 'blocks', and a final 30-metre scramble is all that is needed to reach the top of the mountain.

The peak, as its name suggests, is covered with snow for much of each winter. Also, the route over the summit blocks is iced up during the colder months.

▶ Return the way you have come.

Maltese Cross Route
Hike C9

Route: *From Dwarsrivier to Sneeuberg hut*
Distance: *13 kilometres*
Duration: *2-3 hours (there); 1 hour (back)*
Grade: *Fair*
Booking Authority: *Algeria Forest Station (Tel. (02682) ask for 3440) and Dwarsrivier farm (Address: Nieuwoudt Brothers, Dwarsrivier, P. O. Cederberg 7341) (permit needed)*
General Information: *Although this route goes uphill most of the way, it is nevertheless an easy walk, and a most pleasant one too. The Maltese Cross stands only a few kilometres from the start of this hike, which, consequently, is one of the most popular in*

the mountains. Luckily, most of the visitors are what mountaineers call 'gapers' (they stand and gape at the people climbing the cross, usually uttering remarks about the climbers' insanity; the climbers in turn, being the elitist group that they are, hold gapers' comments in contempt) and so after a quick peer at the cross, they return to Dwarsrivier. This walk is essentially the first day of a two- or multi-day walk, and the choice of what to do from Sneeuberg hut is yours. You could simply retrace your route back to Dwarsrivier farm the next day, or you could try the Sneeuberg ascent (Hike C8), or head for Eikeboom (reverse Hike C7).

From Dwarsrivier farm, drive north up the Driehoek valley for a few hundred metres and take the dirt track off to the left. Follow this jeep track for six and a half kilometres to the wilderness-area gate, making sure to avoid the turn-off to the right after four kilometres. This track is a right-of-way so don't worry about trespassing – though a visit to the Dwarsrivier office is a courteous formality.

▶ Park here and continue up the kloof which lies straight ahead of you, keeping to the right-hand bank above the stream for one and a half kilometres.

▶ After this, the gradient of the path slacks off as it approaches Die Trap shale band. On your left, two peaks rise up, the first and higher of the two being The Pup (1 728 m).

▶ The monolithic cross is reached half a kilometre after reaching the level shale band, upon which a conglomeration of sandstone pillars and boulders stand. The cross rises about 60 metres above a rubble mound, which was once all part of a larger rock mass.

▶ The next one-and-a-half-kilometre stretch is virtually flat, before the path goes up, then down, then up and up some more – parallel to the Sneeuberg's eastern baseline. For two and a half kilometres past the cross, all the streams forded flow down to the right into the Bokveldskloof, which feeds into the Dwarsrivier below.

▶ After a short descent and contour, the path climbs, crossing three small stream beds. Finally, the hut looms up ahead, as the path veers to the right away from the Sneeuberg.

Wolfberg Cracks and Arch
Hike C10

Route: *From Sanddrif campsite to the Wolfberg arch*
Distance: *15 kilometres*
Duration: *3-4 hours (there); 2 hours (back)*
Grade: *Severe*
Booking Authority: *Algeria Forest Station (Tel. (02682) ask for 3440) and Dwarsrivier farm (Address: Nieuwoudt Brothers, Dwarsrivier, P. O. Cederberg 7341) (permit needed)*
General Information: *Much has been written and said about the Wolfberg cracks, but ultimately you have to see and experience them yourself to appreciate their magnificence. I would consider this massive crack system to be the most impressive physical feature of the entire Cederberg. Most of this route falls within the private Dwarsrivier farm, from where permits must be obtained to hike and camp. Only the arch itself and the short approach to it lie within the wilderness area. There is no water along the route, and, unless it is raining, you are sure to need it. I last did this route on a very hot December's day, and suffered for carrying only one litre of water.*

▶ Follow the jeep track from Sanddrif campsite (to get to the campsite, turn left onto a jeep track off the road from Algeria, two kilometres after Dwarsrivier Farm) up through the Valley of the Red Gods – in itself a natural feature well worth spending some time exploring. Sandstone pillars and blocks create a landscape seemingly inhabited by a race of stoic, Olympian-type creatures – they gaze at you coldly but pass no judgment. Drive up to a spot where a group of oak trees provide the last shade for parking or picnicking. From here you can see the path ascending steeply towards the cracks – be sure that it will be higher, steeper and more strenuous than it looks.

▶ The path rises relentlessly for 420 metres over a distance of one kilometre, zigzagging up the scree slope with only the occasional waboom (*Protea nitida*) to provide relief. Just take it slowly, and it will be far less painful than if you try to rush up. Keep to the left-hand path as you go, the red rock turrets looming above.

The cracks are a series of deep, narrow clefts (sometimes as much as 100 metres deep), reaching to the sandstone layer below Die Trap shale band, which were formed at the time that the Cape Folded Mountains came into being. At sunset, when they glow a deep crimson, the rock walls make a superb photographic subject. Furthermore, the cracks offer rock climbers some of the highest quality rock in the country, with routes like Celestial Journey, Wolf in Sheep's Clothing and Red Rain standing out.

▶ Once you have reached the western (left-hand) extreme of the cracks, the main gully giving access to the top of the cracks is just around the corner to the right. This gully is strewn with rocks; negotiating it, however, merely involves boulder-hopping, with some minor scrambling. At the top of the main gully, there is an easy chimney that you will have to slither up as best you can (ask a rock climber how to 'chimney').

If you want to see the 'real' cracks, however, you should be prepared for a mini-adventure (anyone with a large girth might have difficulty making it through the unavoidable wormholes on this route).

At the right-hand base of the main gully you will see a cairn. From there, follow the horizontal rock shelf around to the right. This is an exposed but easy traverse, but be warned: if any members of your party are unfamiliar with this route, it could become dangerous.

Once around the traverse, cross the open ground to another cairn and boulder hop and scramble into the narrow but obvious recess above. Once through this very narrow gap you will find yourself in the main crack.

From here all you have to do is follow the crack. It starts off flat and sandy, with a rock bridge arching right over your head.

After a while you have to boulder hop and scramble over chockstones, climb chimneys,

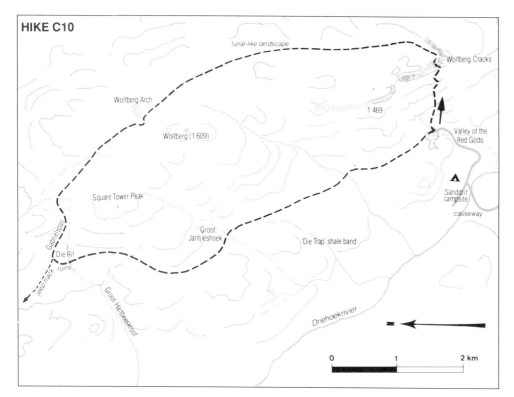

cairn-marked path across the plateau, past the Wolfberg peak, to the arch some six kilometres away. The path follows the basic line along the top of a long cliff that forms the eastern extreme of Die Trap plateau.

The landscape along this section of the walk is quite dry and desolate, with very little growth apart from sparse clumps of restios and lampranthus daisies (a genus of the Karoo-affiliated Mesembryanthemum or 'vygie' family).

The arch itself must be one of the most photographed natural features in the country, especially since access is so easy by way of Gabriëlspas from Die Trap's jeep track south of the Tafelberg (see Hike C12, day 5). The flat floor of the arch makes a fine tea spot.

▶ Return either the same way, making sure to take the right-hand, main gully through the cracks, or else make your way from the arch over the sandy plain to the northwest, and down Gabriëlspas to the left, to the jeep track which runs all along Die Trap shale band. On reaching the jeep track at the ruins of Die Rif farmhouse turn left and continue southwards for seven and a half kilometres to the Sanddrif campsite.

Kromrivier
Hike C11

Route: From Kromrivier farm, up the Kromrivier gorge, to Disa Pool
Distance: 12 kilometres
Duration: 1-2 hours (there); 1-2 hours (back)
Grade: Easy

and squeeze through narrow tunnels. At one point, two consecutive 'wormholes' will have to be negotiated. The second of these is the most problematic: small people will have no trouble, but I had to expel all the air from my lungs, lie on my back and then force myself through by pushing as best I could with my feet and pulling with my hands on handholds at the other end of the hole, all without breathing. Not only do you have to crawl horizontally through the hole, but then climb directly upwards, as the hole is L-shaped.

After that, it's a breeze. Just follow the once-again-easy, shrub-filled gully to Die Trap plateau above the cracks.
▶ Whichever route you have taken, once you are above the cracks, follow the obvious and

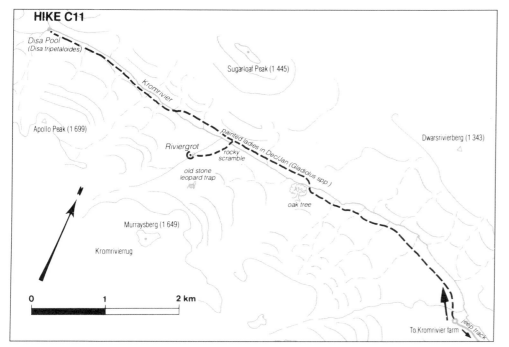

Disa Pool
(Disa tripetaloides)

Sugarloaf Peak (1 445)

Kromrivier

Apollo Peak (1 699)

Riviergrot

painted ladies in Dec/Jan (Gladiolus spp.)

rocky scramble

old stone leopard trap

Dwarsrivierberg (1 343)

oak tree

Murraysberg (1 649)

Kromrivierrug

0   1   2 km

To Kromrivier farm

jeep track

gully on the left. If you look up here you will see a large cave set in the prominent rock band; this is Riviergrot, once used as a shelter by nomadic hunter-gatherers. The inhabitants were, in fact, probably San (Bushmen) as there used to be paintings on the cave walls, though these have long since been vandalized and faded away.

A path leads up this gully to the cave, which is reached by following the cairns through the rocky areas – you can't really get lost. A waterfall pours over the mouth of the cave. In summer when I hiked this way it was reduced to a trickle, but in winter it must make an impressive sight.

▶ If you do not wish to go up to the cave, continue upstream towards Disa Pool. Kromrivier experienced a bad fire some years ago, and the vegetation up the valley was particularly hard hit. But, as is the peculiar way with fynbos, it is after such devastation that the most beautiful flowers flourish. When I walked here in late December the river banks were littered with painted ladies and various ground orchids.

▶ From the pool you can return the same way, or take a path to the right that goes above the cave to a stone leopard trap, and returns to the jeep track at the beginning of the trail.

Booking Authority: *Kromrivier Farm (Address: A. P. C. Nieuwoudt and Son, Kromrivier, P. O. Citrusdal 7340) (permit needed)*
General Information: *This is among the easiest routes described in this book, and is ideal for families with children, especially considering the comfortable (though I think a little overcrowded) accommodation at Kromrivier farm. The walk is gentle all the way, and there is a nice lunch spot at the pool, which marks the turning point of the hike. Watch out for the floral displays at the pool.*

From Algeria drive south past Sanddrif towards the Koue Bokkeveld, turning right at the signpost marked 'Kromrivier'. Get your permits from the Nieuwoudts here before commencing the hike. From the farm, follow a gravel road, across a stream and up the valley for several kilometres, until you reach a grove of pine trees. Park here, and begin your walk.
▶ Follow the path up the Kromrivier, crossing it at the oak tree, and continue up until you are standing opposite the second side

Cederberg Traverse
Hike C12

Route: *Pakhuis to Sanddrif*
Distance: *60,5 kilometres*
Duration: *5 days*

Grade: *Severe*

Booking Authority: *Algeria Forest Station (Tel. (02682) ask for 3440) (permit needed)*

General Information: *In my opinion this is one of the finest hikes in the country, for, not only does it take you through an unsurpassed wilderness area and one of South Africa's finest mountain ranges, but it is really a relatively easy hike. The 'severe' grading is due to the overall length of the hike, the extremes of weather likely to be experienced here, and the area's remoteness. A four-day (46,5-kilometre) variation of this hike – ending at Algeria instead of going to Welbedacht cave on the fourth day – is described; one could even shorten the hike to three days by driving the first stretch from Kliphuis to Heuningvlei. Other variations on the Cederberg traverse have been covered as separate hikes, and still others should be inferred from the excellent 1:50 000 hiking map available at good hiking shops.*

Day 1: Kliphuis to Heuningvlei – 12 kilometres (4 hours)

There is a small but well-serviced public campsite in the Pakhuispas area, called Kliphuis. The traverse begins at a gate, about three kilometres east of the campsite, where a jeep track leads southwards off Pakhuispas. This is opposite to the termination of the Pakhuis ridge, a formation called Faith, Hope and Charity. This jeep track is for use only by conservation vehicles, but it leads the hiker along an easy route all the way to Heuningvlei. If you would rather drive to Heuningvlei, refer to the section at the end of Day 1.

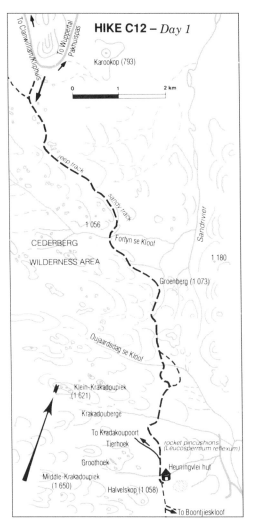

HIKE C12 – *Day 1*

To Clanwilliam/Kliphuis
To Wuppertal/Pakhuispas
Karookop (793)
0   1   2 km
jeep track
sandy track
Sandrivier
1 056
Fortyn se Kloof
CEDERBERG
WILDERNESS AREA
1 180
Groenberg (1 073)
Oujaardsdag se Kloof
Klein-Krakadoupiek (1 621)
Krakadouberge
To Kradakoupoort
Tierhoek
rocket pincushions (*Leucospermum reflexum*)
Groothoek
Heuningvlei hut
Middle-Krakadoupiek (1 650)
Halvelskop (1 058)
To Boontjieskloof

● From Kliphuis, the track to Heuningvlei winds gently uphill, towards a long ridge, for a little over two kilometres. It then passes along the left-hand side of this ridge, until the 'step' (Die Trap) on which the track lies, merges with the general fall-off into the Sandrivier valley to the east.

● After about five kilometres, the track crosses Fortyn Se Kloof, where water is available in all but the very driest summers.

● Having crossed the kloof, the track loops around the general fall of the topography, through three seasonal-river courses, until it passes between two hills the eastern one is Groenberg. This is the watershed between the Sand (flowing north) and Heuningvlei (flowing south) river catchments.

● Keep to the main (right-bearing) jeep track, and so avoid descending to the main Heuningvlei settlement, crossing instead the upper reaches of the Heuningvleirivier, well within the wilderness area. The kloof through which the river flows at this point is called Oujaarsdag se Kloof – an obvious hangover from some historic, probably festive, occurrence here.

● For the next three and a half kilometres, the path skips through some very rocky landscapes, skirting the western perimeter of the valley.

The track is often covered in thick, beach-like sand, which makes walking hard going. Make judicious use of side tracks to save not only your calf muscles, but the ground cover as well.

● Heuningvlei hut backs against a rocky ridge, facing one of the finest remaining stands of cedar trees (*Widdringtonia cedarbergensis*). Directly west of here the Krakadou peaks rise up, showing little of their formidable forms.

You are now in the heartland of the rocket protea's endemic range. Many people are familiar with *Leucospermum reflexum* as a common garden shrub; but few realize how scarce it is in nature – growing only between here and Wuppertal.

To drive to Heuningvlei, you will have to continue over the pass and turn right at the Englishman's grave, towards the Biedou valley and Wuppertal. Pass through the Biedou Valley and over the Heuningvleirivier at Welbedacht farm (one of the most magnificent spring-flower display areas). The road then winds up a long ramp towards a plateau, with some scattered settlements on the right. About 26 kilometres from the Englishman's-grave turn-off, you will see a rural farm; turn off just before it, sharply back to the right. Hereafter the going gets tricky.

The road, more of a track really, is very sandy in places. But don't panic, when you see a sandy stretch ahead, make sure your car is in the equivalent of second or third gear; the idea is to keep a steady speed and course, and, most important, to keep the revs even – neither so high that the wheels will spin, nor so low that you will lose speed and power. Never turn the wheels too sharply when negotiating sand (unless, of course, you have to), as this will cause the car to lose momentum.

About one and a half kilometres from the rural farm ignore the left fork; three kilometres further on you must bear left at another fork which goes towards a small farm on the right – that is not Heuningvlei; one kilometre along a very sandy road, a track forks to the left. Ignore it, as well as a sort of four way crossing another one and a half kilometres further on. Another five kilometres will bring you to a crossing over the Heuningvleirivier. Thereafter turn first left

and then first right, heading for a grove of pine trees on the wilderness area fence line. You can detect the forestry presence here only by a gate and small sign. Heuningvlei hut is to be found by following the jeep track into the wilderness area, to the far end of a large cedar grove. The hut can be seen just north of the grove, on a jeep track coming south from Pakhuis.

Day 2: Heuningvlei to Boontjieskloof – 9,5 kilometres (3 hours)

◗ From Heuningvlei hut, continue along the sandy jeep track for some way. Along this stretch you will be flanked by the stark outline of Krakadou ridge on the right and the Tanqua Karoo in the distance on your left.

◗ After about four kilometres, the road forks: take the right-hand fork, which leads diagonally away from the Heuningvlei valley. Isolated, gnarled cedar trees are fairly common in this area, especially in rocky situations that have been spared the ravages of fire. Two centuries ago these trees formed forests on the rocky slopes and sandy flats of the Cederberg, but their sweet-scented timber fostered a lumber industry among the local populace. It was the woodcutters who built most of the high-quality paths in the Cederberg – for which hikers can be thankful.

◗ Shortly after the fork, the path splits around a koppie: take the left option to avoid going over Groot Koupoort gorge into the Jan Disselsrivier valley. Be on the lookout in summer for poisonous snakes (puff-adders and cobras), though hopefully all you will see are the blue-headed Cape rock agamas and small skinks darting across the track.

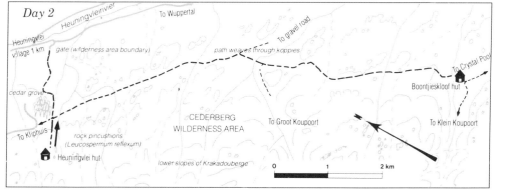

Day 2

▶ The path meanders through fanciful rock formations and impressive boulders. After crossing numerous streams, you will cross a low saddle (about five kilometres from the Koupoort turnoff), and there will be the Boontjieskloof hut nestling in a flat, green valley, backed by a wide, rock amphitheatre on three sides. A perennial stream meanders across the valley from Klein Koupoort, offering some shallow but refreshing pools. The hut here, like all in the Cederberg, is pretty basic compared to National Hiking Way Trail huts, but these huts do offer a (sometimes) flat floor, four walls and a roof against the elements. When the weather turns, which it can do from steaming hot to chilly and blustering overnight, these rustic huts are a welcome sanctuary – just remember they are only available when not used by forestry labourers.

Day 3: Boontjieskloof to Crystal Pool – 12,5 kilometres (5-6 hours)
Although not an unduly long hike, you should allot a whole day to the walk, as it is a sustained, gradual climb all the way to Crystal Pool, along a tortuous path.
▶ From Boontjieskloof, follow the path across the mouth of Klein Koupoort, avoiding all turn-offs to the right. The open 'vlakte' here contain many species of erica and protea.
▶ Thereafter, the path skirts around the poort's southern buttress (missing a left turn to Grasvlei), before entering Skerpioenspoort on the other side of the buttress and parallel to Koupoort.
▶ Skerpioenspoort heralds a three-kilometre-long climb, the agony of which is

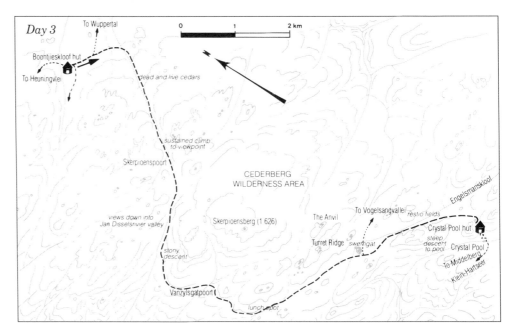

offset by the beauty of the pass: massive red rock walls culminating in the 1 626-metre Skerpioensberg, a puzzle of boulders and outcrops, the grotesque forms of dead cedars, or the welcome sight of large healthy trees, wild flowers and a gurgling brook. During summer, temperatures can exceed 40 °C, while frontal winds are funnelled down the kloof, bringing all manner of tribulations. If the heat is a problem, hike in the early morning and then take shelter from late morning to mid-afternoon. During foul weather, there are numerous natural shelters to choose from.

▶ Numerous false horizons eventually lead onto the real saddle of Skerpioenspoort at about 1 460 metres. From here, the views in both directions are impressive: to the east, the Tanqua Karoo, where a prominent butte focuses one's gaze; to the west, The Dome, Middelberg-Noord and the lesser Warmhoek peak in the middle ground, and the Wolfberg ridge in the background. This is an excellent tea spot, and there are some sheltered spots just before you reach the saddle.
▶ On the far side of the saddle, the path drops down and swings around the lower bases of Skerpioensberg and the abutting ridges.

▶ The third stream reached will be the bottom of Vanzyl'sgatpoort. Here, the path turns upstream, following a gentle uphill valley between Bassonsklip on the right and Turret Ridge on the left. Keep your camera at the ready along here, to record the varied rock forms, the shapes of dead cedar trees and the numerous blooms. Ahead looms Sneeukop, the third highest peak in the range. The shale band known as Die Trap is visible as a broad plinth, upon which most of the higher peaks stand. This area, for me, has all the essential elements of wilderness. I have always been lucky enough to see black eagles in this vicinity, and during my long traverse in the summer of 1989, a breeding pair of mountain raptors was never far away.

▶ At the head of the valley you reach a stream with a couple of lovely pools, one of which is marked 'swemgat' on the map. Be sure to cross the stream near to a lone, large tree on the opposite bank.

▶ The path goes around a low hill on the right-hand (southwestern) side of the stream, and then back along the wide, grassy right-hand bank.

▶ The valley narrows upstream, before emerging once again on a wide grassy plain. The stream continues up Engelsmanskloof, which would take you up to Die Trap at the foot of Sneeukop, where the Sleepad hut is situated.

▶ Follow the path as it swings to the right, away from the stream; Crystal Pool hut is just around the corner (a mere 200 metres away), among a clump of tall eucalyptus trees. Water must be carried from the base of Engelsmanskloof, so fill up bottles and

pots before making for the hut. Unfortunately, the so-called Crystal Pool is to be found past the hut and down a steep, 120-metre ridge. It all depends on how badly you want a swim; there is no place to dip in the stream flowing out of Engelsmanskloof. When washing, remember to move far away from the hut and all running water, as the hut area becomes fouled easily. The path is also badly eroded here, so take due care.

Day 4: Crystal Pool to Welbedacht – 12 kilometres (4 hours)
▶ From Crystal Pool hut, make your way down into Engelsmanskloof around the base of Klein Hartseer.

▶ There is a good path all the way up the right-hand stream bank, and it is a fairly easy, though constant, climb for about one and a half kilometres to the plateau called Die Trap. Here you will hit a T-junction at the base of the impressive Sneeukop peak (1 930 m), the third highest in the Cederberg. Remnants of the old telephone line that once linked all the forestry huts to Algeria can be seen. Sneeukop hut can be found by taking the left-hand path, around the northern base of the peak, for just under three kilometres. But that is not our route...

▶ Turn right, to the southwest, towards Sleepad hut. The path keeps an even contour along Die Trap and reaches the hut after a three-kilometre loop around the base of South Peak. Looking down to your right, the Grootlandsvlakte stretch out below, with Groot Hartseer peak behind to the right and Middelberg-Suid peak up ahead to the right, more or less in line with the Uilsgat Needles.

▶ From the hut, follow the jeep track that runs all along Die Trap, with some gentle ups and downs as it negotiates intermittent stream courses. Avoid the steep path down to Grootland on the right just after leaving the hut.

▶ You pass Shadow Peak (on your left) after two and a half kilometres, then Donkerkloof two kilometres further on. Along this path it can clearly be seen why the The Spout up ahead on the Tafelberg was so named.

▶ Two kilometres after passing Sederhoutkop (at the base of Donkerkloof) you will reach a side-junction that leads off at right angles to the left, towards Langkloof. Pass this, and about 100 metres further on you will reach another side junction, this time to the right, down which you must turn and head over the edge of Die Trap into a gully with a perennial stream.

At this point, Tafelberg is still a few kilometres ahead, but you will be standing opposite the saddle between Langberg and Consolation Peak, which looms up directly in front of the Tafelberg.

▶ Welbedacht cave is easy to spot, a mere 500 metres down the gully on the left-hand side (the 1:50 000 map shows the cave to be situated on a ridge well above the stream but don't be fooled). Welbedacht forestry substation (an old farm house) is situated at the bottom of this gully, where the stream joins a wooded valley at the base of Die Trap.

For the four-day alternative to this hike, one can do the 13-kilometre (5-hour) walk from Crystal Pool to Algeria on the fourth day. From Crystal Pool hut,

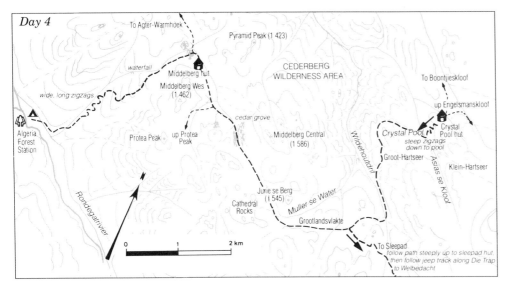

follow the path down a steep slope to the Crystal Pool. The pool gets its name from its sandy bottom that sparkles brightly through the clear water in sunlight. A species of tree erica, *Erica caffra*, grows on the banks of the pool, as well as other delicate riverine flowers.

The path traverses an open plain here, passing some enormous boulders at the far end. It winds on a fairly level course through a series of rocky ridges, heading for the base of Groot Hartseer peak.

From the base of Groot Hartseer, the path drops steeply into the Wildehoutdrif river gorge, zigzagging as it makes a sharp descent for approximately one kilometre down to the river.

From here, it follows the river upstream for another kilometre, with two crossings en route. The path is steep but in excellent condition, being one of the historic woodcutters' tracks.

The trail then turns sharply to the right, and climbs steeply out of the valley. The scenery here is most pleasing, with many colours of bloom covering the valley slopes – white and yellow daisies, lace-like selago flower heads, the bright green of bracken and Cape bamboo (*Elegio capensis*).

Having exited the valley, the path crosses the Grootlandsvlakte. An intermittent stream flows gently across the flats, where the burnt-out trunks of cedars stand forlornly. On crossing the stream, you may see

a large bearded protea (*Protea magnifica*) bush in full bloom, with Sneeukop standing proudly in the background.

A cursory rock shelter can be found at the far end of the vlakte, and from here the path begins an easy ascent up to the head of a stream known as Muller se Water, which flows off to the right. The series of jagged rocky outcrops to the left are collectively called Cathedral Rocks; ahead to the right, two kilometres from Muller se Water, is Middelberg Central peak (1 586 m).

Continue past the head of Muller se Water across the open sandy plain known as Geelvlei. Here you will see some of the few remaining groves of mature cedar forest, but even some of these bear the scars of fire and felling.

About three kilometres from the head of Muller se Water the path descends fairly steeply towards Middelberg West peak. A minor path leads off to the left along here, just before a marshy stream, to ascend Protea Peak (1 486 m) – unless you are looking for more adventure, ignore it.

From here, the path winds down a wide woodcutters' trail (built to exploit the forests on Geelvlei) to the hut on Middelbergvlakte – another place where cedar forests once grew. During midsummer you will probably come across the demure white-and-pink heads of *Gladiolus carneus* blooms, the large painted lady.

From Middelberg hut, follow the path around Middelberg Wes peak (1 462 m), following the stream. If you are stealthy, you could see black ducks paddling in the stream here. These birds are quite common in the region's mountain streams. An infestation of invader wattle trees around the hut has been addressed, but a second generation of saplings is starting to appear – pull out any you see. (From Middelberg hut, a little-used path heads due north and then circles around to complete a circular route from Algeria. I have never done this walk, but from the map it looks as if this could be an extremely satisfying, and rugged, one- or two-day circular outing.)

The path enters a narrow valley overgrown with cedars. Go through the valley to emerge at Boshoek, where fantastic scenery awaits you. The stream falls away sharply to the right into Watervalkloof with a magnificent waterfall below (this can be reached via a side path from Algeria). The vegetation here is very lush, with a range of tones through the greens and reds. With the right light, it offers exciting photographic options.

The path now breaks out along a promontory from Boshoek on the left, and thereafter zigzags steeply down for 600 metres to

Algeria. The pool behind the causeway over the river beckons long before you reach it; follow the call, that swim is bliss.

Day 5: Welbedacht to Sanddrif – 15 kilometres (5 hours)

▶ This a fairly long walk but, as it follows a well-defined track the whole way, it is easy going. From Welbedacht cave, make your way back up to the contour path on Die Trap, and, at the T-junction, turn right.

▶ Follow the path along the base of Consolation Peak with Tafelberg looming up behind it, and descend about 40 metres to cross Waterkloof stream after three and a half kilometres.

▶ The path then rounds a side spur of Corridor Peak, and, for the next two and a half kilometres, keeps on descending to the ruins of the old Die Rif farm, with some large shade oaks (you descend 120 metres from the base of Consolation Peak to Die Rif).

▶ At the farm, the track meets a four-way junction: one path heads down the

Hartbeeskloof, another ascends Gabriëlspas, but our route continues along the jeep track and ascends gently around Square Tower Peak (1 579 m), onto the shale band known as Die Trap. Gabriëlspas climbs up over the range to descend Gabriëlskloof on the far side; on reaching the upper sandy plateau, however, a path heads off diagonally to the right, towards Wolfberg arch.

▶ For the last six kilometres, the jeep track follows a stream as it slowly makes its way down the shale band through the Valley of the Red Gods to Sanddrif campsite. This stretch is all through private land, and, to camp at Sanddrif, a permit must be obtained from the nearby Dwarsrivier farm. Here you can also buy petrol, and a number of excellent cultivars from the local vineyards. The current batch of both whites and reds are immediately drinkable; some crisp, dry whites are subtle and lively (Pinot Gris), while the better reds are good for laying down – which is just what you will want to be doing at the end of a Cederberg traverse!

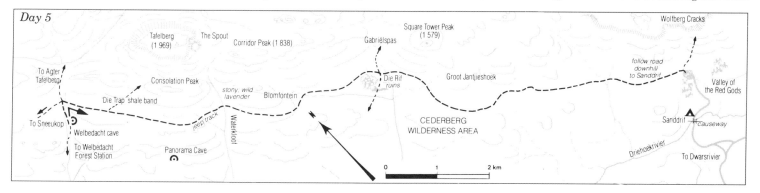

Day 5

GROOT-WINTERHOEK

To me, the most impressive aspect of the rugged Groot-Winterhoek range is its abundance of flowering plants, most numerous of which are the many species of erica. Since a fire in 1988, which ravaged the entire range, the veld has erupted in a blaze of colour. Masses of daisies (genera *Aristea*, *Euryops*, *Senecio* and *Anthanasia*), mauve watsonias, yellow wackendorfias, orchids and a number of Proteaceae provide a festive welcome for those who visit the region. Most Proteaceae, however – the true proteas, the leucospermums, and some of the smaller, less-conspicuous genera such as *Spatalla* and *Aulax* – will take longer to re-establish themselves. Where they have survived burning, the proteas present a magnificent floral display of species such as *cynaroides* (king), *magnifica* (bearded), *nana* (mountain rose), *grandiceps*, *laurifolia*, *nitida* (waboom), *repens* (sugarbush) and *witzenbergiana*, which can be equalled in few places.

Game and birdlife in the Groot-Winterhoek region are nowhere near as obvious as the floral attractions, but hikers are likely to see baboon, grey rhebok, klipspringer and grysbok among other mammals. From spoor and dropping counts, it has been established that at least nine leopards share the territory. The most conspicuous birds are rock kestrels, jackal buzzards, an occasional black eagle, ground woodpeckers and rock jumpers, yellowrumped bishops in the vlei areas, and some frustratingly obscure warblers and cisticolas.

So impressive is the towering Groot-Winterhoekpiek that, until 1892 when the Hex River's Matroosberg was measured at 2 249 metres, it was believed to be the highest peak in the western Cape. In 1899, Dr R. Marloth, who was then vice president of the MCSA, said that as interesting, and worth visiting, as every mountain in the region was, 'there is none which I admire more than the Groot-Winterhoek'.

In 1961, a party led by Jeff Goy set off from Saron up the Vier en twintig Riviere valley, which forms the mouth of Die Hel. The first part – up to the point where the river forks around the main Groot-Winterhoek massif – was reasonably easy. From here, the party followed the right-hand stream, away from Die Hel (by far the easier of the two routes) and on towards Sneeugat. It was a heavy one-day slog up to the first junction at Vier en twintig Riviere, but the next section proved to be an epic.

It included large pools that had to be swum, boulders and waterfalls blocking the gorge that had to be negotiated, and steep-sided kloofs that had to be overcome to reach the Sneeugat valley. The entire circumnavigation of the Groot-Winterhoek took the party a week.

Hiking in the Groot-Winterhoek
As is suggested by the name Groot-Winterhoek, visitors to this wilderness area should be prepared for wind, rain and snow throughout the year, although 80 per cent of the region's precipitation falls between April and September.

The range's two most impressive physical features are its highest and lowest points: Groot-Winterhoekpiek itself, and Die Hel gorge through which the Vier en twintig Riviere river rushes.

The climb up the main peak can be accomplished by a fit party in about 12 hours – but only if they have a good route description. If not, it could take their whole lives. The popular route up the Groot-Winterhoek (2 078 m) is from Sneeugat, above Tulbagh, along Ridge Peak to the true summit. Although this route is a fairly standard climb for experienced mountaineers, I do not recommend it to the general hiker.

Routes in the Groot-Winterhoek wilderness area tend to be – relative to, say, the Cederberg – either easy or extreme. There are 90 kilometres of footpaths in the area, and most of them follow easy contours along the Groot-Kliphuis, Klein-Kliphuis and Vier en twintig Riviere rivers. The others are reserved for well-prepared mountaineers. The first category of hikes will be fully described, while I will give a hint of the other

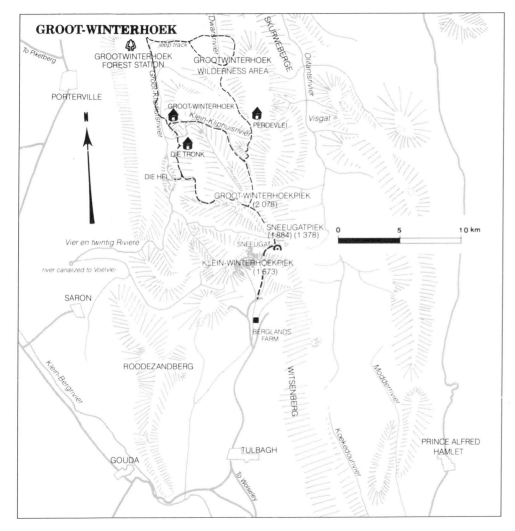

GROOT-WINTERHOEK

possibilities: enough to tempt you but not enough to take away your own sense of mountaineering achievement.

Access to the wilderness area is usually over the Dasklippas above Porterville, but from Tulbagh it is possible to obtain a permit to cross farmland to the Sneeugat area – though this is closed to the public between November and April, when the fruit is vulnerable. Only 12 people are allowed into the wilderness area at any one time, and no-one is permitted to overnight in Die Hel gorge. There are three huts in the wilderness area, all previously farm buildings, and all situated in the vicinity of the Groot-Winterhoek farm. The so-called huts at Perdevlei and Groot-Kliphuis are no more than ruins which afford little shelter in rain or snow. These buildings are the only accommodation in the Groot-Winterhoek, though camping is allowed anywhere except Die Hel gorge.

A number of traditions that made the Winterhoek experience so enjoyable to Dr Marloth are no longer possible. In 1899 he wrote: 'Ask me what is the height of enjoyment and I say to bathe in the foaming brook, the evening meal in the flickering light or the sudden glare of burning heather, the sleep on a bed provided by nature (after a long toil (author's brackets))' at the campsite to which 'boys with our sleeping gear had been dispatched directly'. Well, today you may not light a fire in a wilderness area, you may not pick the vegetation for your nightly comfort, you should never use any detergent in natural water and men and boys must now carry in and out all their own requirements.

Circular Day Walk   *Hike G1*

Route: *East from the Groot-Winterhoek Forest Station*
Distance: *13 kilometres*
Duration: *4 hours*
Grade: Fair
Booking Authority: *Groot-Winterhoek Forest Station (Tel. (02623) 2900) (permit needed)*
General Information: *Before setting out on this hike, it is advisable to consult the fauna and flora display charts while you are getting your permit at the forestry station, to check what you are likely to see en route. The route is simple to follow through the incredibly weathered rock formations on the sandy flats, and it joins a jeep track for part of the way. While the rock formations are similar to those of the Cederberg, the vegetation here is far more lush than the more northerly wilderness region.*

▶ Set off from the forest station along the main path leading southwards towards the Groot-Winterhoekberge, through a break in the fence. After a few hundred metres, having rounded a small koppie, look out for a cairn: this marks your departure from the south-bound route.
▶ Take the path to the left here, and follow it as it moves off in an easterly direction, across a sandy plain at the head of the Groot-Kliphuisrivier valley.
▶ The path crosses two minor streams on the plain; the first of which is easiest crossed near the pump station. The river flows over

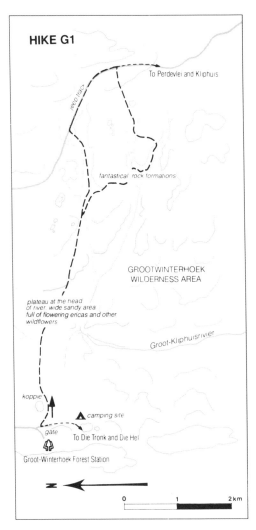

a series of sandstone ridges, creating numerous small waterfalls and pools.
▶ From the pump station, the path heads directly east and is easy to follow. A lone monolithic rock stands up to the right of the path, just a small indication of the spectacular formations that await you. As the path begins a gentle climb, the occurrence of rock formations increases; each one should be closely observed for they are masterpieces of natural, abstract sculpture.
▶ About 200 metres beyond the edge of the open plain, look out for a cairn that marks a path leading off to the right. Take this path and – following the cairns – begin an adventure through a most fascinating landscape of weathered sandstone.
▶ After about two kilometres of this rock-sculpture garden, the path swings around to follow an easterly course, winding its way over rocky ridges and intervening valleys. The sandy valley floors are covered with restios, and interwoven with numerous flowers such as mauve dilatris blooms, white and pink ericas, watsonias, gladioluses, and senecio and other daisy-like flowers. For most of the year, you can stop at numerous places here to quench your thirst with icy mountain water, against a backdrop of the bulky Groot-Winterhoekpiek.

The rocky outcrops create greatly varying microclimates, and consequently you will find aloes, vygies and other succulent plants in one area, bearded proteas in another, and yellowwood trees in yet another.

Rock jumpers, protea seedeaters, marsh harriers, and other bird species may be seen; klipspringers and grey rhebok can also be spotted sometimes, and their abundant spoors suggest that they are fairly numerous. Though snakes occasionally show themselves, it is the skinks, rock agamas and girdled rock lizards that are the most numerous and interesting of the animals here (unless of course you are lucky enough to see a feline predator). Take some time to get to know these harmless reptiles; your patience will be rewarded. They are insatiably curious, and a mating pair can be greatly entertaining as one chases the other round the rocks. Enticing them to you is not a difficult task, especially if a morsel is offered. I have seen large agamas that are used to hikers, running up to a newly arrived group and leaping onto a leg, scaring the wits out of the unsuspecting person.

While you are watching the lizards, a family of dassies may slowly emerge on a sunny ledge to observe you. Here there is something new around every corner – stop frequently, listen and look around you.

A number of tall rocks, with some yellowwood trees growing among them, form a cluster of shady resting places. This is a good place to stop for lunch.

▶ From the rock-cluster the path makes its way up to the top of the ridge, where wonderful views of the surrounding mountains with intermediate landscapes of weathered rock forms are provided. As you wander down to the eastern plain, keep a look out for different types of erica, various proteas, mimetes, other Proteaceae and phyllica bushes. This is a good place to identify some of the lesser known genera of the protea family, as well as some less conspicuous

ground proteas. In damp spots, you should see sundews and orchids hiding between the restio stems.

▶ After crossing another restio-covered plain, the path meets a jeep track. To the right the track leads to the Groot-Kliphuis area, but our way is to the left for about three kilometres, back to the parking area. This section is an easy stroll, but the track is covered with loose sand in places, which makes walking tricky.

▶ After fording a few small streams, the path crosses a more substantial river; look carefully here for the cairn that marks your turn-off to the left. If you reach a gate across the jeep track you have gone too far.

Where the path weaves between the northerly edge of the rock garden and then back across the restio plain, be on the lookout for the rhebok that frequent the area. These medium-sized antelope are the most common species in the mountains, but their shy habits make them hard to spot.

▶ After 10 kilometres, the path rejoins your outward-bound trail, and the last section of the route simply retraces your steps back along the restio plain to the forestry station – a satisfying and easy day's outing.

Die Hel   Hike G2

Route: *From the Groot-Winterhoek Forest Station, down the Groot-Kliphuisrivier, to Die Hel – and then back*
Distance: *30 kilometres*
Duration: *3 days*
Grade: *Moderate*

Booking Authority: *Groot-Winterhoek Forest Station (Tel. (02623) 2900) (permit needed)*
General Information: *The duration given here is designed to give hikers a full day to explore the wonders of Die Hel gorge, in the upper reaches of the Vier en twintig Riviere valley. Otherwise, this hike can be shortened to a two-day outing. The best time to do this hike is in early to midsummer, when water is plentiful and the weather is conducive to wallowing in the huge pool in Die Hel. On this hike, you will never be far from water, and there are numerous pools along the way for dipping in. If I were to give star ratings to hikes, this one would get five.*

Day 1: Forest station to Die Tronk hut – 12 kilometres (3-4 hours)
▶ From the car park near the forest station, follow the jeep track south past the wilderness boundary fence.
▶ Just beyond the fence take the path off to the left, towards a small outcrop of rocks. It is easy to follow the path as it meanders slowly downhill, passing an overnight shelter which can be seen on the left, until the path swings to the right and parallel to the Groot-Kliphuisrivier.
▶ Following the Groot-Kliphuisrivier valley, the path meanders along the river's right-hand bank. The trail is well marked with cairns when it crosses rocky areas. Fantastically shaped sandstone outcrops give a sense of surrealism to the place, exaggerated when weather conditions wash the scene with ever-changing light patterns. In marshy areas, where tall eligia and

leucadendron plants grow, Cape bishops with their black-and-yellow plumage dart about their nests. Raptors include marsh harriers, black-shouldered kites, jackal buzzards, and the occasional black eagle.

▶ Eventually, the path reaches a causeway over the river. A pool below the causeway offers a good swimming spot, where adventurous fingerlings come to nibble you in unexpected places. Shade here makes this a good spot for a snack or lunch.

▶ Cross the causeway, and from thereon follow the jeep track, which winds above the Groot-Kliphuisrivier, on the left-hand side, and then down to cross the bridge on the Klein-Kliphuisrivier just above the confluence of the two.

▶ From the bridge, the track turns away from the valley, up a stony hill to the Groot-

Winterhoek buildings. You may be asked to show your permit to the forester here.

▶ Die Tronk hut is found around a koppie to the left, among a grove of tall eucalyptus trees. The hut is a simple three-roomed structure with no fittings. A third hut is on the far eastern (left-hand) side of the open field across which the first hut faces.

Day 2: Exploring Die Hel – 6 kilometres (2 hours) (for there and back)

▶ From the hut, return to the jeep track, and follow it through the pine plantation (slowly being felled) and cross the small stream at the log bridge which was burned by the 'great' fire. Keep to the jeep track as it follows close to the edge of the rocky ridge on your left. A second track cuts across the open veld to the right and although it looks at first

to be the better route, it soon fades to nothing, and then you will be left to scramble up, down and over numerous rocky gullies and the intervening scrub.

▶ The main (left-bearing) jeep track skirts the top of the west-tending gullies that fall away into the Vier en twintig Riviere gorge. The track narrows to a path that, in some places, is deeply eroded.

▶ Follow this path through the burnt-out protea veld – where watsonia and aristeas now bloom – as it dips around a towering outcrop and into a gully, from where the main gorge of Die Hel can first be seen.

▶ A path enters the gorge below a waterfall, where the river plunges into a huge, dark and mysterious pool. Situated on a ledge above the river is a cave, where faint rock paintings can just be discerned. Not many

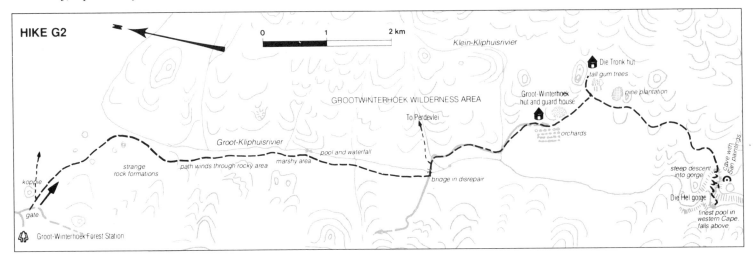

HIKE G2

0   1   2 km

Klein-Kliphuisrivier

Die Tronk hut

tall gum trees

pine plantation

GROOTWINTERHOEK WILDERNESS AREA

Groot-Winterhoek hut and guard house

To Perdevlei

orchards

Cave with San paintings

Groot-Kliphuisrivier

pool and waterfall

path winds through rocky area

marshy area

bridge in disrepair

steep descent into gorge

strange rock formations

koppie

gate

Die Hel gorge

finest pool in western Cape, falls above

Groot-Winterhoek Forest Station

Cederberg

1. *From the top of Skerpioenspoort, looking west between the Boontjieskloof and Crystal Pool huts, you can see the mountains of the Cederberg stretching off into the distance.*
2. *A waterfall in front of the cave near the Kromrivier soothes the fire-ravaged kloof.*
3. *The rocket pincushion* (Leucospermum reflexum) *is a rare member of the protea family, being found only around Heuningvlei and Wuppertal in the wild, though it is a popular garden shrub.*
4. *Seen here from Eikeboom on the Uitkyk-Sanddrif road, the Cederberg Tafelberg slumbers under its winter blanket.*

5

5. *Clusters of mauve 'red-root' (*Dilatris pilansii) *flowers, khaki restios and scarlet pincushions dominate the veld on the Heuningvlei side of the Krakadou peaks.*
6. *Viewed from Die Trap shale band above Welbedacht cave, sunset smears the sandstone cliffs of the Tafelberg, The Spout and Consolation Peak with burnished copper.*
7. *The Anvil, seen here from Engelsmanskloof, protrudes above Chisel Ridge.*

8

8. *After a spring storm at Crystal Pool, a rainbow offers its promise of better things to follow.*

9. *Shangri-la of the Cape mountains, Wuppertal mission village lies in a secluded corner of the Tra-trarivier valley.*

10. *From within the Wolfberg cracks, a hiker peers out across Sanddrif to the ridges flanking the Kromrivier kloof.*

11. *Chisel Ridge looms through the amber twilight gloom, near Sneeukop peak.*

12. *The view north from Welbedacht cave is barred by the ridges and peaks of Middelberg.*

13. *Some of the weird rock formations for which the Cederberg is famous are silhouetted against the sun to appear stranger still.*

14. *A hot day in Wuppertal – where summer temperatures can rise to above 40 ℃ – can be relieved by a trip to Dassieboskloofrivier.*

15. *From Boontjieskloof, the path up Groot Koupoort indicates the beginning of a roundabout route back to Algeria.*

9

10

16

17

16. *Of the forests of* Widdringtonia cedarbergensis *trees that once graced these high mountain valleys, only scattered carcasses remain. It is these Clanwilliam cedars that lent their name to this rugged range.*

17. *Middelberg hut is perhaps the most popular destination for hikers setting off from the Algeria Forest Station. The huts in the Cederberg are old woodcutters' shacks and may be used by hikers only when not occupied by forestry workers.*

18. *Dwarsrivierberg terminates across the Driehoekrivier valley, seen from Uitsig at the top of the Cederberg pass.*

18

Groot-Winterhoek

1. *From the upper reaches of the Groot-Kliphuisrivier valley, the massive bulk of Groot-Winterhoekpiek is diminished by foreshortening.*
2. *Fire is both a destroyer and a regenerator of the mountain fynbos: after a devastating fire in the wilderness area, watsonias burst into bloom at the base of Groot-Winterhoekpiek.*
3. *Rugged rock formations and colourful flower carpets greet hikers throughout the Groot-Winterhoek mountains.*
4. *Pink and orange ericas add bright splashes of colour to the Groot-Kliphuisrivier valley.*
5. *A weary hiker contemplates a plunge into Die Hel's deep pool, surely the most enchanting mountain pool in the western Cape.*
6. *The white bells of* Erica scariosa *decorate the mountainside near the Groot-Winterhoek Forest Station.*
7. *A makeshift footbridge carries hesitant backpackers across a side gully of the Groot-Kliphuisrivier valley.*

6

5

7

8. *The small pink flowers of* Geissorhiza exscapa *are, like all the other species of this genus, confined to the Cape Province.*

9. *The route to Die Tronk hut and Die Hel gorge is punctuated by pools such as this one.*

10. *Hikers descend to Lone Tree Camp in the Sneeugat valley above Tulbagh. The ridge on the right is part of the Witsenberg range, while the base of the mighty Groot-Winterhoek peak looms directly ahead.*

1. Bulbinella frutescens *lilies flourish in the Suurvlak vlei, lying on a high plateau between New Year's, Kromrivier and Hawekwa peaks. Dutoitspiek and Goudini-Sneeukop are seen in the distance.*
2. *Groot Wellington-Sneeukop guards the approach down into the Witrivier valley, between Dutoitskloof and Bain's Kloof passes.*
3. *Junction Pool is a traditional mountaineers' landmark on the Limietberg Trail.*
4. *A nature lover explores above the falls at one of the numerous pools in the Bobbejaansrivier gorge, hunting for red disas.*

5. *On the Klein Wellington-Sneeukop ascent, the vista sweeps up from the junction of the Bobbejaans and Wit rivers, past Bain's Kloof Pass to Limietkop.*
6. *This is how glorious summer hiking days should be spent, resting up in the riverine shade of Happy Valley.*
7. *This little-known and seldom-visited waterfall in the Elandskloof mountains is the site of a proposed hydro-electric dam.*

years ago, these were clearly visible, but humans seem unable to leave be anything unusual. Recent interpretations have shown that San rock paintings such as these are not mere artistic impressions of the outside world. Rather, they are spiritual images through which a clan communicated with the supernatural world of gods and spirits. The artists were always the shamans, and all these paintings were executed while the so-called witchdoctor was in a trance state. The paintings are, therefore, the San equivalent of the icons in a cathedral. These caves are truly holy places and to damage them in any way is akin to desecrating a church. Because of damage that has been done, fires and overnighting in this cave, or anywhere in Die Hel, are prohibited.

▶ The path drops almost vertically down from the cave, covered with loose rocks and scree in places. Care should be taken on your descent to avoid harm both to yourself and to the path.

▶ Once at the gorge bottom, impressive walls rise up on all sides, with huge rounded boulders and potholes marking the river course. If fully prepared for a kloofing trip, it is possible to follow the Vier en twintig Riviere all the way to Saron; if not, content yourself with a stroll down to the second waterfall.

▶ At the huge pool below the main waterfall, shade is provided by numerous water witels (*Brachylaena neriifolia*) trees and one magnificent, spreading yellowwood tree. On the far side of the pool, there is an enormous tunnel-like cave that is home to thousands of bats. The cave extends into the side of the gorge for about 100 metres. It can be reached by swimming the pool, or by a scramble over the far ledge with a final, tricky bouldering move in finger-pinch grips (and a length of fence wire to grab when all else fails).

▶ It is hard to leave the charms of the gorge to gain the upper level, some 130 metres above. The walk back to Die Tronk hut should take little over an hour.

Day 3: Die Tronk hut to forest station – 12 kilometres (4-4½ hours)
▶ The trip back retraces your route all the way to the car park. You are unlikely to find the return trip boring, however, as there is so much to take in that one trip is not enough to appreciate it all.

Perdevlei Semicircular Hike   *Hike G3*

Route: *Groot-Winterhoek Forest Station, via Kliphuisrivier to Perdevlei and Groot-Kliphuis*
Distance: 21,5 kilometres
Duration: 2 days
Grade: Moderate
Booking Authority: *Groot-Winterhoek Forest Station (Tel. (02623) 2900) (permit needed)*
General Information: *Another five-star, easy hike in this seldom-visited wilderness area. The route follows rivers for most of its duration; crosses sandy flats where, in spring, rich fynbos erupts with ericas, geophytic flowers and restios; and wanders through wonderfully weathered sandstone formations. Water is plentiful along the route, and many swimming spots are encountered. The scenery along this hike is exceptional, moving as it does between the rugged Voorberg and impressive Groot-Winterhoek mountain ranges. The 'hut' at Perdevlei is little more than a ruin, and provides scant protection from rain and snow.*

Day 1: Groot-Winterhoek Forest Station to Perdevlei – 11 kilometres (3-4 hours)
▶ From the forest station's car park, follow the path down the Groot-Kliphuisrivier, as in Hike G1. Cross the causeway at Driebosfontein, the halfway mark on the first day's walk. (The path from the causeway to the Perdevlei shelter is a continual, though mostly gradual, eight-kilometre uphill trek.)
▶ Follow the jeep track, keeping a careful look out for the footpath that leads off to the left about 100 metres after you have crossed the causeway (not before, as shown on the 1:50 000 map).
▶ Take this path up a steady gradient to the left of two prominent points, until it levels off on a wide nek. The path becomes hard to distinguish in places, but by following the numerous cairns your safe passage is assured up this natural ramp.
▶ From the top of the ramp, the path descends easily into the Klein-Kliphuisrivier valley, and follows the left-hand bank of the river upstream. The slopes of the river valley are dotted with the gnarled forms of old waboom (*Protea nitida*) trees. These tree proteas may reach a height of 20 metres under favourable conditions. On these slopes, the tectonic folding that gives the

Cape Supergroup of rocks its distinct form, is clearly evident.

▶ After rounding two large spurs, you will be offered a grand view of the valley.

▶ Continue along the path, but do not deceive your feet into believing that the ruins you see now are where they'll be putting themselves up for the night; that place is a good distance on. The stand of eucalyptus trees is, however, a good place to give them a rest.

▶ A little way past the trees, you will reach a junction: the left-hand option proceeds up a side gully to Groot-Kliphuis, whereas the right-hand path keeps parallel to the main Klein-Kliphuisrivier valley – though from here upward it is little more than an intermittent stream or sponge, drying up altogether in late summer. The drainage line is marked by the green stems of Cape bamboo (*Elegio capensis*), the largest member of the restio family. In places, the path becomes indiscernible so you must take heed to follow the cairns.

▶ For the last kilometre, both paths steepen a little, and then climb out of the valley for the final 300-metre climb to the Perdevlei Hut. If you approach the hut stealthily, you may be lucky enough to put a curious steenbok to flight. This antelope's name derives from its brick red colour and not from any preference for stony terrain. You may also see some baboon and genet spoor.

▶ The hut is within a one-minute walk of a large, clear pool, perfect for an afternoon – or full moon, if you have the urge – dip. Remember not to let any detergents get into this uncontaminated water (who wants to swim in someone else's dirty sink?).

*Day 2: Perdevlei to the forester's station –
10,5 kilometres (3-4 hours)*

▶ It is advisable to leave the hut before the temperature gets up, as the initial stage of the second day's outing is up a steep ascent.

▶ Follow the jeep track northwards, zigzagging up the eastern side of a hill, gaining 300 metres in altitude, before crossing over to the western side. About four kilometres from Perdevlei, take the left-hand turn along the jeep track near the top of the climb. The

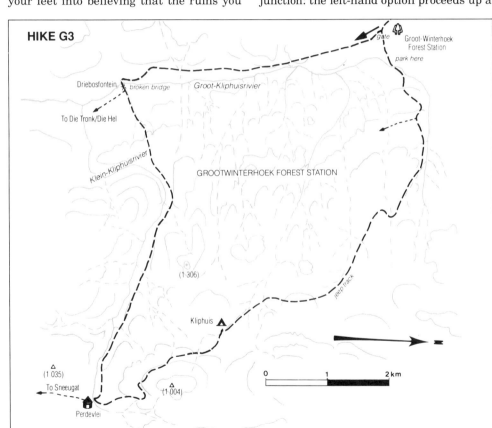

HIKE G3

Groot-Winterhoek Forest Station
gate
park here

Driebosfontein
broken bridge
Groot-Kliphuisrivier

To Die Tronk/Die Hel

Klein-Kliphuisrivier

GROOTWINTERHOEK FOREST STATION

(1 306)

jeep track

Kliphuis

0   1   2 km

△
(1 035)
To Sneeugat

△
(1 004)

Perdevlei

right-hand track will take you to a South African War blockhouse 20 minutes' walk away, and from here the panoramic views are spectacular. The views at the highest point of the climb are quite spectacular, stretching towards the Groot-Winterhoek and over the Swartland towards the Piketberg. You should see *Protea magnifica* bushes along the side of the track – they flower from spring to midsummer.

◗ On the descent to Groot-Kliphuis, the vegetation becomes more grassy, and less like typical fynbos. Various grass species, such as rooigras, do occur in the fynbos zone, but nowhere are they dominant. You will see the gutted ruins of the old Groot-Kliphuis farm up ahead, and you can marvel at the men and women who lived here, eking out precarious livings in these magnificent but unfertile surroundings. Whatever could be raised here would be at the mercy of baboons, leopard and lynx.

◗ Stop and have lunch in the vicinity of the old farm. Water is abundant here, so fill up your water containers, as the final stretch to the forest station will be dry in all but the wettest months.

◗ The last section of the hike is across virtually flat terrain, with little shade and with a glare thrown up from the quartzitic sandstone covering the jeep track. The track winds through bizarrely weathered sandstone outcrops, with the intervening sandy flats carpeted with grasses and restios, and sprinkled with wildflowers. The rock formations here have not been created by sand and wind, or even whipping rain as most people would think. They are the result of chemical weathering, caused by the weak carbolic acid solution formed by standing rain water.

◗ About four kilometres from Groot-Kliphuis, look for the cairn on the left-hand side of the jeep track, which marks your path leading off to the left. This path takes you on an easy and more-or-less direct course for the forestry station. On this final stretch, be on the lookout for grysbok, klipspringers and rhebok. Follow the cairns to make the walk easier, or you could find yourself bundu bashing unnecessarily.

◗ Where you cross the Groot-Kliphuisrivier, you will see a jeep track leading to the forest station; but keep left along the footpath for the easier, shorter route back to your starting point at the car park.

Sneeugat   *Hike G4*

Route: *From Tulbagh, through Berglands farm, to Sneeugat valley and back*
Distance: *13 kilometres*
Duration: *3-4 hours (there); 2 hours (back)*
Grade: *Severe*
Booking Authority: *Groot-Winterhoek Forest Station (Tel. (02623) 2900) and Berglands farm (permit needed)*
General Information: *Sneeugat is a high valley surrounded by the imposing peaks of the Winterhoek and Witsenberg ranges (10 of the peaks are over 1 800 metres high). The scenery is fantastic, with vegetation comprising a number of interesting species, and waterfalls such as the Grand or Tulbagh Falls on the upper Vier en twintig Riviere system. You will need to get permission from the owner of Berglands farm to cross his land – his phone number is obtainable from the MCSA (021) 453412.*

Since November to April is fruit-picking time in the Tulbagh valley, this is also the time that the abutting Klein- and Groot-Winterhoek areas are closed to mountaineers – access to these areas being through orchards and vineyards. Sneeugat bowl is the major catchment area of the Klein-Bergrivier, and its name should suggest something of its character – 'snow hole', nestling as it does in the shadow of the 'great' and 'little winter corner' mountains.

From Tulbagh, take the main road north out of the town. After eight kilometres you will reach a fork; follow the signpost to 'Winterhoek'. At the next fork, follow the sign to 'Misgund'. Cross a river, whereafter the road becomes gravel, and then turn left to the farm marked 'Berglands'. Proceed through the orchards to a reservoir at the end of the road at Berglands farm. You should already have obtained your permit to enter the wilderness area, and made arrangements to cross the private farm land. Check in at the farm house.

◗ Follow the farm road past the sheds, heading towards the mountains for about 100 metres. Our path leads off from the farm road, through an orchard, and ascends a low, stony ridge, all the while looking in the general direction of the Sneeugat nek. For a while, the path keeps to the crest of the ridge between two gullies.

◗ Shortly, you will enter a small, cool glade of yellowwood trees, where moss- and lichen-

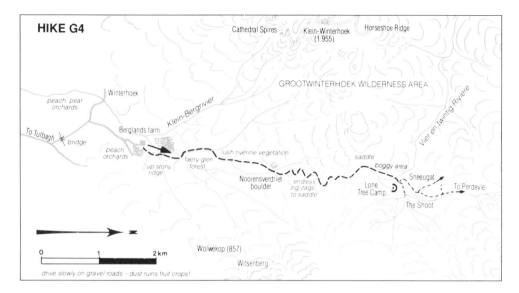

Cathedral Spires — Klein-Winterhoek (1.955) — Horseshoe Ridge

GROOTWINTERHOEK WILDERNESS AREA

Winterhoek

peach, pear orchards

Berglands farm

To Tulbagh — bridge

peach orchards

up stony ridge

faery glen forest

Klein-Bergrivier

lush riverine vegetation

Nooiensverdriet boulder

endless zig-zags to saddle

saddle

boggy area

Lone Tree Camp

Sneeugat

The Shoot

To Perdevlei

Vier en twintig Riviere

Wolwekop (857)

Witsenberg

0   1   2 km

drive slowly on gravel roads - dust ruins fruit crops!

▶ The path descends easily down to the valley, crossing a minor stream before heading east to Lone Tree Camp. The camp is a low overhang with low stone walls built up in front of it. This is a perfect base from which to explore the area: either ascending the Groot- (Hike G6) or Klein-Winterhoek peaks, heading on to Perdevlei (Hike G5) and then the Groot-Winterhoek forest station, or even hiking down the Vier en twintig Riviere valley. The easiest exit, however, is back to Berglands farm.

Sneeugat to Perdevlei
Hike G5

Route: *From Sneeugat down the Klein-Kliphuisrivier gorge to Perdevlei hut*
Distance: *9,5 kilometres*
Duration: *4 hours*
Grade: *Severe*
Booking Authority: *Groot-Winterhoek Forest Station (Tel. (02623) 2900) (permit needed)*
General Information: *This route links the Perdevlei Circular Hike (G3) and Sneeugat (G4). The intervening section, down from Die Hel and up the other main tributary of the Vier en twintig Riviere, is possible to navigate if you are prepared for a full kloofing and slogging trip. This trip has been described in the MCSA Journal (1961), although the first record of a complete circumnavigation of the Groot-Winterhoek is 1928. The section described here is not very demanding and quite spectacular.*

coated boulders create an ethereal 'faery glen'. Cross the boulder field, bearing left to cross a stream, and exit the glade to follow the left-hand stream bank. The massed rock pinnacles of Cathedral Spires and the Klein-Winterhoek buttress rise up on the left. The path crosses a boggy area, through rank vegetation, before recrossing the stream. In springtime, flowers festoon this section of the route: delicate triple-petalled blue irises (*Morea tripetaloides*); *Gladiolus gracilis* blooms; senecio and gazania daisies; and the sweet-scented water-pea blossoms that many people confuse with keurboom (*Virgilia oroboides*).

▶ The path rises up across a steep bank and comes to the wilderness boundary at Nooiensverdriet (girls' remorse) – a massive sandstone boulder planted on a small clearing, which creates a convenient overhang for a picnic or tea break.

▶ Nooiensverdriet marks the approximate halfway point to the Sneeugat nek; although the slope confronting you looks steep, the path zigzags its way up an easy gradient far back into a partly obscured gully that terminates at the nek.

From the nek, you look down into Sneeugat valley, with the larger Witsenberg peaks on your right. From here, Groot-Winterhoekpiek is obscured by its approach ridge, which shows a face of contorted rock strata to the valley. To your left, the Vier en twintig Riviere valley sweeps away to the west.

▶ From Lone Tree Camp, you can choose one of two possible routes to reach the nek between Ridge Peak and The Twins, on the Witsenberg range. The direct route is up the gully parallel to and below the Groot-Winterhoekpiek ridge: this route, although only about two kilometres long, lacks a path and entails bashing your way through dense vegetation. It will take up to four hours to reach the nek in this manner. Your other choice is to ascend the ridge as if you were climbing Groot-Winterhoekpiek. You can ascend the very rocky slope directly opposite Lone Tree Camp to gain the ridge's crest, or you can move a little up the gully mentioned above to a point where you feel the ascent will be easier.

▶ Once you have gained the ridge crest, it is a fairly straightforward route to the nek. Move right, out onto the nek, where you look down the Klein-Kliphuisrivier valley to Perdevlei. The views from here in all directions – across to the Klein-Winterhoek, Groot-Winterhoek dominating like a mini-Everest, the Vier en twintig Riviere valley to the west and Kliphuis to the north, Sneeugat, Medina, Isolated and Arete peaks to the east – are more impressive than anything I have seen elsewhere in the Cape.

▶ From the nek, head down into Sneeugat valley, crossing a boggy area and a stream, and then contouring round to the right to Lone Tree Camp. Over this section look out for the small but beautiful, burgundy-coloured *Protea nana*, which flowers from winter to spring.

▶ Follow the valley floor for just less than a kilometre, and then begin to contour along

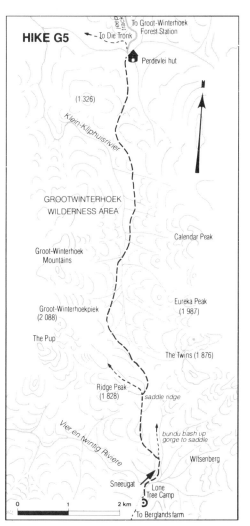

HIKE G5

To Groot-Winterhoek Forest Station
To Die Tronk
Perdevlei hut
(1 326)
Klein-Kliphuisrivier
GROOTWINTERHOEK WILDERNESS AREA
Groot-Winterhoek Mountains
Calendar Peak
Eureka Peak (1 987)
Groot-Winterhoekpiek (2 088)
The Pup
The Twins (1 876)
Ridge Peak (1 828)
saddle ridge
Vier en twintig Riviere
bundu bash up gorge to saddle
Witsenberg
Sneeugat
Lone Tree Camp
0   1   2 km
To Berglands farm

the right-hand side of the gorge, keeping more-or-less to the 1 220-metre contour.

▶ After another three kilometres, you will reach a nek. From here, you look down to Perdevlei, another one and a half kilometres away down an easy slope. In the middle distance, just to the left of the dominant hill, you look out over the Groot-Kliphuis vlakte.

From the hut at Perdevlei, you can proceed either northwards to Groot-Kliphuis along the jeep track, or to the west towards the Groot-Kliphuisrivier, Die Tronk and Die Hel (see bikes G2 and G3).

Groot-Winterhoek Ascent from Sneeugat *Hike G6*

Route: From Sneeugat up Ridge Peak to Groot-Winterhoekpiek and back
Distance: 9 kilometres
Duration: 5-6 hours (there); 2-3 hours (back)
Grade: Extreme
Booking Authority: Groot-Winterhoek Forest Station (Tel. (02623) 2900) (permit needed)
General Information: The times given for this and the following two ascents are for a party of fit and experienced mountaineers, since no-one else should be tackling these routes. I describe them briefly here, as this mountain is extremely appealing to anyone with a sense of adventure, and once you feel competent in the mountains, this peak should be within your capabilities. To reach Sneeugat you will have to do the Sneeugat

walk (Hike G4) from Berglands farm. The Sneeugat ascent of the Groot-Winterhoekpiek is the conventional – and easiest – one, but it is only open from the end of April to the end of October.

This route is only briefly described, as (with one or two exceptions) it should be obvious once you have commenced the ascent. If you do decide to tackle this route, be prepared for every eventuality of weather and route-finding. Finally, if you find yourself in difficulty regarding the steepness of the route, you will certainly have taken the wrong line.

▶ Cross the Sneeugat bowl, fording streams and boggy areas as you make for the steep spur directly opposite you. Once across the valley, bear to the right, climbing the rocky spur that begins the main spur up the peak. Keep to the ridge, crossing a low nek behind the first spur's prominent point, and making a wide figure 'S' as you keep to the main ridge line making for Ridge Peak. Round Ridge Peak to the north (1 826 m), and regain the edge of the ridge leading up towards Groot-Winterhoekpiek.

▶ Once you are at the base of the main peak, move to the right, 'behind' (east and then north of) the peak, with the Klein-Kliphuis-rivier valley stretching off down to your right. If you keep moving around to your left, you will gain easier ground and avoid the southeast-facing cliffs. The final approach is up an obvious gully, which becomes a second gully and leads to the top. Don't attempt this route in icy conditions, as ice axes, ropes and the like will be needed.

▶ Return via the same route.

Groot-Winterhoek Ascent from Perdevlei *Hike G7*

Route: From Perdevlei hut, up Kliphuis gorge to the summit and back
Distance: 13 kilometres
Duration: 7 hours (there); 3 hours (back)
Grade: Extreme
Booking Authority: Groot-Winterhoek Forest Station (Tel. (02623) 2900) (permit needed)
General Information: Few people have scaled this monster peak by way of the alternative routes. However, this should be the second route considered if Sneeugat is not accessible. The final approach follows the conventional line up from Sneeugat, past Ridge Peak (either to the left or right of where this route meets a point, which forms the continuation of the knife-edge from Ridge Peak). To reach Perdevlei, simply do the first day of the Perdevlei semicircular walk (Hike G3). As with all the Groot-Winterhoek ascents, this hike should be avoided if you are not an experienced hiker.

▶ This ascent begins from the Perdevlei hut (see Hike G3). Begin by going due south, climbing diagonally to the right away from the Klein-Kliphuisrivier gorge and into a gully, making for an obvious nek up and slightly to your right (1 230 m). From the nek, you look across the upper Klein-Kliphuisrivier catchment to Groot-Winter-hoekpiek, with the northernmost peaks of the Witsenberg massed on your left.

▶ Having reached the nek, contour along above the Klein-Kliphuisrivier valley, on the Witsenberg's northwestern flank for just over three kilometres, until the valley floor is reached; the floor is quite gently sloped, with the bulky forms of mountains rising up in all directions.

▶ Cross the Klein-Kliphuisrivier and head for a spur to your right. Follow the spur up to a second, linking spur, then veer slowly around to your right, keeping to the easiest spur ridge all the time. You will find yourself climbing up with the major Ridge Peak knife-edge spur in front of you. Move around to the head of the intervening gully, climbing as you cross it to join up at a point along the knife-edge spur's continuation.

▶ From here take the easy line (relatively speaking) sharply to the right, moving up and around to peak's northeastern slope leading into the two gullies which will take you to the summit.

▶ Return by the route you came.

Groot-Winterhoek Ascent from Die Tronk *Hike G8*

Route: Die Tronk hut, via Die Hel to the summit
Distance: 18 kilometres
Duration: 8-10 hours (there); 6-7 hours (back)
Grade: Extreme
Booking Authority: Groot-Winterhoek Forest Station (Tel. (02623) 2900) (permit needed)

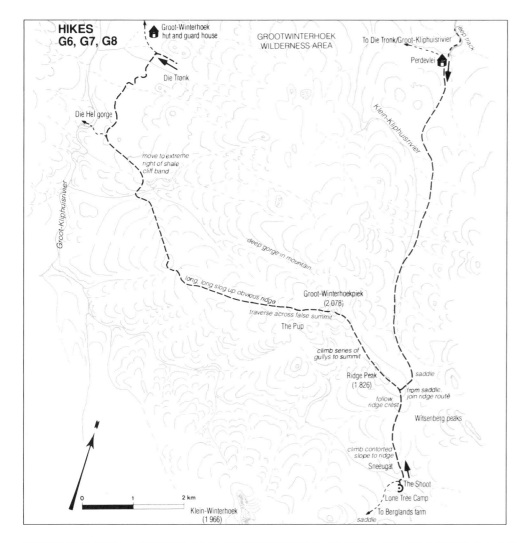

HIKES G6, G7, G8

GROOTWINTERHOEK WILDERNESS AREA

Groot-Winterhoek hut and guard house

To Die Tronk/Groot-Kliphuisrivier

Perdevlei

jeep track

Die Tronk

Klein-Kliphuisrivier

Die Hel gorge

move to extreme right of shale cliff band

Groot-Kliphuisrivier

deep gorge in mountain

long, long slog up obvious ridge

Groot-Winterhoekpiek (2 078)

traverse across false summit

The Pup

climb series of gullys to summit

Ridge Peak (1 826)

saddle

from saddle join ridge route

follow ridge crest

Witsenberg peaks

climb contorted slope to ridge

Sneeugat

The Shoot

Lone Tree Camp

To Berglands farm

saddle

0   1   2 km

Klein-Winterhoek (1 966)

General Information: The route from Die Tronk is very long and a little tricky; to accomplish it in a day you will have to leave at first light, or before. This is a stiff climb, and not recommended to any but the most adventurous of mountaineers – it will take you all day to the top and back and then some, and that is only if you keep a steady pace the whole way. Remember that if you are a slow climber, you will come down in the dark.

◗ From Die Tronk hut follow the jeep track and path towards Die Hel (see hike G2). Where you find yourself standing opposite the upper gorge, make your way over to the east (your left), and head along the easiest route. Make for the spur in front of you and slightly to the right, which is the most obvious line up which to begin your assault. Where the slope becomes noticeably steeper, move off towards your right and into a side gully, which should be crossed at about 500 metres altitude.

◗ Cross the gully and head upwards toward the northwest-facing spur to your right, with the Groot-Winterhoekpiek directly ahead. The spur leads to a high point (1 170 m), before turning slightly to the left to join the main ridge leading up to the summit. From here, the route is more or less straight – on a map that is. In truth, you will be weaving in and out of rocky outcrops, crossing sandy basins, and trekking across burnt out slopes.

◗ The final approach, although ascending about half the total altitude, is the easiest part of the climb in terms of route-finding. The main peak is joined to a lesser summit by a bouldery ridge that must be negotiated.

HAWEQUAS

The Hawequas region gets its name from the main forestry station serving it, which is in turn named after the ridge of peaks looming up above Wellington. The original Dutch spelling given to this Khoi (Hottentot) word was 'Hawekwas'. The area is served by a second forestry station at Kluitjieskraal near Wolseley, but this is mostly a timber concern.

Geographically, the Hawequas could be defined as the mountains flanking the Dutoitskloof and Bain's Kloof passes. Included are the Dutoitsberge, the Hawekwaberge, the Slanghoekberge, the Klein-Drakensteinberge, the Wemmershoekberge and the Limietberge. The two main towns in this area are Wellington and Wolseley, which lie at either side of the Bain's Kloof Pass.

Bain's Kloof Pass was one of the first major passes engineered by that intrepid road builder, soldier, adventurer, geologist and palaeontologist Andrew Geddes Bain. Such was Bain's skill and sense of the aesthetic, that today this pass is a national monument.

One of the main attractions in this area is the short kloofing trips that one can undertake. In the past, hikers and trout fishermen were allowed to overnight in some of these kloofs, but, as in so many other places, a few visitors have so abused their privileges that a ban has been placed on overnighting. Most

hikers and association member anglers believe it is exactly these poachers and litterbugs who spoil the place for everyone else.

The Witrivier, which rises between Groot Wellington-Sneeukop and Kromrivierpiek, is a lively river, gushing down the serene and secluded Happy Valley, through Junction Pool, and over the polished and rounded stones from which it gains its name. But sometimes, in winter, the river takes on a far more fearsome character, as it plunges down its gorge, swollen with the waters from rain and melting snow. It is lethal in this state; in fact, in 1896, four members of a hiking party from the newly formed Wellington section of the MCSA were drowned while attempting a crossing.

In the summer of 1990, I went on a hiking expedition with some companions up Wemmershoekvallei. On the final day of the hike, we could see all of the Hawequas ablaze. What started as a small fire on a farm in Wellington, was fanned by the southeaster, and, over a weekend, had spread over Bain's Kloof, Dutoitskloof and Elandspadkloof, and started making its way up the Wemmershoekvallei. This fire, one of several blazes in the western Cape within a few short weeks, destroyed most of the Hawequas plantations, numerous wild-flower and other farms, and thousands of hectares of exquisite fynbos.

Hiking in the Hawequas
Kluitjieskraal Forest Station controls the northern section of the Hawequas area, where, among other things, horse-riding and canoeing can be enjoyed. The Berg, Wit and Molenaars rivers are canoeing venues, while Kluitjieskraal and Suurvlakte (in the Elandskloof mountains above Voëlvleidam) are delightful places to ride. One may also get a permit from Kluitjieskraal for day access in limited areas of the southwestern Hexrivierberge. With the exception of the two-day Limietberg NHW Trail, only day permits are available to the general public in the Hawequas area.

Accommodation in the area is restricted to the Tweede Tol forestry campsite near the foot of Bain's Kloof, at its junction with Wolwekloof. This is a pleasant but small campsite, where booking is recommended, due to its popularity. Otherwise, the Limietberg Trail offers the only overnight access to non-MCSA members. Caravan and campsites can be found in Paarl and other Boland towns. All the hikes described below fall under the jurisdiction of the Hawequas Forest Station.

Beware – avoid any of the kloofing trips in bad weather, as flash floods occur quite frequently, and are extremely dangerous.

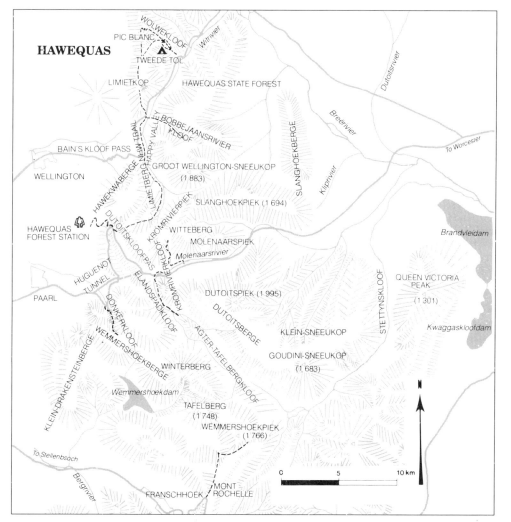

HAWEQUAS

WOLWEKLOOF
PIC BLANC
TWEEDE TOL
LIMIETKOP
HAWEQUAS STATE FOREST
Witrivier
Dutoitsrivier
Breërivier
To Worcester
BAIN'S KLOOF PASS
BOBBEJAANSRIVIER KLOOF
HAWEKWABERGE NEW TRAIL
WELLINGTON
GROOT WELLINGTON-SNEEUKOP
(1 883)
SLANGHOEKPIEK (1 694)
SLANGHOEKBERGE
Klipivier
HAWEQUAS
FOREST STATION
WITTEBERG
MOLENAARSPIEK
Molenaarsrivier
HUGUENOT
TUNNEL
DUTOITSPIEK (1 995)
DUTOITSBERGE
KLEIN-SNEEUKOP
QUEEN VICTORIA
PEAK
(1 301)
STETTYNSKLOOF
Brandvleidam
PAARL
GOUDINI-SNEEUKOP
(1 683)
Kwaggaskloofdam
DONKERKLOOF
WEMMERSHOEKBERGE
WINTERBERG
AGTER-TAFELBERGKLOOF
KLEIN-DRAKENSTEINBERGE
Wemmershoekdam
TAFELBERG
(1 748)
WEMMERSHOEKPIEK
(1 766)
To Stellenbosch
Bergrivier
FRANSCHHOEK
MONT
ROCHELLE
0   5   10 km
N

Klein Wellington-Sneeu-kop Ascent
Hike H1

Route: *From Bain's Kloof village up Deviation Buttress to Klein Wellington-Sneeukop summit*
Distance: *9 kilometres*
Duration: *2 hours (there); 1 hour (back)*
Grade: *Severe*
Booking Authority: *Hawequas Forest Station (Tel. (02211) 62 3172) (permit needed)*
General Information: *This is a not-so-difficult ascent route up a tempting peak – the one that lords over Happy Valley. This is a most pleasant climb to do as a morning or evening's outing, especially as a first-time ascent for new mountaineers.*

▶ The walk starts from Bain's Kloof village at the top of the kloof, but you must obtain your permit from the Hawequas Forest Station in Wellington. Follow the gravel path from the tarred Bain's Kloof road, past the burnt-out hotel in the village to a stile, where a restrictive forestry sign stands above the Witrivier. Descend the easy path to the polished river bed and cross to the opposite bank. Ascend the bank and head off to the left along a natural step, finding a well-worn path that leads around the north-west ridge of Deviation Buttress, heading into the Bobbejaansrivier gully. From the path, take a line up the Deviation Buttress ridge that offers least resistance.
▶ This is a rugged, but easily negotiated ridge, where king proteas burst out of rocky

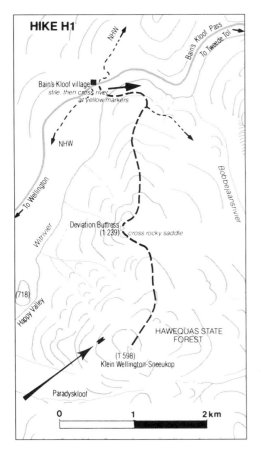

before retreating to the rocky saddle and proceeding up the wide ridge directly opposite you, to climb the 400 metres up to the top of Klein Wellington-Sneeukop.

Bobbejaansrivier   Hike H2

Route: *Up the Bobbejaansrivier gulley's south bank*
Distance: *9 kilometres*
Duration: *1½ hours (there); 1 hour (back)*
Grade: *Easy*
Booking Authority: *Hawequas Forest Station (Tel. (02211) 62 3172) (permit needed)*
General Information: *The hike involves a gradual climb up the gully's left-hand bank to an icy pool set between bands of grey-brown sandstone, all festooned with dripping ferns. Take water with you, as it can be hard to come by on the hike.*

▶ Coming from Wellington (where you have made a short detour to the forestry station to collect your entry permit), take the jeep track at the far (Wolseley) end of Bain's Kloof village to the right for about 50 metres. This will bring you to a wooden stile crossing over a fence, from where white footprints mark the way down to the Witrivier crossing place. Cross the river, continue following the painted footprints across the rocks, and scramble up a steep, loose bank, until a path is reached above the river.
▶ The path crosses some tributaries of the Bobbejaansrivier; do not rely on these for a drink, as water is guaranteed only at the beginning and end of the hike.

▶ The track moves around to the far (north-eastern) side of the northwestern spur of Deviation Buttress.
▶ About four kilometres along this path, you can take a steep side path down to a tiered waterfall and large pool.

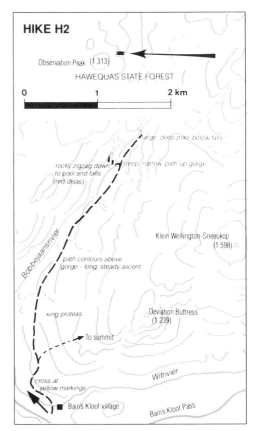

recesses. You will need to use some route-finding abilities to negotiate this natural sloping maze.
▶ Since you are on this ridge, you may as well 'bag' Deviation Buttress peak (1 239 m),

▶ Shortly after passing the side path, the main path begins to steepen as it approaches the largest waterfall in the Bobbejaansrivier gully. The path is cut into the side of a steep slope on the northern side of Klein Wellington-Sneeukop, and tends to become overgrown as well as being eroded, making the journey somewhat hazardous, so take care.

▶ Some boulder-hopping is necessary to reach the pool at the foot of the magnificent waterfall, but the half-hour climb is well worth it.

▶ To get back to your car, simply return along the route you came by.

Wolwekloof Circular Hike 1
Hike H3

Route: *Circumnavigation of lower Wolwekloof (Indicated by markers 5 and 3 on forestry map)*
Distance: *9,5 kilometres*
Duration: *3 hours*
Grade: *Fair*
Booking Authority: *Hawequas Forest Station (Tel. (02211) 62 3172) (permit needed)*
General Information: *This is a popular walk from Tweede Tol, the only camping site in this large area. The entire route is confined to a vast mountain bowl beneath the Limietberge, in the lower reaches of Wolwekloof. The paths are sometimes steep, sometimes loose and slippery and often vague; but without a pack the short distance will be quite easy for anyone with two functioning legs. Take stout walking shoes, though. If you get*

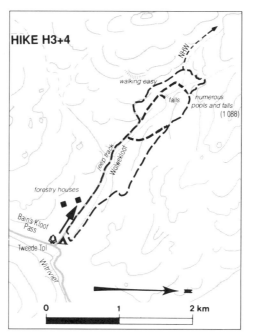

HIKE H3+4

overwhelmed with heat or storm, it is easy to cut the route short and head down to the river or back to camp. It is recommended that you carry water on this hike as watering points are far apart.

▶ A signboard at Tweede Tol's campsite No. 9 marks the beginning of this route. The walk begins with a short but stiff climb, reaching a T-junction after about 500 metres. Turn left, as shown by the board indicating 'Route 5'. Along the first part of this hike it is important to stick only to the

best-defined paths, as there are many confusing false paths. At this stage, this means ignoring all paths but the one leading straight up the mountain.

▶ The path soon enters a hollow, covered in restios and proteas, ahead of which is another steep climb at the top of which is a cool, shady spot. The views seen along this part of the hike will ease the pain of climbing.

▶ From the shady spot, the path leads through two successive restio-filled hollows. The going is fairly rocky, so walk lightly. A word of advice here is to carefully follow the silver arrows painted onto random rocks along the way.

▶ At about the four-kilometre mark, you will come to another T-junction where you must follow the sign saying 'Route 3'. Hereafter you will be required to do some boulder-hopping as the path winds towards the kloof. Along this section it is easy to lose sight of the path, so watch out for those little silver arrows.

▶ As you cross the head of the kloof, the path winds through rock mazes and small patches of indigenous forest.

▶ After following Route 3 for about one and a half kilometres, you will reach yet another T-junction, where you must turn left, heading towards a waterfall which is reached after another five minutes' stroll.

▶ Once at the waterfall, a right-hand turn will keep you on track, descending into the welcoming green valley of Wolwekloof. From here, the campsite is visible in the distance. Although the path is only moderately steep, loose rocks and gravel make the descent somewhat tedious.

Wolwekloof Circular Hike 2
Hike H4

Route: *Circumnavigation of middle and lower Wolwekloof (Described by '3,4, cave and SR' markers on forestry map)*
Distance: *9 kilometres*
Duration: *3 hours*
Grade: *Fair*
Booking Authority: *Hawequas Forest Station (Tel. (02211) 62 3172) (permit needed)*
General Information: *The details for this walk are much the same as for the previous one, following a slightly different combination of paths within the great bowl surrounding Wolwekloof. As the path is rough in some places, it is recommended that you wear sturdy shoes or boots.*

▶ As with the previous walk, begin from Tweede Tol's campsite no. 9, where a signboard indicates the beginning of the walks. The path commences with a short but stiff climb up the side of the kloof. After a 10-minute walk, you will reach a T-junction – follow Route 3 as indicated by the signboard. After another 20-odd minutes, you will arrive at a second T-junction.
▶ Continue along Route 3, until you reach a side junction, where the path to the right will take you down to a waterfall. A visit to the base of the waterfall is worth the effort, and you can rest here for a while.
▶ Back at the junction, turn right to continue to a view site about 100 metres further on. This is an ideal swimming and lunch spot at the top of the waterfall, surrounded by cliffs, and, hopefully, totally secluded.
▶ From here, follow the path indicated as Route 4 (unless the weather is bad, in which case follow the jeep track back to camp). The path basically follows the left-hand bank of the river for about 500 metres, passing numerous large and inviting pools.
▶ After an interesting diversion, the path crosses the river and meets the jeep track (surprise!). When crossing the river, look upstream and you will see a group of rocks looking like a miniature Stonehenge.
▶ If you follow the jeep track, you will eventually come to a gate, behind which lurks a large dog that you would not want to confront. You will have to make for the river, cross and then piece together a path, crossing the river again to reach the campsite.

Elandsrivier Kloof
Hike H5

Route: *Dutoitskloof pass up the Elandspad and back*
Distance: *9 kilometres or longer (If you wish to explore the kloofs)*
Duration: *2 hours (there); 2 hours (back)*
Grade: *Fair*
Booking Authority: *Hawequas Forest Station (Tel. (02211) 62 3172) (permit needed)*
General Information: *This kloof is a paradise for fly fishermen as well as ramblers, as the stream is well stocked with rainbow trout. Unfortunately, overnighting is no longer allowed, for, according to the conservation authorities, unscrupulous fishermen consistently fouled the once-popular cave. Although*

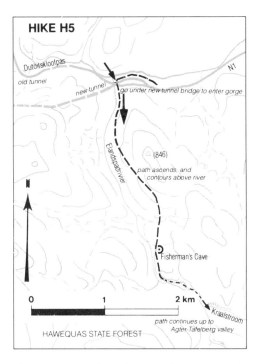

the path ascends and descends quite steeply in places, the hike is generally easy going.

Park in the parking area adjacent to the heavy vehicle stopping site on the Worcester side of the old Dutoitskloof tunnel (approximately one and a quarter kilometres from the new tunnel's northern entrance). Coming from Cape Town, the parking area will be on the left.
▶ From the parking area, walk along the jeep track (heading seemingly away from the

kloof), and at the junction take the left-hand turn to meander along Molenaarsrivier.

The track then veers away from the river and passes beneath the two road bridges where they connect to the tunnel entrances. Once under the bridge the path enters the kloof and keeps to the left-hand bank.

▶ The path ascends to wind around the interconnecting spurs, about 100 metres above the river. The many spurs lend the area a feeling of ruggedness far exceeding the difficulty of the hike.

▶ After about four kilometres, the path winds down to Fisherman's Cave. Just below the cave is a large pool, one of the most famous swimming spots in these mountains. It is highly recommended that you explore the numerous kloofs that converge on the pool area, the main one of which can be pursued for some distance. One word of warning – for this and all the other kloofs – is to avoid them in inclement weather. Flash floods will occur after rain, and these can be devastating, bringing with them an avalanche of water and boulders.

▶ Once you have explored to your heart's content, return to your car by the route you have come.

Donkerkloof   *Hike H6*

Route: From Dutoitskloof pass up Donkerkloof and back
Distance: 10 kilometres
Duration: 2-2½ hours (there); 1-2 hours (back)
Grade: Moderate

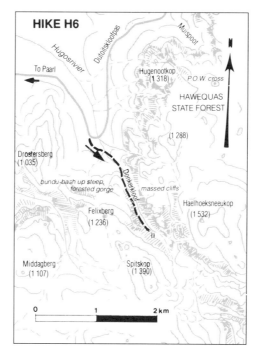

HIKE H6

Booking Authority: Hawequas Forest Station (Tel. (02211) 62 3172) (permit needed)
General Information: This kloof in the Klein-Drakensteinberge is seldom visited, and the so-called path is far from obvious in places. The grade is for the fact that the route is difficult to discern if you choose to carry on past where the markers peter out.

Donkerkloof is found about halfway up the approach into Dutoitskloof, on the old road from Paarl. Where the road makes its last

sharp hairpin bend to the left, you look up into Donkerkloof and its imposing rock walls and spires. The walk starts on the Paarl (western) side of Donkerkloof.

▶ Follow the path upstream, as it crosses from side to side of the river. Although the path is marked by painted white footprints, it can become indistinct in places, forcing you to use your own route sense.

▶ As the path climbs, it approaches some daunting cliff faces. Gaining even more height, you reach a good vantage point from which to take in the views of the Paarl valley. From here you can carry on up the kloof, but the going gets progressively harder.

At this point I'll leave the route finding to you, so that some of the adventure remains. Let it be said, however, that for a sense of adventure and mountain majesty, few places can match these upper reaches. Also, if you do decide to keep at it, a special reward awaits your efforts.

Kromrivier Kloof   *Hike H7*

Route: From Dutoitskloof tunnel up Kromrivier kloof
Distance: 8 kilometres
Duration: 1 hour (there); 1 hour (back).
Grade: Fair
Booking Authority: Hawequas Forest Station (Tel. (02211) 62 3172) (permit needed)
General Information: This is one of the shorter kloofing outings, and consequently one of the more popular ones. Many people, however, miss the best part of the kloof, stopping at a false dead end. The waterfall that

is eventually reached is one of the most spectacular in the region, perhaps surpassed only by the one in Donkerkloof. There is a tricky little scramble on this hike, which can become very slippery in wet weather.

After passing through the Dutoitskloof tunnel – coming from Cape Town – you will reach a fenced-in parking area on your left, the same parking area as for the Elandsrivier kloof (Hike H5).

▶ Park here, and proceed down to cross Molenaarsrivier at a causeway near a suspension bridge. Once across the river, turn left and follow the path a short way to where the Elands and Krom rivers meet. Turn right here up the right-hand bank of Kromrivier.

▶ The path criss-crosses the lower kloof area, offering numerous cooling-off spots. These will be welcome, as, although the river banks are densely covered with bush, the path often climbs above the shade.

▶ The path here is marked by painted footprints, and little exertion is demanded. At one place the path is cut into a gravel bank above the river, where particular care must be taken not to fall or to cause unnecessary erosion.

▶ Where the kloof narrows, the path enters a cool riverine forest, where gnarled roots seem to writhe on the damp ground; sun falls through the high canopy, dappled by falling drops from the damp banks above.

▶ Just after entering the forest, you will come to a cascade in the river, where slippery ledges and low cliffs seem to block your way. If, however, you feel brave enough to tackle this easy – but very slippery – climb, you will

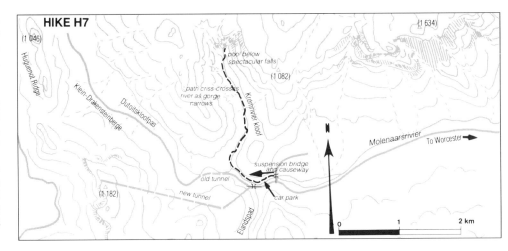

HIKE H7

be well rewarded. Just remember, you have to return the same way.

▶ Once you have passed this section, you will find yourself standing in a mountain enclosure. Across a deep pool, you will see a magnificent 100 metre waterfall.

▶ It is possible to climb by another route, above and around the southeastern side of the gorge, to a point above the waterfall. Otherwise simply return the way you came.

Mont Rochelle   *Hike H8*

Route: *Franschhoek pass to Perdekop*
Distance: *13 kilometres*
Duration: *3 hours (there); $2\frac{1}{2}$ hours (back).*
Grade: *Severe*
Booking Authority: *Franschhoek Municipality (Tel. (02212) 2055) (permit needed)*

General Information: This municipal nature reserve affords access to the wonderful Wemmershoek area. Wemmershoekpiek itself, which crowds over the dramatic Duiwelskloof and Wemmershoek valley, stands 1 766 metres high and is a monarch among mountains. Even though this route description will not bring you to the top of this peak, you will reach a broken plateau of Perdekop, out from which the Wemmershoek ridge projects. When snow falls on the Boland, many 'snow freaks' choose this hike to get their feet cold.

Most of this hike falls within the municipal Mont Rochelle Nature Reserve, the entrance to which is located on the second hairpin bend on the Franschhoek pass, near Die Catspad memorial and signposts, on the left-hand side of the road.

▶ Take the jeep track from the entrance to the left until you reach a locked gate (you can get the key to the gate from the municipality, if you wish to drive your car to the hut to be parked safely). Pass through the gap in the fence and keep left along the jeep track, passing close to some stone buildings. From here, a path runs up the slope ahead and to the left (or you can follow the left-hand stream bank behind the last house). The main path zigzags up the open slope and then begins to contour a way above the stream valley, through rank fynbos.

Tall grubbia shrubs, prickly metallasia, cliffortia and erica bushes will make this an uncomfortably memorable hike if you have chosen to wear shorts. The pink tubes of *Erica Grandiflora* line the path here. In the wet season the area closer to the stream becomes boggy and a nuisance to cross.

▶ The path follows the stream all the way up the valley to a saddle, directly in front of which stretch the Wemmershoekberge. For a breathtaking view of the Wemmershoek valley, follow the path for a few hundred metres to the edge of the gorge.

▶ From the large cairn on the saddle's crest, take the steep path up the ridge on your right, which leads to a series of natural steps, none wide enough to be called a plateau. It is here that you will find snow after a good winter front.

▶ Perdekop is the prominent hill to the northeast, up which the path heads (marked by irregular cairns), skirting around the head of the Wemmershoek gorge. The path ascends rocky slopes and descends through a grassy dell before gaining the Perdekop.

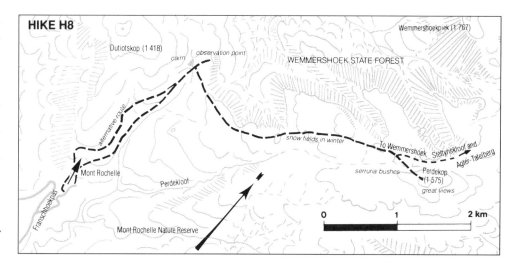

If you plan to take the rather long route around to Wemmershoek, the highest point rising above Wemmershoek valley, take care. Experienced mountaineers will be able to follow the beaconed trail to the summit, but this rarified area is plagued by mists, rain and snow. Unless you feel really confident and there is no threat of bad weather, call Perdekop a good day's achievement and head back down.

Boland Trail – Limietberg Section NHW   *Hike H9*

Route: *From Hawequas Forest Station, via Bain's Kloof village, to Tweede Tol*
Distance: *36 kilometres*

Duration: *2 days*
Grade: *Severe*
Booking Authority: *NHWB (Tel. (021) 402 3093) (permit needed)*
General Information: *This popular trail incorporates the traditional day hike from Dutoitskloof to Bain's Kloof, passing through that favourite venue of mountaineers, Happy Valley. The trail caters for 24 people a day and is the most heavily booked NHW trail in the western Cape, so don't leave your plans to the last moment. Some people find the trail very easy, but the two days in late December on which I chose to walk it were among the hottest I have ever known, and a general lack of water added to my discomfort. In better circumstances, though, the walk can be far more enjoyable, providing some lovely views from the western slopes of the Limietberg.*

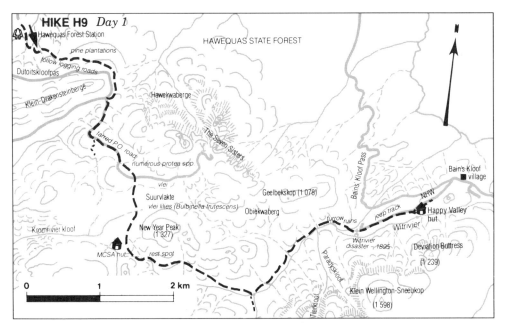

HIKE H9 *Day 1*

Hawequas Forest Station
pine plantations
follow logging roads
Dutoitskloofpas
Klein-Drakensteinberge
HAWEQUAS STATE FOREST
tarred P.O. road
Hawekwaberge
The Seven Sisters
numerous protea spp
vlei
Suurvlakte
vlei lilies (Bulbinella frutescens)
New Year Peak (1 327)
Geelbekskop (1 078)
Obiekwaberg
Kromrivier kloof
MCSA hut
rest spot
furrow ruins
jeep track
Witrivier
Witrivier disaster - 1895
Bain's Kloof Pass
NHW
Bain's Kloof village
Happy Valley hut
Deviation Buttress (1 239)
Paradyskloof
Tierkloof
Klein Wellington-Sneeukop (1 598)

0   1   2 km

Day 1: Hawequas Forest station to Happy Valley hut – 19 kilometres (7 hours)

▶ Start at the Hawequas Forest Station, having announced your arrival to the forester on duty. Fill up with water here for it may be the last you see for a long time. The trail winds up plantation tracks for five kilometres, on a slope leading up to the Dutoitskloof pass. Take care to look for the trail markers and avoid heartbreaking wrong turns (two white feet = change of direction). This part of the trail is fairly steep but not overly strenuous, and does at least afford some shade.

▶ Pass through a gate on reaching Dutoitskloofpas, and follow the tarred post-office track to the left. On a hot day, the dark tar transfers a great deal of heat to your feet, so rest and cool them down if you feel the need.

▶ Where the road levels off – with New Year Peak (1 327 m) visible ahead on your left – you may see king (*Protea cynaroides*) and bearded (*P. magnifica*) proteas, as well as *P. eximia* and a large rocket pincushion (*Leucospermum reflexum*) shrub.

▶ Further on, you will see an ugly tin structure that could be a dilapidated bush shelter, this marks your point of departure from the post-office road, along a more pleasing footpath to the right.

▶ The path crosses a small stream where your thirst can be deliciously quenched, and then heads across the Suurvlakte – one of many montane flats thus named.

▶ Once across the Suurvlakte, the path breaches the shoulder of a valley, before descending into it down some partly laid steps and a boggy, eroded bank, finally crossing the perennial stream at the bottom. A small rock on the far side of the stream gives a little shelter for a lunch spot.

▶ The path now follows the valley, staying on the left-hand bank of the stream. At the 14-kilometre mark, Junction Pool is passed on the right. The pool is formed, as the name implies, when a second stream comes down from between Groot Wellington-Sneeukop and Kromrivierpiek to join the one you have been following. The stream banks are heavily overgrown with riverine species.

▶ Soon after passing Junction Pool, you will meet the Happy Valley jeep track, which leads all the way to the overnight hut at the foot of Klein Wellington-Sneeukop (1 596 m) and Deviation Buttress (1 239 m).

Day 2: Happy Valley hut to Tweede Tol – 17 kilometres (6 hours)

▶ From the hut follow the jeep track northwards, past the plinth commemorating the group of hikers who were drowned in 1896 trying to cross the Witrivier.

▶ After crossing a stile, you will arrive at Bain's Kloof village. Proceed through the village, past the burnt-out old Toll Hotel, and then along the tarred road.

▶ Just before the road curves to the right, the NHW path heads off up to the left, past a water reservoir tank. Climb the path to above the reservoir, where a nice view of the village and backing peaks is gained.

▶ The path winds up the southeastern aspect of the Limietberge for about four kilometres, working its way over to the western side, overlooking Riebeeck-Kasteel and the intervening wheat fields. There is very little shade and water on this section. The small streams are reduced to trickles and then nothing in late summer. Don't rely on them.

▶ Once views over to the west are seen, the path winds through weird rock outcrops, where some relief will be found from the summer heat – or shelter from winter rain. Alternating views of the Witrivier valley, the Waaihoek and the Mostertshoek Twins of the Hexrivierberge to the east open out as you wind along a fairly level stretch of between six and eight kilometres. While walking along this stretch, look out for yellow ground orchids, the brilliant mauve (*Disa racemosa*), king proteas, the yellow hued pine (*Erica pinea*) and mealie (*E. patersonii*) heaths, the small painted lady (*Gladiolus debilis*) and pretty, white chinkerinchees (*Ornisogalum thyrsoides*).

▶ Having rounded the Limietkop (1 174 m), you cross a wide saddle area after the eight-kilometre mark, and head towards Pic Blanc (1 049 m). On reaching the foot of this peak (two kilometres from the saddle), you can choose to carry on up the main path over the summit, or take an easier contour route to the right. This 'easier' route is, however, overgrown and sometimes tricky to follow.

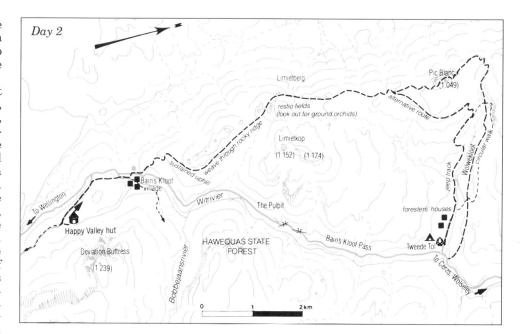

▶ The main path climbs the peak, zigzags down the far northern side, and then descends steeply to cross the head of Wolwekloof. The alternative path contours around the peak's eastern side, before also descending into Wolwekloof.

▶ I took the contour route, and had some difficulty in selecting the main path from the many lesser tracks near the meeting point of the two paths above Wolwekloof. Instead traversing down and to the left on the slope of Pic Blanc, I seem to have headed too steeply downhill too soon, consequently never meeting the main path.

▶ The main (NHW) path skirts around and above Wolwekloof, whereas the alternative route tends to drop down into the kloof's most welcome shade and coolness. If the former route is chosen, you will eventually descend a rocky ridge where pine trees have been felled; if you choose the latter route you will eventually meet up with a jeep track, as the path contours and moves above a waterfall. The track leads to a gate at the forester's house, but you must head down to the river, cross it and meet up with a path that follows a little above the river on the left-hand bank, crossing again on reaching Tweede Tol.

CAPE PENINSULA

The first recorded ascent of Table Mountain was in 1503 by the Portuguese admiral, Antonio da Saldanha, while en route to the East. The Dutch colonists who first settled here appear to have spent precious little time on this sort of recreation, for their aim was the far more serious business of commerce, agriculture and trade. With the British occupation of the Cape, however, it soon became a popular pastime to scale the great Table from town, by way of Platteklip's beckoning gorge.

The fashion really took hold after Lady Anne Barnard, the colony's most chronicled socialite, took a picnic on top of the mountain, with the great baskets being carried up by slaves. In the 1700s, three famous European naturalists, Carl Thunberg, Anders Sparrman and François le Vaillant enjoyed trips up Table Mountain. Le Vaillant managed to negotiate a five-day traverse along the peninsula's mountain spine – a walk that is commemorated in this volume.

An interesting anecdote to our story is one on Joshua Penny, RN. Penny was an American who had been press-ganged into joining the Royal Navy. When, in 1799, his ship, HMS *Spectre*, docked in Table Bay, Penny jumped it and made for that great grey monolith that stands guard over the bay. For 14 months he slept in a cave near Fountain Ledge, below the upper cableway station,

living off the land. 'I never enjoyed life better than when I lived among the ferocious animals of Table Mountain,' he later wrote.

By late last century, a new breed of climber emerged in the Cape. These men and women forged the first rock-climbing routes on the mountain. By the time the MCSA was formed in 1891, many of the mountain's classic rock routes had already been opened. Not only is Cape Town our mother city, but Table Mountain can also claim to be the nursery of the country's rock-climbing fraternity (which is not to suggest that the ascents are always easy!).

Today, it has been claimed, Table Mountain is the most climbed mountain in the world. It has been declared a national monument and, although not sacred in the sense of Mount Fujiyama, occupies a special place in the hearts of all Capetonians. How sad, then, that even this has not stopped people from defiling its slopes with eroded paths, litter, ugly developments and fire.

The Cape Peninsula is not as florally rich as the Hottentots-Holland mountain range, yet its statistics are impressive: it is the size of the Isle of Wight, or half the size of New York City, and has more plant species than the entire British Isles (Table Mountain alone has some 2 500 recorded species). Since the first of its plants (a blue sugar-bush, at first classified as a new species of

thistle) was taken back to Europe by a Dutch sailor in 1597, the Cape's flora has impressed botanists and delighted gardeners the world over.

While human encroachment has stopped short of endangering the peninsula's fynbos component, it certainly has brought the once-extensive forests to the brink of extinction. Dense Afro-montane forests, with giant yellowwoods (*Podocarpus latifolius*), white pear trees (*Apodytes dimidiata*), towering lichen-covered stinkwoods (*Ocotea bullata*), red alders, spreading assegai trees (*Curtisia dentata*), Cape beech (*Rapanea melanophloeos*) and Cape holly (*Ilex mitis*) trees, once arched over singing rivers and fern-frilled glades. First the forests of Hout Bay were plundered by shipbuilders; then, as the colony at the Cape grew, the demand for hard wood saw the forested slopes of Table Mountain flattened. Still, a walk along the Contour Path, or any of the many paths that lead through Newlands Forest, reveals a magical sylvan world that leads one far away from the city's urban din.

Although almost all of the peninsula's wild animals (lions, leopards, antelope, hippos, buffalos, and even migrant elephants) were not compatible with urban life, the birds remain. The Cape fynbos is not known for its abundance of bird life, but Table Mountain has an impressive 150 recorded

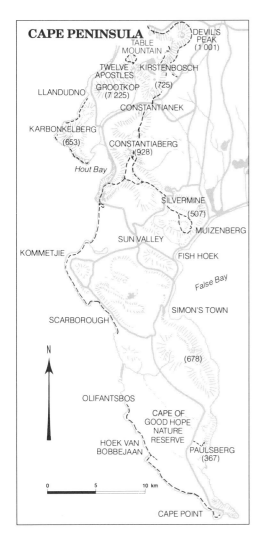

CAPE PENINSULA

DEVIL'S PEAK (1 001)
TABLE MOUNTAIN
TWELVE APOSTLES
KIRSTENBOSCH
GROOTKOP (7 225)
(725)
LLANDUDNO
CONSTANTIANEK
KARBONKELBERG (653)
CONSTANTIABERG (928)
Hout Bay
SILVERMINE (507)
MUIZENBERG
SUN VALLEY
FISH HOEK
KOMMETJIE
False Bay
SIMON'S TOWN
SCARBOROUGH
(678)
N
OLIFANTSBOS
CAPE OF GOOD HOPE NATURE RESERVE
HOEK VAN BOBBEJAAN
PAULSBERG (367)
0   5   10 km
CAPE POINT

species. Orange-breasted sunbirds, Cape sugarbirds, red-winged starlings, rock pigeons, doves, grassbirds and a few species of cisticola are the most common. The most impressive, however, are the black eagles which soar the ridge winds, the white 'windows' on their wings, and crosses on their otherwise black backs flashing as they swoop and turn. Their diet consists almost exclusively of rock hyraxes (dassies), though in the Cape of Good Hope Nature Reserve, the small antelope which find sanctuary there help to vary the eagles' diets.

Hiking in the Cape Peninsula

There are literally hundreds of ascent routes up Table Mountain, ranging from the simple Platteklip and Nursery gorges, to climbs that are graded upwards of H (that is very serious rock climbing indeed). Many of the old ascent routes have been closed off by the city's parks and forests department, due either to degradation or to their inherent danger. Others still, while they are known to the real mountain lovers, I will not reveal here; many are steep and prone to erosion so that excessive use would soon make them unpassable. Any route that I consider to be dangerous to the average hiker has also been omitted.

At the last minute, I also deleted the route description for the Kloof Corner ascent, when I decided that this was really a climb and not a hike. Since this route was climbed by Victorian ladies in straw bashers, high-heel boots and long, many-pleated skirts, I consider it within most people's ability, but without a good knowledge of the route you could get into a lot of trouble (and in mountaineering terms 'trouble' is a bad thing). This is a spectacular route, and one that I would highly recommend to anyone who can handle the exposure and has a good route description to follow. People who venture off the main paths on Table Mountain without a sound knowledge of the routes, should have their estates and wills put in order.

Local conservation authorities are wisely hesitant to develop hiking huts within the mountain reserve area, but I believe that public pressure should be brought to bear on the various local authorities for the development of such facilities in suitable sites: at lower altitudes, or perhaps in or near forestry plantations.

Table Top   *Hike P1*

Route: *Up Platteklip gorge across Table Mountain to Kirstenbosch*
Distance: *10 kilometres*
Duration: *4 hours*
Grade: *Severe*
Booking Authority: *None*
General Information: *If you do only one walk in Cape Town, this should be it. The route up Platteklip gorge is fairly strenuous, but then you are not really in a rush, and if Lady Anne Barnard could do it, so can you. If you get your timing right, you can do the whole climb in shade. Enjoy the knowledge that this route has been used by just about every famous person who climbed the mountain, from Admiral da Saldanha to General Jan Smuts (John Lennon went up by cable*

car). Remember that every year hikers get lost or trapped here (usually through negligence), and some end up dead. Save yourself and the mountain rescue teams trouble, and go prepared: give the southeaster due consideration and, no matter what the weather conditions, take something warm to wear, preferably a lined windbreaker, and something to drink. Also remember that the walk is linear, so transport will be needed to and from either end of the walk.

▶This route starts at the sign marked 'Platteklip Gorge' on Tafelberg Road, about one and a half kilometres after the lower cableway station (if you are really keen, you can start at the stairs just to the right – as you look up the mountain – of the lower cableway station; climb them to the contour path and follow that to Platteklip gorge). From the sign, your route heads straight up the mountain. The path is steep and unrelenting, but it is well constructed and virtually paved. The stone steps were obviously built for giants, and will tire you out if you try to take them too fast. As with longer hikes, you should never try to maintain a pace that leaves you gasping for breath.

▶ Cross the Contour Path (see Hike P6), where a stream is overhung by shady bushes. In summer, the gorge from here on can become very hot indeed. The City Parks personnel have their time cut out trying to maintain paths on the mountain and stop erosion – please help them by following the main, zigzag route *around* the fences, and do not contribute to unsightly degradation by taking short cuts. You should see orange-

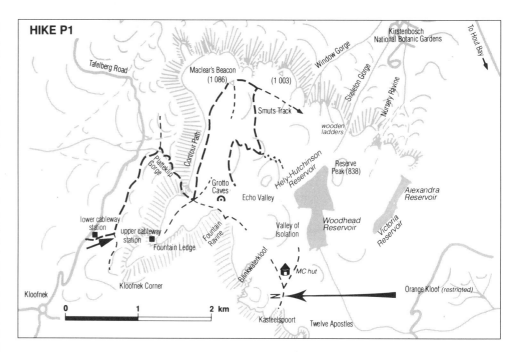

HIKE P1

breasted sunbirds flitting about the blooms on the lower slopes; I have seen black eagles swooping by here, being harassed by a lanner falcon, and squadrons of starlings.

Just before reaching the top of the gorge, it is possible to traverse a way out on the right-hand (facing up the mountain) wall to gain a spectacular view of the city. Don't go beyond the limit of good sense for the drop here is unforgiving.

▶ On reaching the top of Platteklip, follow the signpost to Maclear's Beacon. The vegetation on top of the mountain is noticeably different from that on the slopes; poor soils, and the force and desiccating effect of the wind, act as a bush cutter, keeping the fynbos cropped and similar to the Afro-alpine vegetation on top of the Drakensberg escarpment. The summit is marked by seepage areas en route to Maclear's Beacon, where grassbirds, neddickys and other cisticolas can be seen. You may also be lucky enough to see a malachite sunbird, its metallic green plumage and long tail flashing in the sunlight. Ponder Maclear's Beacon awhile, remembering that this astronomer royal and his team made the opening ascents of many of the western Cape's highest peaks – and all in the course of their work.

▶ From Maclear's Beacon, descend into Echo Valley, where some of the area's best stands of mature fynbos are to be found. Large king proteas (*Protea cynaroides*), sugarbushes (*P. repens* and *P. neriifolia*), waboom (*P. nitida*), *P. grandiceps* and various leucadendrons (cone bushes) reach their flowering best from spring to late summer.

▶ The path here zigzags, follows a fence for some way, and is often overgrown; stay on the main path, which is signposted at pertinent junctions. The valley is a special place, as not only is it botanically rich, but a wonderful sense of isolation encapsulates this unexpected wilderness.

▶ The Echo Valley path leads automatically around Hely-Hutchinson Reservoir (no swimming permitted – we have to drink that water) to a signpost near Breakfast Rock, at the top of Skeleton Gorge.

▶ From Breakfast Rock, head down the gorge to the Contour Path. Turn left along the Contour Path to cross the gorge, turning right just after crossing to go diagonally down to the Kirstenbosch parking lot.

Skeleton Gorge   *Hike P2*

Route: *From Kirstenbosch up Table Mountain*
Distance: *3 kilometres*
Duration: *1 hour (there); 45 mins (back)*
Grade: *Moderate*
Booking Authority: *None*

General Information: This simple but exciting route up Table Mountain's forested, eastern flank was Jan Smuts' favourite walk. Although the route is hard to miss, the top of the gorge is blocked by boulders and, in wet conditions, with water gushing down, it may become dangerous. If the watercourse becomes impassable, it is possible to scramble out on the right-hand side of the gorge, but this too may be dangerous. Otherwise it is a fairly steep but very beautiful hike. You will need to carry some money with you to pay the entrance fee to Kirstenbosch.

▶ The route begins in the Kirstenbosch National Botanic Gardens, and is well signposted. From the Kirstenbosch car park, proceed past the tearoom and hall, then turn right up the Arboretum. From here, head directly towards the mountain and into the gorge. The profusion of paths and tracks may at first confuse you, but just head uphill for the obvious place and you won't go wrong.

▶ Bypass the Braille Trail on the edge of Newlands Forest, and join Smuts' Track. The massive wild almond (*Brabejum stellatifolium*) trees you will see are remnants of Jan van Riebeeck's hedge that he had planted here to mark the edge of the Dutch settlement. The odd signpost should help you on your way.

▶ Soon after entering the natural forest, your route comes to a Y-junction with the uppermost Kirstenbosch road: if you kept to the gravel road turn right here for about 40 metres and then left, heading directly upwards once more; if you went straight up the path where the road swung away to the left,

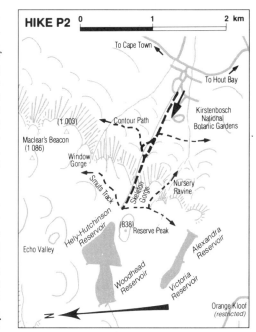

then just carry on up, and over a T-junction. Another 100 metres will bring you to a signpost at the Contour Path.

▶ Cross this and follow the well-constructed path up the left-hand bank of the gorge. In wet conditions, an impressive waterfall is formed here, at the foot of Smuts' Track. In drier conditions, you can boulder-hop up the river bed for much of the way.

▶ The path keeps to the left-hand bank of the gorge, moving close to the river and then veering away from it. At an altitude of about 500 metres, some tricky cliffs must be overcome: many thick roots and two wooden ladders are present to help you up. It may be slippery along this section when wet.

◗ Once above the cliffs, you have to boulder-hop up the side of the stream bed, until the gorge widens out near the top. Keep to the right-hand bank, moving further to the right to round a cascade blocking the gorge about 150 metres further on. Although you are near the top of the gorge, don't turn off until you reach the signpost.

◗ From the top of Skeleton Gorge, you can explore anywhere on Table Mountain; you can return by the same path, or return to Kirstenbosch via the easier Nursery Ravine a few hundred metres to the south of Skeleton Gorge (follow the sign around the back of Breakfast Rock).

Apostles' Traverse   Hike P3

Route: *Along the Pipe Track, up Wood Ravine, to Grootkop and back.*
Distance: *14,5 kilometres*
Duration: *5 to 6 hours*
Grade: *Moderate*
Booking Authority: *None*
General Information: *This is a longish but fairly easy hike that is suitable even for a hot summers day. There is, however, no water to be found on the hike, so carry according to the weather (in summer, preferably 2 litres for each adult). If you start from the upper cableway station, the walk becomes easier, but be sure you know the way or have a map, for even with signs it is easy to get lost on top of Table Mountain. Heat can quickly give*

HIKE P3

way to cloud and rain, so you should be prepared for a change in the weather.

◗ Start at the beginning of the Pipe Track, next to the Waterworks building at Kloofnek. Pass the filtration plant and head for

Camps Bay along this most pleasant walk. In summer, start early (no later than 07h30) and you may witness exciting lighting conditions when the buttresses and ravines are backlit. Pass the Kasteelspoort sign, and continue along a jeep track past the stone pipe housing and concreted breakpressure tank, to the signpost marking Wood Ravine, which, needless to say, is wooded. Do not continue on to Corridor and Slangolie ravines, as they are now closed off.

◗ Climb the steep, pleasant (though slightly eroded in parts) path. About two thirds of the way up Wood Ravine, the bush shrinks to wind-cropped fynbos, and the top of the gorge opens out onto the Back Table area. The T-junction with the path running between the Western Table and Grootkop is marked by a signpost pointing down Wood Ravine. Turn right here to follow the well-demarcated path all the way up Grootkop. Avoid the numerous side paths, such as those going down to the right to Corridor, Ascension and Slangolie ravines, or left to Disa Gorge.

◗ The path along the Apostles' skyline resembles a roller coaster, going down through the tops of successive ravines and up over buttress summits. The sandy track passes through interesting rock formations and over areas that, in winter, are very boggy; in summer the vegetation seems sparse and near dead. The approach up Grootkop is not straight, but by way of the less severe left-hand skyline, which avoids the rock bands facing you as you approach.

◗ As you reach the final approach to the peak, the path will fork: keep left along the main path, and continue past some huge boulders. After passing the boulders, turn right up to the summit.

▶ To return, retrace your steps along the upper Apostles' path, then continue past the turn-off into Corridor Ravine to the top of Slangoliekloof – where an easy rock scramble must be negotiated, with great views down into the ravine itself.

▶ Do not descend into Slangolie: carry on along the table top instead, passing a signboard warning you of a dangerous descent, and continue past the Wood Ravine sign to the sign marking the Kasteelsport descent. If you wish, you can descend to the Pipe Track here, otherwise, simply carry on over into Blinkwater Ravine and up again to gain the Western Table at the head of Platteklip gorge. From there, head a short way left to the cableway station and ride down to Tafelberg Road. Remember, however, that the walk from the top of Kasteelspoort to the cableway station is generally uphill, with numerous ascents and decents along the way – and precious little water (you can get water from a tap near the Mountain Club huts, opposite the top of Kasteelspoort).

Apostles' Circular Walk
Hike P4

Route: *From Kloofnek, along Pipe Track, up Apostles and back.*
Distance: *11 kilometres*
Duration: *3½ to 4 hours*
Grade: *Moderate*

HIKE P4

Booking Authority: *None*
General Information: *This is a good walk for a summer's day; make an early start and you can complete the hardest part in cool shade. The Pipe Track alone is a very pleasant walk with imposing views of the Twelve*

Apostles, Camps Bay and the coast. Remember to take a windbreaker along; after the ascent you might be wet with perspiration and clouds and a wind on the summit will make you very cold and miserable. Probably the best time to do this walk is in summer, when a northwesterly wind bring clouds of cool, moist sea air swirling around the buttresses and playing in and out of the ravines. The early morning sun dramatically backlights the ridges, and highlights the streamers of cloud.

▶ The route begins at Kloofnek, where a tap at the roadside can be used to fill water bottles, for, in summertime you are unlikely to find any water along this hike. Take the granite steps up to the right-hand side of the waterworks buildings and gardens. After a short climb, the route levels out and becomes a gravel path. This is the Pipe Track – as you will no doubt gather from the pipe aqueducts along the way. For the first several hundred metres, the path is lined with stone pines *(Pinus pinnea)*, and you will pass a water-filtration plant, which looks more like an old school hall, up on the left.

▶ Shortly thereafter, the path traverses a few ascents and descents as it contours beneath the cliffs of Kloofnek Corner. About a kilometre from the start, the natural vegetation becomes more and more dense, as the path moves into the sheltered areas between Fountain and Blinkwater ravines. From early summer, the veld comes alive with colour: the tightly bunched composite flower heads of *Athanasia parviflora*, a rounded daisy-bush with feathery green leaves; the delicate purple-and-mauve blooms of the wild geranium *Pelargonium cucullatum*; the white and golden puff-balls of *Leucospermum conocarpodendrum*. Early settlers called this bush the 'kreupelhout' because of its gnarled limbs. It is a fire-resistant plant that grows on granite-derived soils.

This area of rank vegetation is a popular haunt for birds such as Cape sugarbirds, sparrow-like Cape Buntings with their distinctive head stripes, and tiny neddickies. The neddickies fall firmly into the category of 'lbj's' – little brown jobs. They can, however, be identified by their diminutive size and monotonous 'weep, weep, weep' and 'teep, teep, teep' song. When alarmed, they will fly to a conspicuous perch, flick their short tails and give an alarm call that sounds like someone running their fingernail across the teeth of a comb.

▶ At the two-kilometre mark, a sign points up Blinkwater Ravine, but this dangerous path has been closed off, so ignore it and carry on. Just a little further along, two consecutive paths – the first one vague and the second more definite – lead diagonally up to the left, towards a cave in the sandstone cliffline of Porcupine Buttress. Some 500 metres further on, a signpost shows the way up Kasteelspoort – the actual ravine of which is obscured by Kasteel Buttress. This is not your route however. You must head for Wood Ravine, about one and a half kilometres further on. (Midnight Lover's Cave is found a little way up the Kasteelspoort path, and off to the right).

▶ About 200 metres further on, the gravel path reaches a concrete jeep track that comes up from Camps Bay. This is a continuation of the Pipe Track, so follow it past the concrete apron that is an outlet at the bottom of the Woodhead Tunnel water pipeline. Shortly hereafter, the jeep track reverts to a gravel path and heads up a short climb, before descending past a eucalyptus thicket. The path then levels off again, and passes a stone breakpressure tank. Wood Ravine is reached 250 metres after this tank, where the path heads steeply uphill (petering out at the bottom of Slangoliekloof).

▶ Your route takes an even steeper line, up Wood Ravine, which is marked by a rusty but easy-to-see signpost on the left. The once-well-laid path has seen little maintenance in recent years, though apparently this is soon to change. As it is, take care when climbing some of the large stone steps that are beginning to work loose. You are not so likely to hurt yourself as to cause the path harm. This is a pretty gorge, where lilies such as the attractive chincherinchee (*Ornithogalum thyrsiodes*), with its small, white flowers, illuminate the dank, green gorge.

▶ The path climbs up the left-hand side of the gorge, veering further left about a third of the way up towards the first line of cliffs that is encountered. Remember that the river shown on maps does not run in summer. The stark forms of dead trees stick out of the low, confined riverine forest – these may be aliens (probably gums) whose spread has been curtailed. About two thirds of the way up, the gorge narrows and becomes shallower, and the gradient lessens. You pass the small, dark grotto from where the stream springs, when it does. Cliffs rise up on either side, forming an impressive approach to the top of the gorge – Wood Buttress is on your left and the Antler and Spring crags of Spring Buttress on your right.

▶ After a climb totalling 425 metres, you come to the Grootkop path, where a signpost points back down Wood Ravine. In the low fynbos scrub here, grassbirds can often be seen sunning themselves. These robin-size warblers are rufuous to pale-buff coloured, with buff and black streaks and dark moustaches. The tail is diagnostically long, and appears tattered in flight.

▶ With Grootkop away to the right, you can see the three Mountain Club huts in front and slightly to the left, and the stone wall of Woodhead Reservoir at the top of Disa Gorge straight ahead. The top of the Back Table area is to me a wonderfully desolate place, with windswept boglands, gorges and dams, caves and views over most of the mountainous Cape Peninsula.

▶ Turn left here along the sandy path for 500 metres, until you reach the small gully that marks the top of Kasteelspoort (before this a path leads off to the left, to the old cableway station, but there is no way down from there). The well-made path down Kasteelspoort has recently been upgraded by the construction of stone blocks in wire cages – that act as steps and erosion barriers – as well as short barbed-wire fences to block off short cuts. The path is very easy to follow, on natural and man-made steps – if you find yourself on loose gravel, you have taken a wrong turn. This is easiest done where the path reaches a flat rock deck; your route continues down from the far left-hand edge.

▶ From here on down, I always come across paper, plastic and broken glass, more than enough to fill all my pockets. Observation leads me to conclude that the main culprits are the large parties of youngsters – complete with ghetto-blaster radios playing full-volume – who hike here on weekends, and who probably haven't given a thought to the problem they are causing.

After descending for about 200 metres, the path begins to veer off to the right, and, from the base of the Kasteel Buttress cliffs, it takes a diagonal course back to the Pipe Track. Just below the 340-metre contour, where the Jubilee and Barrier ravine streams converge, the path crosses a wooded gully, and from here the Pipe Track is just a hop and skip away. Turn right to follow the Pipe Track for four and half kilometres back to Kloofnek.

(Note: Although no permit is needed to do this walk, it does carry a price: the Pipe Track and Kasteelspoort route is a popular one and consequently strewn with litter. The price you must pay to walk this route is to pick up at least one piece of litter and put it in the bin where the Kasteelspoort path meets the Pipe Track.)

Lion's Head   Hike P5

Route: *From Sea Point, up Signal Hill to Lion's Head*
Distance: *10 kilometres*
Duration: *2-2½ hours (there); 1½ hours (back)*
Grade: *Moderate*
Booking Authority: *None*

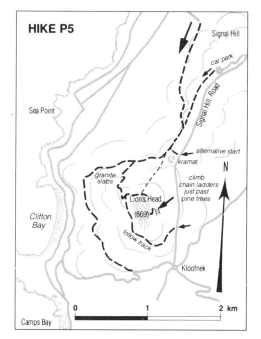

General Information: The first section of this hike is along a broad path, on a gradual slope; it ends, however, up a steep rocky face that is negotiated with the help of a chain. Don't be put off, however, this hike is ideal for family groups. On full-moon evenings, this is an ideal place for a champagne picnic. Take lots of water with you on this walk, as the route is dry.

▶ The walk starts at the steps at the top of Clifford Road (off High Level Road) in Sea Point. Climb the steps and you will emerge

at a wind break of eucalyptus trees. Walk up through the trees and take the path leading off to the right, then zigzag up Signal Hill. Keep to the most well-defined path or you will cause unnecessary and unsightly erosion – and get lost.

▶ You will eventually come to a broad, near-level path, that leads to the gravel parking lot on top of Signal Hill. Just before reaching the top, take a short (10-metre) detour to a bench, from where you can admire the view of Sea Point and Robbeneiland. The large, rounded shields of rock protruding above Sea Point are part of a granitic batholith, similar to the outcrops on which Chapman's Peak Drive lies. When weathered, these rocks form a rich clayey soil, on which the tall silver trees (*Leucadendron argenteum*) on the hill's southeastern slope flourish.

▶ From the parking lot (you can drive here from Kloofnek), the Lion's Head path heads off in a southerly direction. The vegetation on Signal Hill is mostly grassy, so fynbos flowers are not much in evidence here.

▶ Follow the path as it curves gently, ignore the junction a little way past the car park, and continue straight until a fence blocks your way. Do not cross the fence; instead follow the path as it doubles back and gently climbs – the last 20 metres of the climb are fairly steep.

▶ At the top of the slope you will reach another junction; turn left, in the direction of a tree jutting out from Lion's Head. The path is more or less level, having been cut into a reddish shale band.

▶ Circle the lower slope of Lion's Head, until you find yourself looking down into the city bowl area. On reaching a wooden bench, take a rest before tackling the steep climb that awaits you.

▶ A little way past the bench, you will see a chain hanging down from the cliff face above; climb it for about four metres. From here you may be confused as to where the route goes.

▶ Continue straight up, aiming for a pine tree that sticks out above you. You will have to negotiate four ledges and short cliff faces in all, but you avoid the last one by using the chain ladder provided. On reaching the third cliff face, you will be rewarded with a grand view of Clifton, and Camps Bay.

▶ From the top of the cliffs, it is a matter of a series of straightforward rock scrambles – follow your own route – to the top. If you have brought food with you, this is a wonderful spot to take a leisurely lunch.

▶ Return the same way, or, at the first junction you meet on the 'up' path, go steeply down to avoid the main path's many meanderings. This latter route is steep and heavy on one's feet, and since it passes close to some precipitous drops, take extra care. You will join the main path about 150 metres above the car park.

Table Mountain Contour Traverse
Hike P6

Route: *Lower cableway station to Constantianek*
Distance: *18,7 kilometres*
Duration: *6 hours*
Grade: *Moderate*

Booking Authority: *None*
General Information: *This route may be broken up into a number of shorter variations, for which you should consult a detailed map to check out all the options. When talking of scaling large mountains, climbers speak of 'rubbing noses' with the peak, getting a feeling for its possibilities. In the case of Table Mountain, a circumnavigation is the best way to 'rub noses'. You can include the Pipe Track hike for a long but fulfilling day's hike, but a complete circumnavigation is unfortunately not possible due to private property restrictions above Hout Bay's Longkloof, and the hydrological and botanical research area of Orange Kloof, which is closed to the public. For anyone with an interest in climbing history, the names encountered along this hike should evoke intense nostalgia. The walk is linear, park a car at each end, for transport.*

▶ Purists will make their way up from Kloofnek to the Contour Path at Kloof Corner, but most people will prefer to start at the stone steps leading up behind the lower cable station. The steps reach the Contour Path at the start of the India Buttress route, and you must turn left here and head towards Platteklip gorge.

▶ After a little more than a kilometre, you will reach the gorge (complete with signposts); cross it and continue along the contour. The path is very easy from here, heading along stony ground and occasionally making use of natural rock ledges.

▶ About half a kilometre beyond Platteklip you will reach a small, wooded gully, with a tiny waterfall. Just after passing this serene spot, the path divides. You can, if you wish, follow the upper path – the middle traverse around Devil's Peak – as it zigzags upwards, passes Woodstock Cave, and descends to the King's Blockhouse. (There is an even higher traverse route, but that is for people who know the area well.)

▶ Otherwise, take the lower traverse path to the left, as it drops down a little to just above Tafelberg Road. Directly opposite the Eastern Table edge, the path crosses the saddle path coming up from the road. Carry on around Pine Buttress – a grove of gum trees is, fortunately, all that remains of the alien species that once grew in this area. Be careful here, as the path may become slippery and infirm.

▶ On reaching Oppelskoprug, the path turns away from the city bowl; the views from this point are quite grand. It should take you about one hour to cover the four kilometres from the cableway station to here, unless you are stopping frequently to admire the views, and the flora.

▶ The path now rounds Oppelskoprug, turning away from the city bowl area. Suddenly the view changes altogether and the feeling is one of greater isolation. Earlier felling has left the dried-out logs of pine trees littering the steep slopes of Devil's Peak (1 000 m). After rains the stream pouring down from Minor Peak (862 m), past the Woodstock Cave, can become a rushing torrent and difficult to pass. As it is, this aspect of the mountain is quite boggy in places for most of the year. Remember to pull out any acacia seedlings you see along the way.

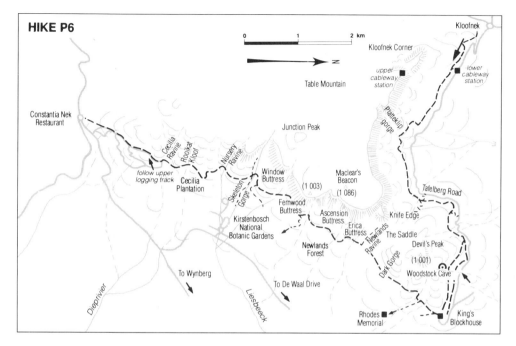

▶ The path passes high above the ruins of the Queen's Blockhouse and then onto the more complete King's Blockhouse. Cannons point out from this historic military installation towards Table Bay, and a plaque recounts the fort's story.

▶ Take the steps steeply down from the cannons' mounts to the lower track and then pass through the stile at the edge of the Groote Schuur Estate. You now reach a three-pronged fork: keep to the upper path and continue through the plantation, crossing two log bridges.

▶ The path curves around the eastern buttress, into the First and Second Waterfall ravines, and out of the estate through a second stile before entering the indigenous Newlands Forest.

▶ For the next few kilometres, the path passes formations with names that echo from the past, glorious age of mountaineering: Newlands, Rooiels, Grassy, Ascension, Wormhole, and Hiddingh ravines; Erica, Wormhole, and Fernwood buttresses.

▶ After passing a large square rock, the path ascends into Kirstenbosch in two steep

sections. It drops again almost immediately, losing all the gained height, and then descends once again down an easy zigzag.

▶ The path then winds on down Window Gorge and around the cliffs of Window Buttress (out of sight), before finding a new contour to follow into Skeleton Gorge. Trees along this section are marked with name tags to help identification.

▶ The path veers to the right into Skeleton Gorge, Jan Smuts' favourite route to the top of the mountain. After crossing the apex of the gorge, you will reach the path known as Smuts' Track heading upwards. Cross this and follow the Contour Path as it emerges into a patch of mountain fynbos with the glorious national botanic gardens falling away below you.

▶ After four shallow loops through the fynbos – where you will see keurbooms (*Virgilia oroboides*), wabooms (*Protea nitida*), and mountain cedars (*Widdringtonia nodiflora*) among the many tall fynbos plants – the path ducks back into forest as it enters Nursery Ravine. A zigzagging path goes up on the right-hand side of the ravine, right next to the river, eventually reaching the mountain top right next to Castle Rocks. You could end the hike here and follow the ravine down into Kirstenbosch.

▶ If, however, you prefer the elegant solution of completing the entire walk, then continue along the Contour Path, to emerge again on a fynbos slope. Where the path approaches the tall eucalyptus trees that mark the edge of Cecilia Plantation, keep to the level path, which shortly becomes a track and then a gravel road. The contour route within

Cecilia State Forest is marked by small concrete blocks imprinted with a running figure. The path crosses Rooikatkloof and then the better-defined Cecilia Ravine, where some pleasing indigenous forest remains within the pine-dominated plantation.

▶ Keep to this track, above a private house, and soon you will descend to Constantianek, where tea and scones, or (perhaps more to the point) a beer, await you in the restaurant's pleasant tea garden.

Karbonkelberg Traverse
Hike P7

Route: *Hout Bay to Llandudno around the coast*
Distance: *12 kilometres*
Duration: *6 hours*
Grade: *Moderate*
Booking Authority: *None*
General Information: *Although it involves some tricky traversing around cliffs if tackled at the high tide, this is one of the most satisfying walks on the peninsula. The waves' constant drumming on the rocks creates soothing music for the duration and there are numerous coves for bathing if you begin to overheat. The tricky traverse around the steep cliffs of The Sentinel gives a tougher grading to what is essentially a level path. The walk is linear, so be sure to organize transport to and from the beginning and end (parking at the end is in Leeukoppie Road; follow the signs to Llandudno and Sandy Bay from Victoria Road).*

Plan your hike to coincide with the low tide for the first section, so that you can boulder-hop across the rocky seashore around The Sentinel, thus avoiding a climb as high as 20 metres above the sea. This higher route, although feasible, is potentially dangerous and not for those who have a fear of heights and slippery rock ledges. At the best of times this is not an easy hike, and you should set aside the better part of a day to complete it. There are short cuts, such as the path over the saddle between The Sentinel and Kapteinspiek back to Hout Bay.

▶ This hike begins at a rubbish dump at the southern end of Hout Bay harbour, near the Old Cannon battery – but persevere, as after this the scenery only improves. Follow the path around The Sentinel as it rises to follow the line between vegetation and boulders. By virtue of perspective, the looming cliffs of The Sentinel appear to be overhanging the sea at a precarious angle.

▶ The route skirts The Sentinel's impressive baseline with the cliffs rising to a high point of 331 metres above you. The path continues to curve around to the right, crossing the boulders to Badtamboer point. It then leads across a scree of tumbled granite and sandstone boulders which, in places, have been weathered into fantastical shapes, and passes a headland and a small cove, into which the waves thunder and send up great columns of spray into the air. As the tide rises, the waves push up into the cave-like head of the first ravine, when hikers have to run a watery gauntlet.

▶ Yet another headland is crossed, the path crosses a second cove, above the head of which a decent cave provides shelter in bad weather. Beyond this the path rises, with a line of minor cliffs falling away below. Negotiate this section with care, and then descend to a stony beach.

▶ Ahead is a one-kilometre stretch of rocky beach, where spray-fed, bright-green vegetation reaches down to lichen-painted boulders; proceed over the boulders to the rocky promontory, beyond which lies Seal Island. On the landward side of this headland there is a freshwater spring, the area around which is littered with the rubbish left by generations of fishermen. In springtime, however, the seepage area is a garden of arum lilies and other wildflowers.

▶ Just beyond Seal Island, a path makes its way over the saddle between the two peaks, back to Hout Bay, but you must carry on along the shoreline below Kapteinspiek and Karbonkelberg, taking care when and if you need to negotiate your way around ravines.

▶ Along the slopes of the Karbonkelberg there are three major and one minor ravine to be crossed. Where you round a corner to lose sight of Chapman's Peak behind you, the path rises to about 150 metres to skirt easily around a wide ravine, after which the route is up-and-down for about 200 metres.

▶ Now descend the path into the second ravine: soft greenery and a rock overhang surround this small, box-like canyon. This is approximately the halfway mark of your walk and makes for a good lunch stop.

▶ From the bottom of the ravine you have to climb for about 15 metres to a beacon. From the beacon, you descend in two stages down the cliffs back to the high-water mark.

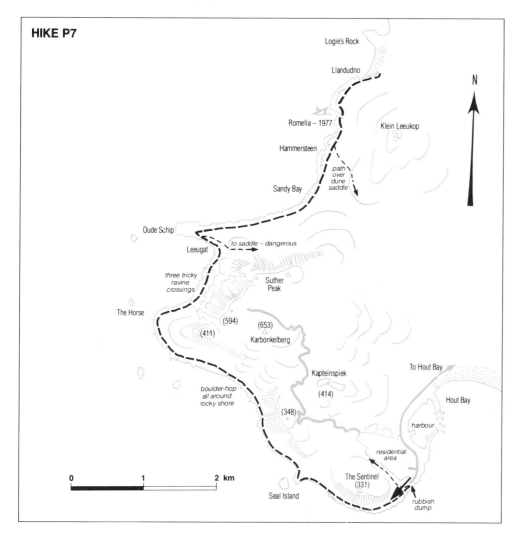

HIKE P7

Logie's Rock

Llandudno

N

Romelia – 1977

Klein Leeukop

Hammersteen

path over dune saddle

Sandy Bay

Oude Schip

to saddle – dangerous

Leeugat

three tricky ravine crossings

Suther Peak

The Horse

(594)

(653)

(411)

Karbonkelberg

Kapteinspiek

To Hout Bay

boulder-hop all around rocky shore

(414)

Hout Bay

(348)

harbour

residential area

0   1   2 km

The Sentinel (331)

Seal Island

rubbish dump

After a stop, turn the sharp corner and take heart – the way across the precarious-looking cliffs that rise up from the Brako ravine is really easy. Make for the top end of the ravine, and do not try to cross it near sea level. Traverse across the 30-centimetre-wide ledge about 150 metres above sea level.

Having crossed the ravine, descend back to sea level down a little gully. From here, follow the shoreline for about 100 metres until you reach what looks like the hardest ravine of all (it's not, and it's the last one). For this one do not do as before, by trying to go up and around the ravine, but head down and across the cannonball-like beach boulders and lo! – you're across.

Follow the rock beacons along a boulder beach, where you may see a shell midden, as well as gnarled bits of driftwood. After about 10 minutes, you will come to Bakleiplaas, where the coast begins to curve around to the right, leaving behind the cliffs of the Karbonkelberg. Passing Duikerpunt, where seals often come ashore to rest and bemoan their lot, make your way across the rocky beaches and through coastal bush for about two kilometres to the small rocky peninsula known as Oude Schip.

To the south of the point is Leeugat bay, where on the dark and stormy night of 5 August 1909, the steamship *Maori* struck the rocks. Three lifeboats were lowered from the ship, but only one reached safety.

From here to the beach at Sandy Bay the going is much easier than the previous section: irregular blue-painted marks on rocks plot the route through the bush and over boulders.

For about an hour the path skirts through the bushy slopes, passing Shorty's Cave (Shorty being a Strandloper-type fisherman who used the cave in the 1940s and '50s), through a narrow gap between two boulders, and continues along the bush-sided path parallel to the coast, before descending to a large boulder, out of which grows an umbrella-like milkwood tree. Pass the point where a white cross indicates an aerial survey mark, and follow the boulder-bush line to Sandy Bay proper – one of the most beautiful beaches in the Cape.

Cross the nearly one-kilometre-long beach, pass the rocky area known as Hammersteen, and on past Nudist Beach. From here the path goes through the bush to Sunset Rocks, where the *Romelia* lies wrecked. This, and its sister ship the *Antipolis*, were being towed to Taiwan as scrap metal in 1977, when they both broke away from the towing vessel during a storm.

Finally, the path reaches Leeukoppie Road. This marks the end of the hike where, hopefully, you have arranged for a vehicle to take you home again.

Silvermine Two Peaks Walk

Hike P8

Route: *Silvermine circular hike*
Distance: *9,5 kilometres*
Duration: *3-4 hours*
Grade: *Moderate*
Booking Authority: *Cape Town Department of Parks and Forests (no permit needed)*

General Information: This walk provides access to some of the finest scenery in the western Cape. Two summits, Noordhoekpiek and Constantiaberg are visited on the way, and the summit views from these peaks are the best in the peninsula. Constantiaberg is the prominent, rounded peak between Die Ou Kaapseweg and Constantianek, with the tall radio mast on its summit. Its central situation affords it the very best vantage point between Cape Town and Cape Point. A small entrance fee is charged at the Silvermine Nature Reserve, so take money with you.

To reach the start of the walk, take the Silvermine Nature Reserve entrance at the top of Die Ou Kaapseweg pass, then drive straight up the tarred road, and park at the parking lot near the reservoir.

Walk up the paved track to the reservoir, and cross the dam wall. When you reach a junction, take the left-hand track. Carry on uphill until you reach a junction at a jeep track. Bear right here to pass a fire lookout and carry on along a ridge towards Noordhoekpiek. Along this section you can take in the breathtaking views down the pastoral Noordhoek valley to the village of Kommetjie in the distance.

Once on top of Noordhoekpiek, to which the jeep track ascends all the way, you will be rewarded with the finest view possible of Hout Bay. No matter what the weather – as long as you are afforded a view at all – Hout Bay must be one of the scenic splendours of South Africa. What a pity that the forests that once spread up the valley were decimated by the early colonists to supply wood

for ship repairs, building timber and fuel. The rock buttress that lords over the bay entrance is The Sentinel, while Kapteinspiek and the Karbonkelberg stand further back and higher, to the right and left of The Sentinel respectively.

Follow the jeep track down Noordhoekpiek as it descends to cross a plain. From here, you can head back to the reservoir the way you came. Otherwise, where the jeep track makes a sharp right turn, carry straight on up the southern slope of Constantiaberg ahead. After toiling for some time up the zigzag path, you will join the tarred post office track that leads up to the summit of the peak.

Despite the somewhat unnatural setting with PO tower 140 and its necessary degradation, the 360° views from up here are – as I have suggested – quite wonderful. If we want to be a technologically developed country, we will just have to accept communications structures on many of the most prominent peaks across the land. After all, no-one wants to be without their FM and shortwave radio reception, television, telephone, modem, fax and telex link-ups.

Head back along the road for a few hundred metres, and then take the left-bearing path down the ridge to the Elephant's Eye Cave. From the cave you are afforded views of Constantia and Lakeside below, and the southern suburbs and Cape Flats beyond. This huge cleft in the mountain above Tokai forest, is reputed to have once been the stronghold of a Khoi tribe led by a woman. Looking up to the cave from below will give you an idea of how its name came about.

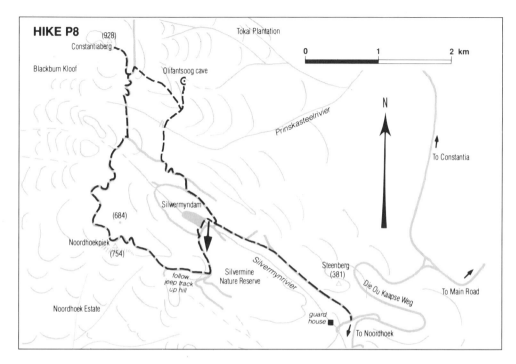

HIKE P8

(928)
Constantiaberg
Blackburn Kloof
Olifantsoog cave
Tokai Plantation
Prinskasteelrivier
N
To Constantia
Silwermyndam
(684)
Noordhoekpiek
(754)
follow jeep track up hill
Silvermine Nature Reserve
Silvermynrivier
Steenberg (381)
Die Ou Kaapse Weg
To Main Road
Noordhoek Estate
guard house
To Noordhoek

0   1   2 km

▶ Follow the path past another fire lookout until it rejoins the jeep track leading back to the reservoir.

From the cave it is also possible to steeply descend the Tokai Nature Trail to the state forest below. If you take this route, you will move out of the montane fynbos belt and into the forest belt, where indigenous forest remains in the moist ravines – locked between pine plantations. There are 37 kilometres of nature trail still to be explored within the state forest area if you have the urge.

Kalk Bay Caves and Waterfall
Hike P9

Route: *Die Ou Kaapseweg to Kalk Bay and back*
Distance: *10,5 kilometres*
Duration: *3-4 hours*
Grade: *Fair*
Booking Authority: *Cape Town Parks and Forests Department (no permit needed)*

General Information: *The name of this area, Silvermine, dates back to 1687, when Simon van der Stel, in one of his many efforts to find the legendary mineral wealth of Africa, had his miners dig in the area for silver – of which they found nought. Although the route description begins on Die Ou Kaapseweg, it could just as easily begin on Boyes Drive above Muizenberg, or, for a much longer walk, from Tokai State Forest below Constantiaberg. For people wanting to explore the peninsula between Table Mountain and the Cape of Good Hope Nature Reserve, I suggest that this is the place to go. From here, other walks will suggest themselves, mainly within the Silvermine Nature Reserve. Because of my line of work, I am forever asked to suggest hiking venues; and yet in the western Cape it takes little imagination to 'discover' that one's doorstep is the first step to many an outdoor adventure.*

Take Die Ou Kaapseweg up from Tokai towards Noordhoek. The road levels off on top and passes the main Silvermine Nature Reserve gate on the right-hand side of the road. Where the road curves to the left and begins its descent to Noordhoek, turn off and park in front of the reserve gate.
▶ From the gate, a gravel jeep track leads off into the reserve, heading in an easterly direction. Follow this track for several hundred metres as it turns to the right, to the left, and then to the right again.
▶ The next several hundred metres is an easy stroll on the contour to a pretty waterfall on the Silvermynrivier. It is worthwhile exploring the gorge below the waterfall.

A short distance past the waterfall, take a turn-off to the right to make your way around a hill, rather than head straight onwards up a gully to a saddle. The walking is easy and the views across the sandy plain to Chapman's Peak and Noordhoek beach are extensive.

For about one and a half kilometres after the turn-off, the track keeps more or less to the contour, providing a lovely jaunt through leucospermum-dominated fynbos. When the jeep track forks, go left and continue, past the path leading off to the right about a kilometre further on.

The path maintains its course, veering to the left around the hill, and then begins to ascend a wide amphitheatre to a saddle. Where the gradient of the path up this wide and shallow amphitheatre begins to ease off – nearly two kilometres from the jeep track turn-off – take the path to your right. This path goes uphill towards the Kalkbaaiberg (516 m). After an ascent of about 40 metres, the path veers off to the right, levels off for a few hundred metres, and then turns to the left and begins a steeper ascent to a saddle between Kalkbaaiberg and Klein-Tuinkop (492 m) on your left.

Descend on the other side of this saddle, passing both Kalkbaai and Ridge (502 m) peaks on your left and Klein-Tuinkop on your right, to the Amphitheatre; here narrow valleys lead off to both left and right while you stand, surrounded on all three sides by sandstone ridges and peaks. Make for the far side of the left-hand valley – Echo Valley – to descend for one and a half kilometres down it.

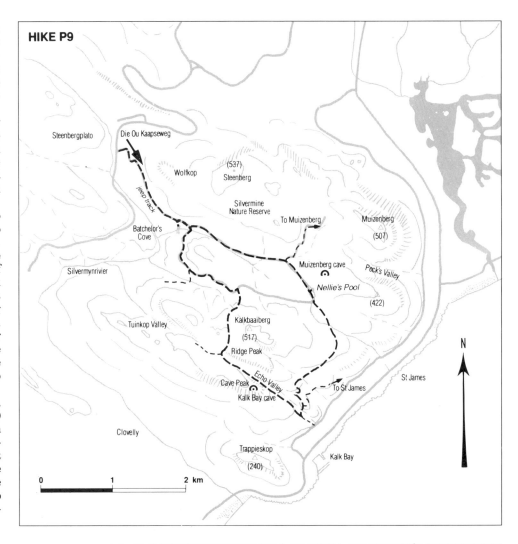

HIKE P9

By turning right and then immediately left you will find yourself on the ridge walk overlooking Fish Hoek. While taking in this sweeping vista you will pass the Oread Halls and the very long Boomslang caves on your left and right respectively. In all there are over 80 caves lying in the sandstone cliffs hereabouts. Do not try to explore too deeply into the caves, as some are very deep and dangerous, and over the years many people have come to grief in this way.

▶ From the bottom of Echo Valley, turn left to ascend a slope for about 100 metres to reach Oukraal. From here you take the steep zigzags up Jacob's Ladder, where a track comes up from St James. Keep to the main track here and avoid the path that leads off to the left into the Spes Bona bush. On reaching the 300-metre contour, the path levels off and crosses a sloping plateau, going in the direction of Muizenberg. It then veers around in a wide arc to the left across the plateau, and is soon met by a track coming in from the right.

▶ Keep to the left, to pass Nellie's Pool, with Muizenberg cave on the ridge opposite. Here you regain the Steenbergplato, which is the old name for the Silvermine Nature Reserve area at the top of Die Ou Kaapseweg.

▶ From here you pick up a broad jeep track. The track breaches a low saddle to Junction Pool, where it meets another path coming in from the right. You, however, must carry on in a northerly direction, keeping left to avoid the restricted military area.

▶ About one kilometre beyond Junction Pool, there is a picnic spot where a stream has been dammed. You are now less than a kilometre from the Silvermynrivier waterfall and have a little over a kilometre to go to return to the starting point.

Kanonkop
Hike P10

Route: *Bordjiesdrif road to Kanonkop, up Paulsberg and back*
Distance: *6 kilometres*
Duration: *1½ hours (there): 45 mins (back)*
Grade: *Fair*
Booking Authority: *Cape of Good Hope Nature Reserve (Western Cape Regional Services Council) (permit needed)*
General Information: *There are three main attractions on this short hike – first there is the signal cannon, after which Kanonkop is named; then there are the views from Paulsberg over all of the Cape of Good Hope Nature Reserve; and finally there are the magnificent wildflowers that make the veld sparkle with colour for much of the year. You will need to pay a small fee at the gate (R2-00 per vehicle and R2-00 per person), where you will also receive your permit. The reserve is open for day visits only; after the Kruger National Park it is the most visited conservation area in the country. There is a restaurant in the reserve, which serves lovely tea and scones.*

▶ This hike has been recently rerouted, and now begins about 200 metres after the turn-off to Venus Pools, from the Bordjiesdrif road (Buffelsbaai). The path begins at Bynes (bee hive) and follows the general contour towards Kanonkop, near the end of this it ascends approximately 100 metres over a distance of several hundred metres, to gain the site of the old signal cannon, perched on a lichen-splashed ridge of low rocks. The cannon is found at about 230 metres, pointing towards Cape Point and overlooking Buffelsbaai and most of False Bay.

▶ The vegetation here comprises a typical fynbos mix of mainly restios, small erica bushes, leucadendrons and the occasional medium-sized leucospermum, with helichrysums, pelargoniums (geraniums) and other bulbous plants recognizable only when they are in flower.

▶ From Kanonkop (not a kop at all) backtrack for about 20 metres, and then turn right at a cairn towards a big hill – Paulsberg. There are two routes to the top of this hill, one via a ridge on the sea side of the hill, and the other via a saddle on the land side. To follow the 'sea route', bear right to the ridge at the base of Paulsberg and then head diagonally back and up to follow just behind the ridge edge all the way up, looking out for the occasional cairns. Near the top, where the way is partly blocked by rocky outcrops, you can scramble over the ledges and loose boulders – taking care with loose blocks – or you can move further around to the left, away from the sea, and make your way up through the low scrub.

▶ To take the other route, bear left from the cairn, and head towards the saddle. At the second prominent boulder (about two metres high), you should see a vague path leading off to the right, past a cairn. From here, you should move diagonally up to the left for the first half of the climb, and then curve slowly to the right, heading for the lower right-hand shoulder of the hill. If you are lucky you will be able to follow cairns and a basic path all the way up through the increasingly dense bush. If you miss the cairns, you can't really get lost, just head for the top by taking the line of least resistance.

❿ Near the summit, the vegetation becomes progressively more lush. This is due firstly to the cloud and mist inception, but possibly also to the fact that fire penetration has been limited up here. On the rocky outcrops red crassulas (*Crassula coccinea*) show their brilliant, red flower heads. The odd king protea (*Protea cynaroides*) sprouts around the summit, but the dominant shrub here seems to be the common sugarbush (*P. repens*). Beware the blisterbush (*Peucedanum galbanum*) which can provoke nasty sting rashes in some people.

The views from the top are grand on a clear day, when you can survey all of False Bay, the Hottentots-Holland mountains on the far side of the bay, Cape Point, and the rocky ledges below known as The Cauldron. The Venus Pools are found on the ledge area, nearest to Buffelsbaai.

❿ To return, make your way back to Kanonkop, heading first for the saddle behind (west of) Paulsberg, which is littered with large, geometric boulders. From here, follow the narrow, erratic path to Kanonkop directly to the south. From Kanonkop, take the path steeply down to the Venus Pool road, heading for the spot marked 'Booi se Skerm' on the 1:50 000 map. Turn right up the tarred road, passing the old lime kiln site on your way back to the starting point.

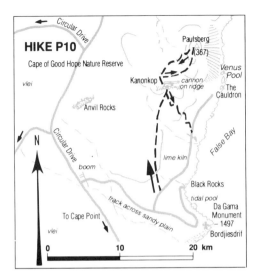

HIKE P10
Cape of Good Hope Nature Reserve

Cape of Good Hope *Hike P11*

Route: Hoek van Bobbejaan to Cape Point
Distance: 12 kilometres
Duration: 4 hours
Grade: Easy
Booking Authority: Cape of Good Hope Nature Reserve (Western Cape Regional Services Council) (permit needed)
General Information: This is an easy stroll along the scenic Cape Point coastline (get your permit at the entrance to the Cape of Good Hope Nature Reserve), where you experience a diversity of habitats from sandy to rocky shores, rock pools, headlands and cliffs. Anyone wanting more of a challenge can extend the walk by starting at

Olifantsbospunt, near the Skaife Education Centre. If you do decide on this longer variation, you will pass a shipwreck close to the centre. Baboons frequent this area, having become used to human 'handouts'. Avoid them totally, especially if you have food, as they can become a problem – even dangerous. You might also see bontebok, mountain zebra and eland. This is a linear walk, so take two cars for transportation.

❿ From the parking area at Hoek van Bobbejaan, take the jeep track that winds down to the sea from the right-hand side (facing the sea) of the area. This spot is much fancied by fishermen, so for the first part of your hike this odd breed of person may stand a guard of honour for you. It will take about 20 minutes before you reach the rocky shore, where you will see the remains of a liberty ship. These flimsy vessels were mass-produced in the USA during the Second World War, as troop and cargo carriers, and in their convoys they were easy prey for the German U-boats that prowled these waters. The *Thomas T Tucker* wreck at Olifantsbospunt is also a liberty ship.

❿ Immediately to your right, you will see a fence. This is the boundary of Brightwater farm. The landowners agreed to have their farm included in the reserve on the condition that they alone reserved the right to use it for holiday purposes.

❿ Turn left along the shore and head for the Cape of Good Hope where, apparently, Bartolomeu Dias planted a cross on his voyage in 1488. A somewhat overdone replica can be seen near the reserve's restaurant.

The first part of this walk involves a fair amount of boulder hopping. While it is a great area for beachcombing, remember that this is a reserve and that it is illegal to remove anything – look and touch only. The beaches and rocky areas are rich in shells and shell fragments, various types of seaweed, driftwood and other 'treasures' from the sea. Make sure to explore the rock pools along the way.

The bird life along this section of the coast is varied, including even fish eagles and black eagles among the recorded species. Perhaps the most interesting coastal bird, and one that you are likely to see, is the black oystercatcher, with its bright red legs and stout bill. Being highly visible and active, these birds seem to be common along our shores, though they are, in fact, rare to the point of being endangered. There are thought to be fewer than 5 000 of these birds left in their natural habitat, from the Cunene River mouth along the coast to the Transkei/Natal border. Oystercatchers are highly sensitive to disturbance, especially while breeding and nesting. Oystercatchers are known to breed around the Klaasjagers estuary in the reserve.

You may choose to boulder-hop over most of the rocky shoreline, or follow the rough footpath on slightly higher ground; this path sometimes widens to become a vague jeep track. The path is alternately sandy (and tedious to negotiate), and welcomely grassy.
You will pass the Kommetjieberg (381 m) and Groot-Blouberg (267 m), then on to Muishondbaai (mongoose bay) and Platboompunt (flat tree point) – a name

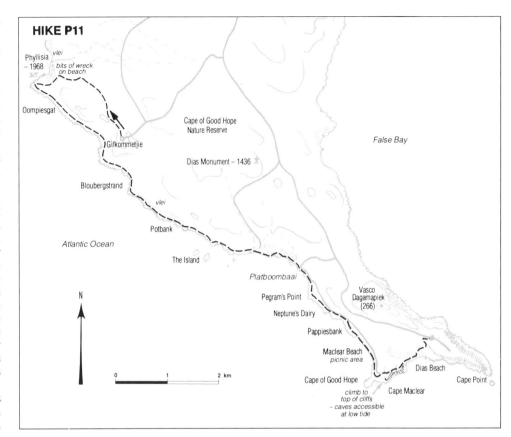

HIKE P11

presumably referring to the milkwoods that grow in the area. Here you can see a rocky island out at sea. Along this stretch you will negotiate many rocky points, between which lie the sweeps of wave-sculpted beaches, beaches for which the Cape is famous. You can choose between boulder-hopping, following the rough path between the beach and scrub line, or walking along the tar road that leads towards Maclear Beach. On reaching this beach, Vasco Dagamapiek (560 m) rises up on your left.

▶ Continue until you reach the parking area, and then follow the footpath that leads from the far end of the area up the 'Cape of Good Hope scenic route'.

▶ The path rises steeply for 400 metres, and then passes through a fine stand of coastal fynbos, with magnificent views over the Cape of Good Hope. Cape Point is to your left (if you are facing seaward), and the rest of the reserve and the coastline before you and to your right. Some 45 minutes from the lower car park, you will reach another, larger car park at the base of the Cape Point headland. This is the end of the hike.

If you have never been there, then a short walk up to the lighthouse and viewpoint at Cape Point are highly recommended – just don't let anyone kid you that from here you can see the two oceans meeting. That is a romantic notion, though it does seem to draw the crowds.

Le Vaillant's Peninsula Traverse
Hike P12

Route: *Cape Town to Cape Point*
Distance: *60 kilometres*
Duration: *3 days*
Grade: *Severe*
Booking Authority: *Cape of Good Hope Nature Reserve (Western Cape Regional Services Council) (permit needed)*
General Information: *The name that I have given to this somewhat contrived trail celebrates the 18th-century French naturalist who accomplished this feat during his stay at the Cape in 1783. One factor making it easier for him 200 years ago than it is today, was the absence of private property and restricted reserve land – so he could walk and camp where he wished. For years now the many public authorities who control land on the peninsula (city council, regional services council, provincial conservation, state forestry, and various town councils) have spoken about developing a trail down the full length of the peninsula, but so far nothing has been done. The main problem is overnight facilities – there are none. You must plan your overnight stops before setting out. My aim here has been to describe a basic route across public land, connected by public roads where necessary. The route is perhaps not ideal, but it is feasible, though you will have to break the walk between Kommetjie and the Cape of Good Hope Nature Reserve. My recommended walk takes three days, and has been planned to make use of already existing facilities.*

Day 1: Kloofnek Corner to Constantianek – 18 kilometres (8 hours)
▶ The route starts at Kloofnek Corner, conveniently near Stan's Halt youth hostel (from the Kloofnek circle go down the Clifton road to Stan's Halt). Climb up the corner to the Contour Path and traverse around the front of Table Mountain to Platteklip gorge (of course, you could bypass the first uphill slog by taking the cable car to the summit of Table Mountain). Climb the gorge and then follow the sign to Maclear's Beacon. From Maclear's Beacon take the path (signposted) to Skeleton Gorge.

▶ From the top of the gorge carry on past Castle Rocks and Nursery Ravine, giving wide berth to the upper plantations and Alexandra and De Villiers reservoirs. Once past the line of the back table, keep to the forestry bridle path. Two hundred and fifty metres after crossing a bridge (at the top of Spilhaus Ravine), double back to the left and descend into the Cecilia Plantation. Thereafter, stick to the uppermost track of this road system to emerge at the Eagle's Nest promontory (421 m). From Eagle's Nest, there is a direct path to the nek.

At the nek, you can stay at the Houtkapperspoort holiday cottages (tel. (021) 794-5216), or proceed down into Hout Bay, which has a range of accommodation in the town. You can catch a bus back up to the nek for day two's fun.

Day 2: Constantianek to Kommetjie – 20 kilometres (8 hours)
▶ The path begins a few hundred metres beyond the Constantia Nek Restaurant on the road to Hout Bay, and the starting point is clearly indicated by a signboard on the left-hand side of the road. The path makes for a firebreak, that cuts a way up directly behind the restaurant, up the main ridge of the Vlakkenberg.

▶ On reaching the wide plateau on top of Vlakkenberg, carry straight on (south), making for the gully that leads in the direction of the Constantiaberg (928 m).

▶ Follow the upper Bokkemanskloof down towards the plantations of Tokai State Forest to your left. Make for the fire break to make an easy pass around the right-hand side of the plantation, eventually coming to the telecommunications road that heads for the masts on the Constantiaberg. The road is met just short of three kilometres from the nek. Follow the road for about the same distance, avoiding short cuts where the road twists and turns.

❱ Where the road makes its final hairpin bend to ascend the final ramp up the mountain, leave it and make for the jeep track one kilometre across an open plain below you to your right by heading around the top of a shallow valley on your right-hand side. Where you meet the track, bear right and follow it around the base of Noordhoekpiek (754 m) for about two and a half kilometres to where the track heads off to the east, and a firebreak leads you down for one and a quarter kilometres to the saddle between Noordhoek and Chapman's peaks (going behind the pinnacle that stands above the Noordhoek valley amphitheatre).

From the saddle, your path takes the steep line down a gully to the northwest. The going is made easier by virtue of the firebreak that clears a way above the left-hand stream bank, going downhill.

❱ When the path meets Chapman's Peak Drive, turn left to proceed up the gentle 600-metre slope to the main viewsite. From here, follow the road all along the Chapman's Peak cliff line: take care not to obstruct traffic on the narrow road.

❱ From here it is a four-and-a-half-kilometre slog downhill to the Noordhoek turn-off. Turn right at the turn-off, and another one and a half kilometres along the road will take you to the Red Herring tearoom.

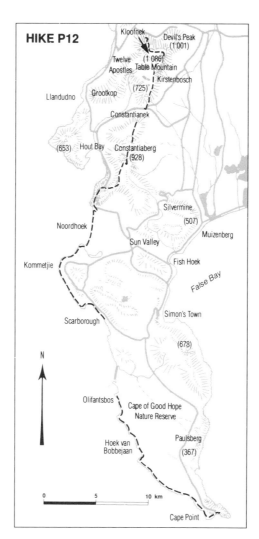

HIKE P12

❱ This makes a welcome stopover, but our route continues ... Proceed to the beach parking area and onto the beach for a four-kilometre slog over the soft sand of Noordhoek Beach to Klein Slangpunt. Depending on conditions, you can either follow the surf line, or keep to the harder surface of the near-dune flats.

❱ Pass the wreck and continue down the beach until you have crossed the Wildevoelvlei stream mouth (don't drink the polluted water here), then cut to the left inland of the rocky point – unless you wish to explore the rocky coastline.

❱ The first place you will arrive at in Kommetjie is our destination – Imhoff caravan and camp site. There are two other caravan and camping grounds, as well as a hotel, in Kommetjie.

Day 3: Kommetjie to Cape Point – 30 kilometres
❱ Now is the point that you are going to have to break your walk. Drive from Kommetjie (under your own pre-arranged steam) to the reserve gate, and then to Olifantsbospunt on the west coast. From here, simply follow the coastline down to Cape Point (for a fuller description from Hoek van Bobbejaan, see the Cape of Good Hope walk (Hike P11)).

Alternatively, you could walk from Kommetjie to Scarborough along the sea road, past misty cliffs, and then head for the reserve gate under your own pre-arranged steam (private car, hitch-hike or whatever). From the gate you can hike the 15-kilometre-stretch along the main reserve road to Cape Point.

BOLAND

The Boland hiking region is dominated by the long Hottentots-Holland range, which merges with a number of other ranges (the Groot-Drakenstein, Wemmershoek, Franschhoek, Stellenbosch, Jonkershoek and Kogelberg ranges) to create a swirling vortex of folded ridges and peaks. These various constituent ranges are often lumped together under the name of Hottentots-Holland, but I prefer to call them by the more general name of the Boland mountains.

These were the first mountains that blocked the way for European settlers interested in exploring the interior of southern Africa. The curious name of 'Hottentots-Holland' is said to have been coined by scouts sent out by Jan van Riebeeck to explore the land east of Table Bay. After crossing the daunting Cape sand flats, these scouts came into a beautiful valley at the foot of some mountains. Here they found hundreds of Khoi (Hottentots) congregated on the banks of the Eersterivier, so they called it the Hottentot's 'Holland', or home. Earlier, Van Riebeeck had named the range the 'Mountains of Africa' – a name I would have preferred to have had preserved.

The three major towns of the region are Stellenbosch, Franschhoek and Grabouw. Around these towns – in the pleated valleys below the Boland peaks – many of the country's premier wine estates were founded. The ornately gabled Cape-Dutch homesteads of prosperous wine farmers seem to echo the forms of the folded crags that rise up majestically behind them. This is one place where man has created something to complement the beauty of his natural surroundings.

The Boland Mountains are graced with the richest flora of all the fynbos biome, not because the soils here are more fertile than elsewhere (in fact, quite opposite is the case), but because of the extraordinarily high rainfall in the area. Winter rainfall averaging around 1 500 millimetres at the Nuweberg rain gauge (and considerably higher than this on the peak above) is supplemented by heavy snowfalls in winter, and regular mist-inception – softening the desiccating effects of the blustering southeaster – in summer.

Included among the floral species of the Boland mountains are some extremely rare and beautiful plants; the marsh rose (*Orothamnus zeyheri*) and blushing bride (*Serruria florida*), for instance. Ironically, many of the loveliest and most delicate of all the flowering fynbos plants grow in the most exposed upper reaches of these mountains, lashed in winter by snowstorms, and singed in summer by harsh sunlight and searing southeasterly winds.

It is not only these rarities that you should look out for, however, as there are really so many floral delights to find. Apart from the famous proteas, the widespread leucadendrons (conebushes) and leucospermums (pincushions), as well as the Proteaceae family's lesser-known genera – *Diastella*, *Aulax*, *Sorocephalus*, *Serruria*, *Mimetes*, and *Spatalla* – are represented by numerous species. Most proteas flower from autumn to spring – reaching a peak in winter. Spring, though, is best for the overall fynbos bouquet, but even mid- to late summer has its charms – painted ladies, delicate orchids of many shapes and shades, and of course that most glorious of all the members of this family, the king protea (*P. cynaroides*), being on show at that time.

Though nowhere abundant in the fynbos region, birds are more plentiful in the Boland than in most other mountain areas. While the actual species differ little from those representative of the entire region, they seem to be more frequently observed here, especially at the higher altitudes. Some of the smaller species you are likely to see are: brilliant orange-breasted sunbirds, flitting around the erica blooms; Cape buntings, sparrow-like seedeaters recognized by the black and white stripes on their heads; little Cape siskins; and various warblers such as neddickies, Victorin's warblers (an endemic species), grassbirds, and grey-backed and Levaillant's cisticolas.

Hiking in the Boland

The standard warning, that mountain weather is unpredictable, is particularly applicable to the Boland mountains. Hiking in this region without equipment to withstand the fiercest storms can turn a pleasant hiking trip into a fight for your life. Indeed, in most years, at least one death is recorded in these mountains, and the cause is often hypothermia. I have set out on the Boland Trail in midsummer, only to be forced back by a blizzard coming in from the southeast, along the Hottentots-Holland mountains. This is the only time I have ever turned back on a hike, but I saw no point in continuing on my hands and knees for another 20-odd kilometres, forcing my way into stinging, horizontal rain. So I spent the rest of my weekend swimming and basking in the sun on a Betty's Bay beach.

The only overnighting opportunities offered in the Boland mountains are on the Hottentots-Holland section of the Boland NHW Trail. There are five huts on the trail – Eikenhof, Landdroskop, Shamrock Lodge, Boesmanskloof and Aloe Ridge – and bookings must be made through the NHWB office in Cape Town (Tel. (021) 402 3093). There are, however, numerous one-day hikes from the various forest stations that control the area: Jonkershoek, Grabouw, Nuweberg and La Motte. Horse-riding is permitted in the La Motte State Forest in the Groot-Drakensteinberge, while all-terrain bicyclists (ATBs) can obtain permits to enter all four state forest areas, as long as they keep to existing forestry roads (contact ROMP club for more details: Tel. (021) 439 6740).

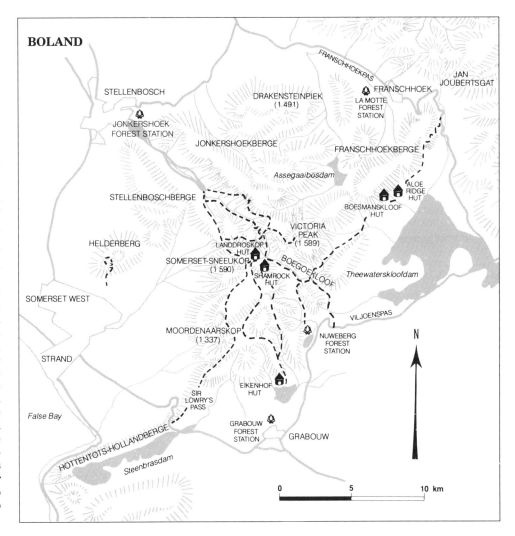

BOLAND

STELLENBOSCH

JONKERSHOEK
FOREST STATION

STELLENBOSCHBERGE

HELDERBERG

SOMERSET WEST

STRAND

False Bay

FRANSCHHOEKPAS

DRAKENSTEINPIEK
(1 491)

JONKERSHOEKBERGE

Assegaaibosdam

JAN JOUBERTSGAT

FRANSCHHOEK
LA MOTTE
FOREST
STATION

FRANSCHHOEKBERGE

ALOE
RIDGE
HUT
BOESMANSKLOOF
HUT

VICTORIA
PEAK
(1 589)

LANDDROSKOP
HUT
SOMERSET-SNEEUKOP
(1 590)
SHAMROCK
HUT

BOEGOEKLOOF

Theewaterskloofdam

VILJOENSPAS

MOORDENAARSKOP
(1 337)

NUWEBERG
FOREST
STATION

N

EIKENHOF
HUT

SIR
LOWRY'S
PASS

GRABOUW
FOREST
STATION

GRABOUW

HOTTENTOTS-HOLLANDBERGE

Steenbrasdam

0   5   10 km

The Hottentots-Holland section of the Boland Trail is a well-conceived and well-planned trail, offering numerous options in a limited, but beautiful mountain area. Book well in advance for this trail as it is one of the most popular trails of the NHW system. Indeed, at peak times of year, the paths, and especially the huts, can become unpleasantly crowded. Such is the demand, however, that some people have lobbied to have the trail opened to even more people – Landdroskop and Shamrock Lodge huts combined can sleep 70 people! This does not make for a high-quality mountaineering experience perhaps, but then, if it is solitude that you want, you should hike at off-peak times.

Whatever the circumstances, this outstanding trail should not be ignored. There are two routes to the Landdroskop hut (from Sir Lowry's Pass (Hike B1) and Eikenhof (Hike B2)) and five from it (back to Eikenhof (Hike B3), to Jonkershoek (Hike B4), to Nuweberg Forest Station (Hike B5), to Boesmanskloof and then Franschhoek (Hike B6), and down Boegoekloof (Hike B7)). These routes will be discussed separately as the first seven hikes.

The Boland is easily accessible and so, after Table Mountain perhaps, this is the area most people will explore first. I have described some of the most obvious and popular hikes, but day permits can be obtained for any of the state forests, and it is then up to you to get a good 1:50 000 map and explore beyond (when booking for the NHW trail, a trail map is provided for each member of the hiking party, the cost of which is included in the trail fee).

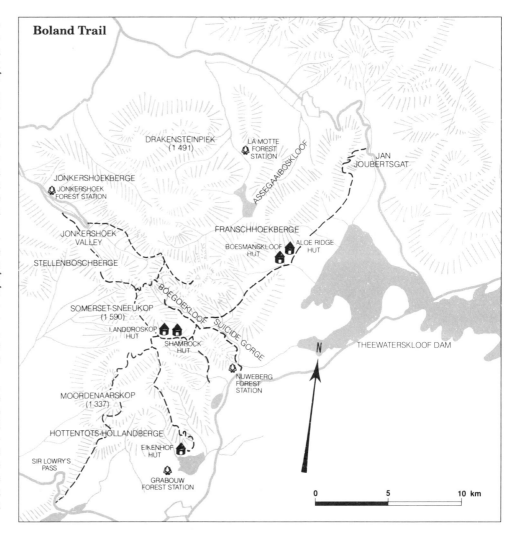

Boland Trail

Sir Lowry's Pass to Landdroskop NHW
Hike B1

Route: *Sir Lowry's Pass car park to Landdroskop*
Distance: *23,1 kilometres*
Duration: *9 hours*
Grade: *Extreme*
Booking Authority: *NHWB (Tel. (021) 402 3093) (permit needed)*
General Information: *This was the original start of the Boland Trail; it involves a demanding day's hiking, which can become worse if the weather closes in. In fact, because of its unpredictable weather, this route has developed something of a reputation for epic hikes. It is exposed to the full might of north-westerly gales in winter, and blustery south-easterly ones in summer; some ill-equipped hikers have succumbed to hypothermia on this route, so make sure that you don't add your name to the trail's obituaries. If you are well prepared, however, this is an outstanding hike. Although the hike does not include any major ascents, anyone who has completed it in adverse weather will agree that it warrants the 'extreme' grading.*

▶ At the top of Sir Lowry's Pass, a forestry sign indicates the newly built security parking place at the beginning of the trail. From here, you follow a jeep track steadily up towards the Gantouwpas. The NHW path takes a sharp turn to the right, away from the jeep track to the beginning of the Gantouwpas (where a power line crosses the mountains). The top of the pass is marked by mounted cannon (just off the path) which were used to announce the arrival of ships at Table Bay. The ruts made by old wagon wheels can be seen here, and the spot has been declared a national monument.

The Gantouwpas, originally a game trail, became the first route used by Europeans to cross the Boland mountains, when, in 1653, an expedition led by Hendrick Lucas was sent to buy cattle from the Khoi. The pass continued to be used until, in 1823, it was replaced by a more accessible one just to the west – named after Sir Lowry Cole, governor at the time.

The NHW map conveniently indicates the major plant communities along the trail; communities A and B being encountered along this stretch. Clusters of hairy, crimson fire heath flowers (*Erica cerinthoides*); sticky, red and green/yellow-tipped rosettes of Masson's heath (*E. massonii*), brown-bearded, white bunches of *E. plunkenetti* and *E. imbricata* bells line the path. Various genera of everlastings are common along the edge of the jeep track, including red, white and yellow species. Growing on the track you may see the delicate violet flower head of the slender, three-petalled iris, *Morea tripetala*. The fynbos veld is dotted with king proteas (*Protea cynaroides*), and the prostrate, yellowish-green, cup-shaped ground rose, *Protea acaulos*.

▶ From the top of the Gantouwpas, the path leads uphill along the main axis ridge of the Hottentots-Holland range, towards the communications tower on Hans se Kop. Keeping to the general incline, the path rounds the 'kop' to the right, dropping down to meet Buys se Pad, an historic road, now used for access to the tower.

▶ Follow the road around to regain the edge of the range at Groot-Waainek. If this nek does not live up to its name, you will be rewarded by spectacular views over the Cape Flats and False Bay; if it does, you will be battling your way through turbulent clouds brought by the winds.

▶ Once again, the path loops away from the ridge to round Moordenaarskop (1 337 m and 1 340 m), zigzagging up the steepest section. On gaining the eastern side of this mountain, you look down into the dark, forested depths of Wesselsgat kloof, 500 metres below (the Stokoe's Pass route up from Eikenhof can be seen on the opposite side of the gorge).

▶ From here, continue curving around to Klein-Waainek, another view site. After this, the path winds in and out, up and down, as it negotiates five major spurs (passing the emergency shelter at the 13,75-kilometre mark), with numerous lesser loops, keeping more or less to the 1 200-metre contour. Looking down into the funnel of Wesselsgat on your right, you will see numerous waterfalls. You should also see specimens of *Mimetes argenteus*, the silver bottlebrush that is endemic to this range. This showy plant is also the trail's emblem.

▶ At the 18,75-kilometre mark, the path reaches the seepage area called Guinevere, where the restio *Chondropetalum mucronatum* is dominant. Looking down from the watering point at Guinevere, you can see the river tumbling down the Witwatervalletjies,

HIKES B1, B2, B3

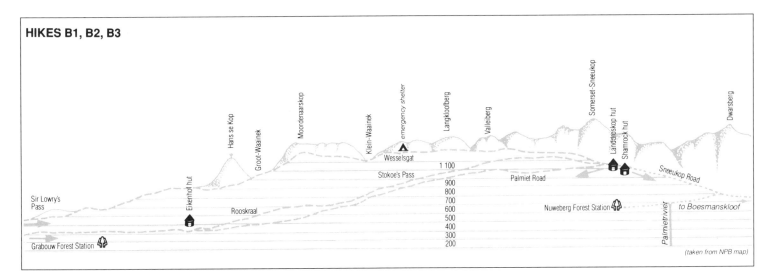

(taken from NPB map)

into Wesselsgat. The magical beauty of these colourful flats should explain the reference to Arthurian legend.

▶ From here, the path rounds Landdroskop peak (1 515 m) and begins its final descent towards the Landdroskop and Shamrock huts. In summertime, the dark pink blooms of the large painted lady (*Gladiolus carneus*) line the path between scratchy restios, blombos (*Metalassia muricata*) and climber's friend (*Cliffortia* sp.) bushes. In spring, it is the red-and-yellow-tipped clusters of Masson's heath that line the paths.

▶ On approaching the final flats where your path joins the Eikenhof route, the huts can be seen straight ahead. The path, however, still executes a one-kilometre-long loop around to the left before reaching its

conclusion. You may sleep in either hut, depending on your preference and the available space. Here, as elsewhere, don't waste the tank water, as hikers after you need it too; i.e., no showers or letting the tap run while you do your ablutions. Also, be considerate enough not to mess the drinking areas with food scraps and soap.

Eikenhof NHW
Hike B2

Route: *Eikenhof hut to Landdroskop hut*
Distance: *14,2 (+ 5,5) kilometres*
Duration: *6-7 hours*
Grade: *Severe*
Booking Authority: *NHWB (Tel. (021) 402 3093) (permit needed)*

General Information: *This is a fairly steep hike, but only of moderate distance, allowing you to stop and appreciate the route's floral spectacle. In my experience, this route offers the richest botanical experience of the entire trail – even though the first four and a half kilometres are through a pine plantation. The path begins at the Eikenhof hut – a converted farmhouse beside the Eikenhof reservoir, with flush toilets, shower and fireplace. However, you will have to park at the Grabouw Forest Station car park – some five and a half kilometres away – and then follow Apple Garth and Bon Acres signs, keeping left past Grabouw Country Club to the forestry gate. From there it is a short stroll around the dam to the hut, starting point of your hike.*

▶ From the Eikenhof hut, follow the painted footprints (two feet indicating a change of direction) along the gravel logging roads, where the tall pines afford valuable shade while you gain some altitude. As you emerge from the plantation – at about 660 metres – Nuweberg peak (1 280 m) rises up to the right. The path climbs fairly steeply from here to a drinking spot, and, from there, through some rocky shale and sandstone scree areas, where the path has been eroded in places.

▶ At the six-kilometre mark, the path begins to climb steeply, before levelling off for a short while, passing through a wooded gully where *Elegia capensis* stems grow up to three metres high.

▶ After climbing diagonally across an open slope, the path heads up Stokoe's Pass. Some neanderthal hikers prefer to take a short cut up a steep slope on the right, thereby bypassing the best part of the route. They also ruin it for other hikers by causing needless erosion and consequent bad feelings. In two trips I have recorded five species of protea in bloom (*Protea cynaroides*, *P. lacticolor*, *P. stokoei*, *P. neriifolia*, *P. acaulos*), the finest specimens of *Mimetes argenteus*, numerous leucadendrons, gladioluses, ground orchids and the shocking blue clusters of aristea stalks among others.

▶ On reaching the end of the pass, one gains a viewpoint down into the mysterious depths of Wesselsgat kloof and across to four peaks rising in altitude from left to right: Moordenaarskop (1 337 m), Langkloofberg (1 338 m), Langklippiek (1 359 m) and finally Valleiberg (1 385 m).

▶ From Stokoe's Pass, the path follows a rocky ridge, zigzagging up the steeper sections. The path passes around the back of Nuweberg, only 80 metres from the summit. The highest rainfall in South Africa is recorded on this peak, averaging 3 300 millimetres annually.

▶ A vlei is crossed, where the water-loving restio *Chondropetalum mucronatum* grows in dense tufts, then the path drops down to another vlei area, meeting the Sir Lowry's Pass path. Watch out for Christmas painted ladies (*Gladioulus undulatus*) in summer.

▶ The huts, complete with fireplaces (you may be pleased to hear), are just a short stroll away from here.

Eikenhof Return NHW

Hike B3

Route: *Landdroskop hut back to Eikenhof*
Distance: *12,6 kilometres*
Duration: *4 hours*
Grade: *Moderate*
Booking Authority: *NHWB (Tel. (021) 402 3093) (permit needed)*
General Information: *This is the shortest and easiest section of this trail's layout. For this reason, it is much favoured by weekend hikers. To my mind, however, it has less to offer from a scenic point of view than the other sections, though some interesting plants can be seen. Parts of the upper slopes have recently been logged, and this, I feel, detracts from the wilderness character one expects of such an area.*

▶ From Landdroskop, take the Sir Lowry's Pass route, passing a turn-off to the right to Jonkershoek. One kilometre from the start, you will reach a fork. Take the left-hand prong here, and follow the track along what is called the Palmietpad. The first five kilometres involve a very easy descent, passing the twin upper tributaries of the Palmietrivier (with the Nuweberg to the right), and proceeding along a narrowing mountain peninsula called The Sphinx. Various species of protea and erica are visible along this stretch, as well as some other common but not easily identified plants such as the sturdy but sparsely branched shrub *Priestleya vestita*, with its clusters of small, hairy, overlapping leaves and compact yellow flower heads.

Another is the fountain bush (*Psoralea pinnata*), a feathery-leafed shrub growing to a height of up to four metres in damp places, with sweet-smelling lilac-and-white flowers. *Podalyria montana*, a member of the pea family, is a stout shrub with pink-and-white flowers. The flowers are sweetly scented and many people mistake this for the larger, and somewhat more widespread keurboom (*Virgilia oroboides*).

▶ One kilometre from The Sphinx, you reach the plantation zone, on the approach to which a curious ericaceous plant can be found flowering from spring through to autumn; this is the heuningblom (*Retzia capensis*). This many-stemmed shrub is densely covered with long, thin, rolled leaves, between which the red-and-white-tipped, cigar-shaped flowers emerge. This is the only species of its genus, and it is

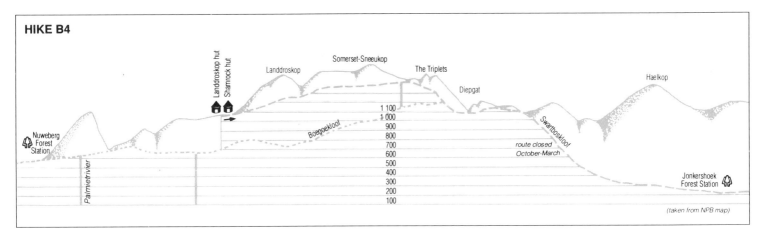

Landdroskop hut
Shamrock hut
Somerset-Sneeukop
Landdroskop
The Triplets
Haelkop
Diepgat
Boegoekloof
Swartboskloof
route closed
October-March
Nuweberg
Forest
Station
Palmietrivier
Jonkershoek
Forest Station

1 100
1 000
900
800
700
600
500
400
300
200
100

(taken from NPB map)

endemic to the mountains between here and the Riviersonderend range.

▶ Just before entering the plantation area, the path joins a logging road, and from here it is a matter of merely following the painted footprints, though you still have another 450 metres of altitude to lose before reaching the end of the trail. Some sharp descents occur on the road, the last one leading to the pleasant river forest vaulting the Keeromsrivier, where the gurgling waters entice you to strip off and take a refreshing dip.

Landdroskop to Jonkershoek NHW
Hike B4

Route: *Landdroskop hut to Jonkershoek*
Distance: *17,6 kilometres*
Duration: *7 hours*

Grade: *Severe*
Booking Authority: *NHWB (Tel. (021) 402 3093) (permit needed)*
General Information: *This route can be shortened by about two and a half kilometres if you arrange transport to meet you where the path joins the Jonkershoek circular drive. The route's mountain scenery is its outstanding feature, as it passes most of the range's highest points and offers views of all the major peaks in the area. If you are going to see any wild animals in the Hottentots-Holland Nature Reserve, this is the most likely place that it will occur. Predators such as leopard, caracal and black-backed jackal are fairly frequent visitors, while smaller animals like genets, mongoose (small grey), grysbok, grey rhebok and klipspringer are perhaps more common than sightings would suggest. This route should be avoided in stormy weather as Landdroskop is frequently covered in snow during winter storms; some years back, a group of boys froze to death in a snowstorm here. This route is closed during the fire hazard season (October to March).*

▶ From Landdroskop hut, take the path towards Sir Lowry's Pass for about 400 metres through a seepage area. Then take the turn-off to the right, where an unusual species of protea can be seen flowering in spring. *Protea caespitosa* brings forth a delicate pink flower from amid its tufted, long, cabbage-like leaves. The flower itself is surrounded by a cluster of dried, papery brown leaves. This ground-hugging species is found only on the highest mountains, in isolated patches above the snow line.

▶ For about one and a half kilometres the path ascends diagonally across the eastern flank of Landdroskop (1 515 m), to the apex of the Riviersonderend valley. From the viewpoint on the watershed between the Landdros and Riviersonderend kloofs, you can see the suburbs of Somerset West far below to the left (west), and the complex ridges of the various Boland ranges stretching off to the right.

▶ The path turns sharply around the head of the valley at 1 240 metres, through a messy scree area, and contours towards a slope, up which the path zigzags for a stiff 140-metre climb over more scree. The path flattens out just after the three-kilometre mark (at 1 400 metres), and a further kilometre's walk along a flat, though rocky, stretch brings you to a nek, with Somerset-Sneeukop (1590 m), the highest peak in the reserve, rising up on your left. The dominant protea species along this route is the milky-white *Protea lacticolor*, but – if it is summer – you may also see the delicate, salmon-pink flower heads of *P. grandiceps*.

▶ Keeping to the contour around Somerset-Sneeukop, the path reaches a drinking spot at the source of Boegoekloof's uppermost tributary, which, at 1 420 metres, is the highest point reached on this trail. From here, you can look over into Staircase and Nuwejaars kloofs, both at the head of the Lourensrivier.

▶ The path then descends into Boegoekloof's wide gorge and around the first of two spurs that form buttresses to The Triplets peaks on the left. At the first buttress, the path levels off for nearly a kilometre, during which a number of scree fields are crossed.

▶ Approaching the second spur, the path begins an easy descent, which soon turns into a steep zigzag ending on a watershed between Boegoekloof and Jonkershoek valley. A right-hand turn here will take you towards Guardian Peak (1 227 m) and the top of the Kurktrekker pass.

▶ Your path, however takes the left-hand option for an easy two-and-a-half-kilometre hike along the ridge joining the Stellenboschberge (to the north) with the main Hottentots-Holland range. At the nine-kilometre mark, you will reach a magnificent viewpoint, from which you can see the Nuwejaarskloof falling steeply away into the forested Diepgat to the left, and the Jonkershoek River valley disappearing away to the right. This is a recommended tea spot, unless greater shelter is needed in bad weather conditions.

▶ After going gently downhill for one kilometre, passing the oddly named Pic-Sans-Nom (1 162 m), the path begins its steep and final descent through Swartboskloof. It is a sustained, knee-jarring, four-kilometre haul from Pic-Sans-Nom to the junction of Swartboskloof and the Jonkershoek circular drive which marks the end of your hike.

Nuweberg NHW   Hike B5

Route: Landdroskop hut to Nuweberg Forest Station
Distance: 20,5 kilometres or 7,2 kilometres
Duration: 2 hours or 7-8 hours
Grade: Fair and severe (respectively)
Booking Authority: NHWB (Tel. (021) 402 3093) (permit needed)

General Information: The routes between these points include sections of, respectively, the Boegoekloof (Hike B7) and Boesmanskloof (Hike B6) hikes. The route via Boegoekloof is something of an epic, and is closed in the wet season (April to September). It is, however, a fantastic hiking route and compares with the best, offering, as it does, both open montane vistas and enclosed gorge settings. The shorter route follows the Sneeukop Road jeep track all the way to Nuweberg.

To follow the Boegoekloof route, take the Sir Lowry's Pass path for about 400 metres before turning right along the Swartboskloof/Jonkershoek path. Continue along this for eight kilometres, up a scree-riddled series of ascents past Somerset-Sneeukop and The Triplets. After a sharp descent from The Triplets, turn left at the junction on the saddle between The Triplets and Guardian Peak, away from the Swartboskloof path, and head eastwards to Guardian Peak (1 227 m), descending easily to the nek that separates Kurktrekker pass from Boegoekloof; this is just on halfway and it is marked by a direction sign. From here on, the going is (almost) all downhill, the first five kilometres following the Riviersonderend valley (see Hike B8), and thereafter linking up with the Sneeukop Road.

▶ The Sneeukop Road route is an easy two-and-a-half hour ramble, all downhill, on a well-defined jeep track through very rugged mountainlands. Where the jeep track executes any of its numerous hairpin bends, do not be tempted to take short cuts, lest the bad luck of a broken-leg curse befalls you*.

HIKE B5

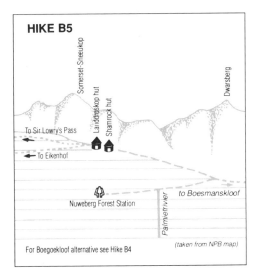

Somerset-Sneeukop

Landdroskop hut
Shamrock hut

Dwarsberg

To Sir Lowry's Pass

To Eikenhof

Nuweberg Forest Station

Palmietrivier

to Boesmanskloof

For Boegoekloof alternative see Hike B4 *(taken from NPB map)*

▶ For three and a half kilometres, the road winds down above the Riviersonderend valley, between the opposing bastions of Nuweberg on your right and Dwarsberg on your left. At three and a quarter kilometres the road levels out into a mountain bowl, where it forks and the Boesmanskloof path heads off to the left. Keep right, following the road that veers away from the Riviersonderend valley. The road heads down the Palmietrivier valley, and into the Nuweberg plantation before finally reaching the forestry station there.

* Author's note: It is a universal mountaineering law that berg adders lie in wait for unsuspecting hikers on all mountain short cuts.

Franschhoek NHW *Hike B6*

Route: *Landdroskop hut to Franschhoekpas*
Distance: *29,6 kilometres*
Duration: *2 days*
Grade: *Severe*
Booking Authority: *NHWB (Tel. (021) 402 3093) (permit needed)*
General Information: *This is a most pleasant route, passing innumerable rivers, through very rugged territory all along the southwestern slopes of the Franschhoekberge. The mountain pools are sprinkled with disas and gladioluses in summer, and often the upper peaks are snow-dusted in winter. Weatherwise, this is one of the kinder routes of the Boland Trail: you are sheltered from the worst forces of winter gales, and are never high enough to be bothered by the clouds brought by the southeast summer winds. One detraction, I found, was the inordinate amount of litter along this route, as well as the resurgence of alien acacia plants along some of the rivers. The second day's route starts out fairly easy, but, after six kilometres, it begins to climb, getting progressively steeper until you reach the aptly named Purgatory Nek. Very important is the fact that the NHW path no longer crosses the Laaste Vlakte, but takes a sharp turn to the right at Purgatory Nek to head down Jan Joubertsgat to the historic bridge on the old Catspad. This is due to the new owner of this land not wanting hikers to cross his territory. The turn-off is poorly signposted and the map has not yet been updated, but you have been warned.*

Day 1: Landdroskop hut to Boesmanskloof hut – 17,6 kilometres (6-7 hours)
▶ Leave the Landdroskop hut and proceed along the Sneeukop Road jeep track for three and a half kilometres. Along this section, the hiker is completely enclosed by a diorama of sun-washed ridges and peaks, one behind the next, creating a wonderful sense of isolation. The vegetation along here is dominated by restios and the cotton-wool flower heads of various Bruniaceae plants.
▶ Where the road levels out and reaches a T-junction in a wide bowl at Eensbedrogen, follow the path veering left, towards the main valley. Five hundred metres further on, you will reach a T-junction; turn to the left again, crossing a side stream and then the Riviersonderend at the Eensbedrogen pool. This is the first of numerous river crossings on the route, complete with suspension bridge and numerous swimming holes upstream. Shade and shelter are afforded by typical fynbos-associated riverine bush, providing a good excuse for a tea stop. Downstream of this crossing is the start of the Suicide Gorge (Riviersonderend Canyon) kloofing route.
▶ From the Eensbedrogen pool, continue onwards for another kilometre – climbing steadily – until you reach the suspension bridge at Red Hat Crossing on the Boegoekloof river. Take a good rest and enjoy the splendours of this gorge, for from here you are faced with a steep uphill zigzag, followed by a steady climb, before Stony Nek is reached about one kilometre from the bridge. Common plants here are the two species of grubbia: *Grubbia tomentosa* found

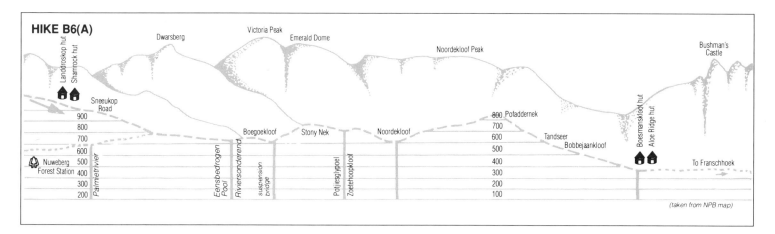

HIKE B6(A)

(taken from NPB map)

on the drier rocky slopes; and *G. rosmarinifolia* found along stream banks and around vleis (*G. rourkei* from the Kogelberg completes the family). Grubbia plants are many-stemmed shrubs which grow up to two metres high; their lanceolate leaves and berry fruits lead some people to mistake them for a form of wild olive.

▶ From Stony Nek, the path contours for several hundred metres, before dropping down to Pootjiesglypoel (slippery-feet pool), and then crossing two side streams. All these stream banks are sprinkled with the confetti of *Disa tripetaloides* flowers in summer. At this last stream, drink your fill and then fill your water bottle, for there is no more water between here and Boesmanskloof, a taxing six and a half kilometres away.

▶ A two-and-three-quarter-kilometre, sustained, but never very steep, climb from the second stream takes you up Noordekloof,

past Die Krulle (the curls), to Poffaddernek. From the nek you look down the impressive Bobbejaanskloof and the steep slope called Tandseer (toothache), across to the Tierkloof falls and down into Boesmanskloof. Grit your teeth, because you have to descend this steep, loose, zigzagging path for four kilometres. Finally, you will round The Spindles and Die Ridder (the knight), to see a suspension bridge leading across the wooded kloof to the twin huts of Boesmanskloof and Aloe Ridge. Bliss. Just upstream of the hut is found a delightful little pool in which to soothe your tired body. The aloes around the hut, which give the area the name of Aloe Ridge, are *A. plicatelis*.

Day 2: Boesmanskloof hut to Franschhoekpas – 12 kilometres (5 hours)
▶ The path follows the base of the Franschhoekberge, veering left from the huts and

heading slightly uphill. Once it has broached a low rise, it crosses a flat stony area into the barely defined Klipspringerkloof, before executing a few shallow curves in and out of side-stream gullies to Sweetwater Pool, at the three-kilometre mark. Look out for a large, dark boulder in the path that is sliced through by numerous thin, vertically parallel, white quartz veins.

▶ After one more kilometre the path climbs around a koppie (512 m) and then rises again to cross three streams. This is the beginning of the (at first gradual) climb to Purgatory Nek; but a few 'running in' kilometres are yet to come.

▶ Intermittent streams and a few permanent, swift-flowing rivers are the prominent feature of this area. For a while, the path skims just above the Aan-de-Palmiet-Valley plantation, and then, at around the six-kilometre mark, it curves off to the right, up

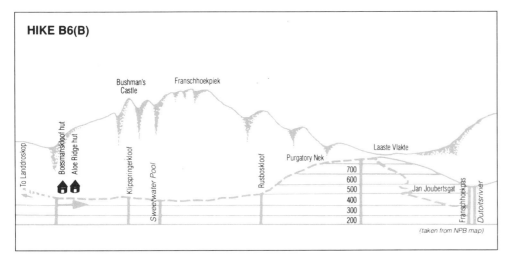

HIKE B6(B)

To Landdroskop · Boesmanskloof hut · Aloe Ridge hut · Klipspringerkloof · Sweetwater Pool · Bushman's Castle · Franschhoekpiek · Rusboskloof · Purgatory Nek · Laaste Vlakte · Jan Joubertsgat · Franschhoekpas · Dutoitsrivier

700
600
500
400
300
200

(taken from NPB map)

and away from the cultivated realm, into Rusboskloof. This pretty gorge, with its shallow, rounded pools is the last watering place on the trail so, with five kilometres still to go, take your fill here.

▶ Taken slowly, with time allowed to observe the varied flowers along the way (everlastings, yellow heliopteris daisies, delicate white corymbium flower clusters, brightly coloured watsonias), Purgatory Nek's two-kilometre climb need not be the hellish experience it is often described as being.

▶ On reaching the nek, the landscape opens out across a wide field of golden-green restios, dabbed with bold blue splashes of *Aristea major* flowers, clustered around the stiff, branched metre-high stems.

▶ Remember to take the right-bearing path here, following the steeply zigzagged path

down the quartz-strewn slope into Jan Joubertsgat kloof. From Purgatory Nek, you look across the Franschhoekpas to the massive forms of the Wemmershoek range forming the skyline. The path meets the Franschhoekpas road on a tight hairpin bend at the Jan Joubertsgat bridge, where there is room for vehicles to pull off the road. Transport from here is a matter of personal arrangements, for there is no real alternative to this unsatisfactory end point (parking your car here would be inviting theft).

Boegoekloof
Hike B7

Route: *Landdroskop hut to Nuweberg Forest Station*
Distance: *20,5 kilometres*

Duration: *7 hours*
Grade: *Severe*
Booking Authority: *NHWB (Tel. (021) 402 3093) (permit needed)*

General Information: *This kloof was one of the first – and certainly the best – collecting grounds for the aromatic, oily leaves of the boegoe bush* (Agathosma crenulata), *which were used by the early colonists as a natural remedy for many illnesses and to flavour brandy. In a preindustrial age, boegoe was an important product and much effort was expended in the kloofs, gathering the plant. Many of the paths later used by mountaineers were pioneered by the boegoe gatherers, and this hike is perhaps the most typical of all. Although this walk has been treated as part of the Boland Trail NHW, it is possible to do it as a day hike (you will need to get a permit from the Nuweberg Forest Station), starting on the Jonkershoek Panorama Walk (Hike B9) and following the sign pointing the way above the Kurktrekker. Both routes are closed between April and September, the wet season. The route is linear (well, semi-circular anyway), so be sure to arrange transport to the beginning and at the end of the walk.*

▶ Start the hike at Landdroskop hut and proceed along the Jonkershoek path (see Hike B3). The path passes Somerset-Sneeukop and The Triplets, and then zigzags steeply downward. When you reach a fork, take the right-hand path towards Guardian Peak and down to the saddle between Boegoekloof and the Kurktrekker pass. From here, just follow the sign pointing down Boegoekloof to the right.

Cape Peninsula

1. *A replica of the old signal cannon points out over Buffelsbaai towards Cape Point. Cannons such as this one were positioned at strategic points all over the western Cape to warn off approaching ships – be they 'men of war' or the passenger and trading ships that were the life-blood of the colony.*
2. *From the summit of the Paulsberg in the Cape of Good Hope Nature Reserve, one gains a 360° view of the southern peninsula.*
3. *This part of Table Mountain is seldom seen by the cableway tourists: Hely-Hutchinson Reservoir – one of five similar reservoirs – lying between the tops of Skeleton Gorge and Kasteelspoort.*
4. *On a narrow coastal plain confronting False Bay, the crimson blooms of* Brunsvigia orientalis – *the candelabra flower – grow from an underground bulb. The flowers have but a short life, whereafter they seed, die and then roll about in the wind.*

2

3

5. *False Bay blurs behind a close-up view of an* Anapalina pulchra *bloom on Paulsberg, in the Cape of Good Hope Nature Reserve.*

6. *This view down Kasteelspoort to Camps Bay can be seen from the site of an old cableway station that was used to transport materials and machinery during the building of the mountain reservoirs. There has been some talk of rebuilding this as a tourist facility.*

7. *One way of reaching the top of Table Mountain is by taking the cable car; another is to scale the 'Africa' face. Alternatively, you could refer to this book for a compromise.*

8. *On the ridge above Blinkwaterkloof, a hot and thirsty hiker surveys (from right to left) the Twelve Apostles, Grootkop, Orange Kloof and Hout Bay, Kommetjie, Chapman's Peak and the Constantiaberg.*

9. *The cool waters of Buffelsbaai appear enticing after a hot walk in the Cape of Good Hope Nature Reserve. The sharply pointed peak in the background is Paulsberg.*

7

8

9

Boland

1. *Seen here from Guardian Peak, the Stellenbosch (left) and Jonkershoek (right) ranges flank the Jonkershoek valley.*
2. *At the end of the rainbow, Boesmanskloof and Aloe Ridge huts await weary hikers en route to Franschhoek on the Boland Trail.*
3. *On a clear day atop the Helderberg you can see... well, Gordon's Bay at any rate.*
4. *Many people regard Jonkershoek as the most beautiful valley in the Boland Mountains – but only those not familiar with the more impressive Assegaiboskloof. It is here that the Bergrivier rises and the blushing brides grow.*
5. *The Gothic forms of Third Ridge and Banghoek peaks peer over the Bergrivier saddle between the Jonkershoek valley and Assegaaiboskloof.*
6. *Spikes of* Aristea major *blooms mark the final stretch on the Boland Trail, three days and nearly 60 challenging kilometres from Sir Lowry's Pass.*
7. *Landdroskop, wrapped in a gossamer veil of cloud, can be seen here over the shoulder of Stony Nek.*

8. *Sunrise over the Landdroskop and Shamrock huts dusts the landscape with golden light. In the distance are the Groenlandsberge and the Langeberg.*

9. *Rusboskloof is one of the numerous rivers encountered between Eensbedrogen and Die Krulle.*

10. *From Pofaddernek, the National Hiking Way snakes down to Boesmanskloof.*

8

9

10

Langeberg

1

1. *Bushes of* Leucospermum oleifolium *decorate the countryside at Die Galg above McGregor. The Boesmanskloof hike to Greyton begins here.*

2. *For seasoned mountaineers it is never too cold or too wet for a tea break, especially when the stop is in the enchanting Zuurplaats valley on the Swellendam Trail.*

3. *The Kruispad is the shortest and easiest of the three possible routes from Proteavallei to Wolfkloof in the Marloth Nature Reserve.*

2

3

4. *The newly described* Disa cardinalis *can be found near the Nooitgedacht hut.*
5. *King proteas, ground orchids, erica species* pulchella *and* curviflora, *gladioluses and flamebushes are among the plants that you will see flowering in the Swellendam Trail's Drosterspas.*

6. *Large animals are uncommon residents of the fynbos, which is dependent on insect pollinators for its regeneration. This partly accounts for its flowering exuberance, as well as its wealth of insect species, their prey and arachnid predators.*

7. *It would be well worth your while to take an extra day to explore the Wolfkloof and allow yourself to experience the abundance of fynbos there.*

8. *The Proteavallei hut is prime real estate in the Langeberg mountains. From the hut, you can see Misty Point – living up to its name in this picture.*

9. *From above Boskloof hut, the shortcut path back to Koloniesbos can be seen taking a diagonal line up to Twaalfuurkop.*

Overberg

2

3

1. *Buffeljags bay is the start of the walk to Quoin Point along the wreck-littered southern Cape coastline.*
2. *In a large eucalyptus tree overlooking the Kleinrivier estuary at Hermanus, a Cape eagle owl guards its nest. Tucked underneath its parent was a single snow-white, puffball chick.*
3. *The vegetation seen here is typical of the limestone fynbos that occurs between Cape Agulhas and Kaap Infante.*
4. *There are many wrecks along the southern Cape coast: this one being a salvage vessel that was wrecked near Quoin Point in 1946.*
5. *Leucadendrons (conebushes), mimetes (flamebushes) and restios (reeds) line the rest of the ridge in the Harold Porter National Botanic Gardens overlooking Betty's Bay.*

4

5

6. *Cape cormorants are the most common avian residents of the Cape shoreline.*
7. *Ancient limestone deposits have been eroded to form calcrete cliffs on the eastern shore of De Hoopvlei, near to the historic homestead.*
8. *The De Hoop coastline near Koppie Alleen comprises extensive dune fields, calcrete cliffs and intertidal pools and shelves that for decades have been protected from human exploitation.*

▶ For the first kilometre, the path is an easy downhill stroll, with Somerset-Sneeukop rising up to your right and Dwarsberg and Victoria Peak to the left. The path then cuts back on itself to descend into a steeper part of the kloof, and crosses the upper reaches of the Riviersonderend. The path criss-crosses the river in this, the most impressive part of the kloof. This area sports a rich growth of riverine trees and tall tussocks of the restio *Canamois virgata*. This is also where boegoe is at its most prolific, the place to which boegoe pickers of old sought access. There are 14 species of boegoe occurring in this area, representing only a small portion of the total 145 species of *Agathosma* found in South Africa.

▶ Just short of three kilometres from the start, the path reaches the Dwarsberg pool, which is a most inviting swimming spot when the kloof traps the summer's heat. Dwarsberg (1 523 m) rises almost vertically from this point, creating a dramatic backdrop for your pleasure. Above you a waterfall splashes the Dwarsberg's lower reaches.

▶ The path carries on along the river, passing an old boegoe pickers' camp at about the three-kilometre mark (where the path veers away from and then back to the left-hand bank of the river).

▶ It continues to criss-cross the river until about a kilometre from the Dwarsberg pool, when it begins to climb gradually away from the right-hand bank for two kilometres – passing two more waterfalls in the process. At the five-kilometre mark you will find yourself standing nearly 100 metres above the river bed.

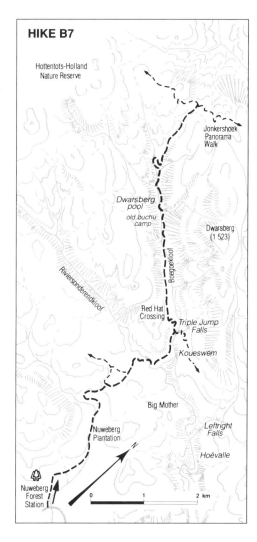

HIKE B7

Hottentots-Holland
Nature Reserve

Jonkershoek
Panorama
Walk

Dwarsberg
pool
old buchu
camp

Dwarsberg
(1 523)

Boegoekloof

Riviersonderendkloof

Red Hat
Crossing

Triple Jump
Falls

Koueswem

Big Mother

Nuweberg
Plantation

Leftright
Falls

Hoëvalle

Nuweberg
Forest
Station

0   1   2 km

▶ Now, as you have probably anticipated, you must zigzag steeply down to the river, where a suspension bridge vaults the Triple Jump Falls. In this densely overgrown valley you will find mountain water pea (*Podylaria montana*) and water witels (*Brachylaena neriifolia*) trees stretched over the flowing river water.

▶ Don't cross the bridge; instead head right (westward) along the NHW path, above the river and around a spur where brunia plants and mountain cedars (*Widdringtonia nodiflora*) predominate. A kilometre of easy contouring will bring you to another river crossing, with a swimming hole found above the crossing. From this point, the Suicide Gorge route disappears around a tricky corner; don't follow the river unless you wish to end up at Viljoenspas, as, once you have committed yourself to this route, there is no coming back.

▶ Follow the path down, always keeping left, to the Sneeukop Road jeep track that joins Nuweberg Forest Station with the Landdroskop hut. Proceed down the jeep track, crossing the Palmietrivier, through the plantation, to the forest station.

Suicide Gorge   Hike B8

Route: From Nuweberg, down the Riviersonderend canyon, to the Villiersdorp pass
Distance: *17 kilometres*
Duration: *7 hours*
Grade: *Extreme*
Booking Authority: *Nuweberg Forest Station (Tel. (0225) 4301 / 4785) (permit needed)*

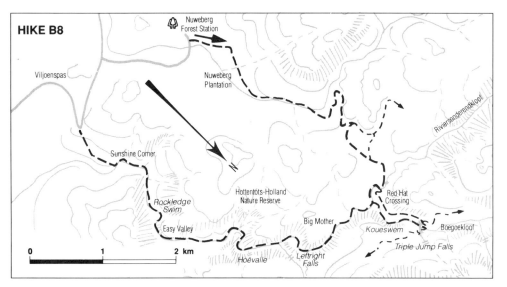

HIKE B8

General Information: *Like Boegoekloof, permits to this spectacular gorge trip are issued only from October to the end of March. You would not want to do the walk at any other time, for the water – in which you will be immersed for most of the day – becomes unbearably cold in winter. Also, the gorge is narrow and deep, and sunshine becomes a rare commodity at water level, even on a clear day – in fact, unless you have a clear day for your trip, abandon or change your plans. At any time of the year, a wetsuit (preferably with short arms and legs) is recommended. This hike is potentially highly dangerous, involving numerous compulsory jumps of up to 15 metres into deep, dark pools. If you have a bad back, avoid it.*

▶ Your starting point is the Nuweberg Forest Station (just off Viljoenspas between Grabouw and Villiersdorp) – also the place from which to collect your permit. The path follows the Sneeukop Road, through the plantation, past a picnic place on the right, and up the left-hand bank of the Palmietrivier.

▶ Two and a half kilometres from the start, the road crosses the river and then swings to the left, back to the right, and left again, winding its way for over a kilometre to the top of this ridge. Where the road breaches the ridge and enters a wide valley, take the right-bearing path along a stream's right-hand bank towards the Riviersonderend.

▶ After about 700 metres, a path comes in from the left; cross the stream here to the

formation called the Eensbedrogen pillar, thereafter going up and down again to a bridge crossing the Riviersonderend. Carry on along the NHW path, climbing for one kilometre into Boegoekloof. This is where our trip really begins, so don your wetsuits, waterproof your cameras and victuals, and brace yourself...

▶ Keeping to the right-hand bank, make your way downstream below the suspension bridge – rounding a tricky corner by way of a narrow ledge – until you are faced with only one alternative: to jump into that dark and forbidding pool. From here, you will follow the canyon's eccentricities for about eight kilometres with, if I remember correctly, five compulsory jumps varying between four and seven metres high. If you choose to be macho, you can increase the minimal height of jumps in places, but if you are really dismayed by the prospect of jumping, it's too late. Actually, in most places you can slip and slide your way into the pools.

▶ Near the end of the well-defined canyon, the path loops away from a pool where a jump is not absolutely necessary; if you do choose to jump this one, check it out first from below as there is a dead tree stump lurking just beneath the water.

▶ The last part of the trip involves boulder-hopping and swimming down some lesser pools until the river emerges out of the canyon. Soon thereafter you will reach a weir, where you should exit the valley through the plantation, meeting Viljoenspas at a hairpin bend. Transport from here back to Nuweberg Forest Station is up to you to organize (you can park your car at Viljoenspas, but it is an open road, so you're inviting theft).

Jonkershoek Panorama Walk
Hike B9

Route: *Circular walk up Swartboskloof*
Distance: *17 kilometres (12,5-kilometre and 12-kilometre alternatives)*
Duration: *7 hours (5-6 hours for alternatives)*
Grade: *Severe to extreme*
Booking Authority: *Jonkershoek Forest Station (Tel. (02231) 5715) (permit needed)*
General Information: *I regard this as the finest, most spectacular day outing in the western Cape, and rivalled only by hikes in the Natal Drakensberg. This is a long and fairly strenuous walk to complete in one day, and you may prefer to do only the first or the last half of the walk. The Jonkershoek Valley is a fire-protected botanical research area, and is therefore closed from October to March (fire-hazard season). Although water can be found at numerous places on the hike, it is advisable to carry a bottle per person, for the going can be hot and thirsty. Purchase your permit from the guard at the forestry gate (R1-50 per person).*

This hike will be described as two separate ones, both using the Kurktrekker pass as a descent; to do the entire walk as one, begin up the Jakkalsvleirivier path to the Jonkershoekberge ridge and descend by way of Swartboskloof – you may be exhausted but

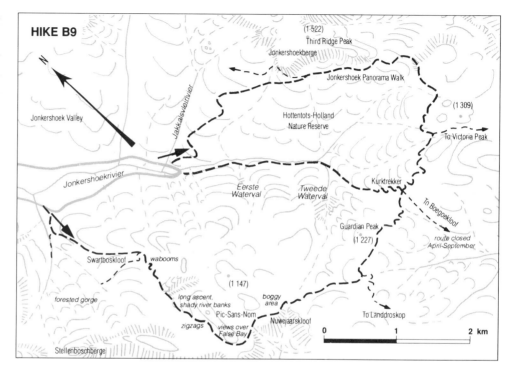

HIKE B9

you won't be disappointed. If you do decide to do the whole walk, you are advised to make an early start on this hike as it is tough going and long. This route is closed during the fire hazard season, from October to March (inclusive).

▶ The Jonkershoek circular drive about-turns at a concrete bridge over the Jonkershoek River (there is a parking space just before the bridge on the eastern side). A few metres back from the bridge a sign marks

the beginning of the panorama walk, pointing up the Jakkalsvleirivier. Take this sometimes badly eroded path up through recently burnt protea veld, where you can see the charred remains of what were some of the largest mountain cedars (*Widdringtonia nodiflora*) in the western Cape.

Fire is used, somewhat controversially, as a management tool for veld conservation, and to improve water yields. This particular fire was, however, an unscheduled one, ruining decades of research in a specially protected area. At the same time, observations of the effects of fire on this mature community helped to dispel many myths about the benefits of regular burning. But ideas are slow to change and habits even slower; we can therefore expect veld managers to continue with their wasteful burning programmes for some time yet.

▶ The Virgin and First, Second and Third Ridge peaks loom ahead, their gothic forms towering above the high contour path. The path executes two zigzags before taking a diagonal course up to the right to meet the contour path. If you miss the main path on the zigzags, just carry on directly – and steeply – up a lesser path until you reach the contour path.

▶ The contour path is fairly sandy and stony, winding in and out of a few stream gullies, where the only shade for many miles is found. Enjoy this level section, for, after little more than a kilometre, the contour path begins its ascent towards the Bergriviernek, negotiating some seepage areas and loose, steep ground on its way. You may be lucky enough to see the last showing of the April fool or blood flower (*Haemanthus coccineus*) or, lower down, the splendid white belladonna lily (*Amaryllis belladonna*). White-necked ravens (larger and bulkier than crows, with prominent primary feathers), rock kestrels and even the occasional black eagle may be seen soaring or hovering above the nek.

▶ On reaching the nek you will be greeted by what must surely be the most spectacular panorama in the western Cape. Third Ridge and Banghoek peaks on the left throw lofty spires and buttresses skyward, and then plummet down into the fertile beyond of Assegaaiboskloof. On the right, teetering cliffs define the view. Behind you, the more gentle, but equally attractive, valley of Jonkershoek frames the northwestern picture. It is possible to descend into the inviting depths of Assegaaiboskloof, but that is another story: the only known community of the most beautiful of all flowers, the blushing bride (*Serruria florida*), is found there (and one day, my son, all that will be a dam).

▶ From here, the climb continues, taking a fairly dramatic route along the cliff line (not for your average vertigo-sufferer). After a while, the path heads for the higher ground to the left, gaining the top of a ridge. A magnificent view down the Jonkershoek valley provides some compensation for the odd moment of anxiety you may have experienced on the way here.

▶ On crossing a marshy gully (about a kilometre from the top of the ridge), where the path goes 'upstream' for a short way before veering off to the right, a path carries on up the gully and broaches a summit plateau, where the view suddenly opens out to reveal the entire mountain stronghold of the Boland. Directly ahead, across a peat bog, Victoria Peak (1589 m) regally dominates the landscape to the southeast, rising up from the high plateau like a crown.

▶ From this gully, the path veers off to the right to regain the skyline overlooking Jonkershoek, with Guardian Peak (1 227 m) directly ahead. The path then descends onto a restio-cloaked, boulder-strewn saddle, with Boegoekloof dropping off to the left (south). The saddle makes an appropriate, though waterless, lunch spot, as long as the wind is not blowing (it can become something of a wind funnel).

▶ From here you have the option of descending the Kurktrekker pass into the Jonkershoek River gorge (described at the end of this route description), or retracing the Swartboskloof route, which follows.

▶The Swartboskloof route is signposted, a little over two kilometres from the causeway bridge at the apex of the circular drive, on the Jonkershoek valley's southwestern flank. The first few hundred metres go gently uphill, towards the wooded kloof on the right. On nearing a river, however, the path deviates away from it to the left to follow the Swartboskloof river valley. There are numerous scientific instruments along the way, which should not be tampered with. A large tract of protea veld here has been burnt by a fire that swept the valley head a few years back.

▶ For much of the way the path follows the right- and then the left-hand river bank within the sheltering canopy of the riverine forest. About two kilometres from the start, the path joins a contour path, and then executes a series of tight zigzags as it negotiates the steep side of the kloof. Near the top of the kloof, the path criss-crosses the now-less-eager stream, finally reaching the top at 1 100 metres.

▶ The path then continues on a slight uphill course towards Pic-Sans-Nom (1 162 m) before curving round to the left, past the peak's summit to overlook Nuwejaarskloof, at the head of the Lourensrivier. Looking across the forested Diepgat gorge, you will see the Somerset-Sneeukop (1 590 m), with The Triplets (1 457 m, 1 515 m, 1 503 m) in front and to the left; the views afforded from here and for the following few kilometres almost equal those from around the Bergriviernek. The path skirts and then moves away from Diepgat, heading towards Guardian Peak. The route is pleasantly level, despite its negotiating a kilometre-long ridge between The Triplets and Guardian Peak.

▶ A little after the 10-kilometre mark, a junction is reached where the NHW trail from Landdroskop comes in from the right, and the panorama walk path proceeds to the left (remember that we have just reversed the last part of the Boland Trail, Landdroskop to Jonkershoek NHW (Hike B4)). Take the left-hand path towards Guardian Peak, heading for its summit. The path avoids the summit by curving to the right and then descending, quite steeply at first, for one kilometre to a saddle between Boegoekloof and Jonkershoek. Here you will reach a junction; take the path to the left down the Kurktrekker pass.

▶The Kurktrekker pass is a nasty little piece of work, zigzagging down a loose eroded slope into the Jonkershoek River gorge. Although this is not marked as a path on the NHW map, it does exist and is clearly defined, if in poor condition. I would not, however, recommend using this path as an ascent route, for the protection of both yourself and the environment.

▶ Where the path enters the forested zone, a side river comes down from the right. Don't be fooled into crossing this river; keep to the left, and you will enter the main gorge. Now cross the river, and continue down its left-hand bank. As you cross the river you will see a path leading up to Tweede Waterval: don't take it unless you know the route, as it involves a tricky rock scramble.

The banks of the river are decorated with large rooiels (*Cunonia capensis*), witels (*Platylophus trifoliatus*), Cape holly (*Ilex mitis*) and wild almond (*Brabejum stellatifolium*) trees. Before the gorge opens out, near Eerste Waterval, the path has been cut into the river bank, and a wire railing is provided in one spot.

▶ A little less than two kilometres from Tweede Waterval, Eerste Waterval can be seen high up on the left, on a tributary. The final one and a half kilometres is along flat and sandy ground, moving away from and above the river until the last easy descent to the road just below the bridge.

Victoria Peak Hike B10

Route: *Jonkershoek Panorama Walk to Victoria Peak*
Distance: *22 kilometres*
Duration: *4-5 hours (there); 3-4 hours (back)*
Grade: *Extreme*
Booking Authority: *Jonkershoek Forest Station (Tel. (02231) 5715) (permit needed)*
General Information: *This is the second highest peak in the Boland mountains – at*

1 589 metres only one metre lower than Somerset-Sneeukop. With an early start, this walk is a good day's outing, and certainly a prized ascent for anyone who, like me, feels they have to climb a mountain 'because it's there'. Victoria Peak's central situation in the Boland mountain vortex, and its superior altitude, make it a prize well worth attaining. Of all the peaks in this area, this is the one I consider to be the finest (non-technical) climb. Return by way of either of the Panorama Walk routes (see hike B8).

▶ To reach Victoria Peak by the easiest route, follow the panorama walk route along the Jonkershoek mountains to Bergriviernek, between the Jonkershoek and Assegaaibos valleys, and up to the high plateau at the head of the Jonkershoek valley (see hike B9). Where the panorama walk path heads inland to negotiate a rocky gully, take the path up that gully where the panorama walk path crosses the gully and heads off to the right back towards Jonkershoek valley.

▶ A short walk will take you up onto a wide plateau that is guaranteed to elate you. In the wet season, this plateau becomes a large bog, so bring your best gaiters or be prepared to muddy your boots. Victoria Peak, Dwarsberg and Emerald Dome can be seen straight ahead, while a complete 360° panorama view of the Hottentots-Holland Reserve and its complex array of peaks and ridges is afforded from this spot.

▶ The path gains 30 metres in altitude over the next kilometre, as it passes above Boegoekloof, but this is lost again approaching Victoria Peak. The peak should be

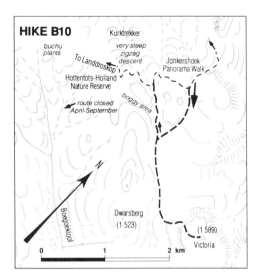

HIKE B10

Kurktrekker

buchu plants

very steep zigzag descent

To Landdroskop

Jonkershoek Panorama Walk

Hottentots-Holland Nature Reserve

route closed April-September

boggy area

N

Boegoekloof

Dwarsberg (1 523)

(1 589) Victoria

0   1   2 km

approached by way of the easy southwestern ridge, but, to lose as little height as possible, don't make directly for this ridge. Rather head slightly to the left of the ridge at first, and then use the slope in the way dictated by your own common sense. You can choose a direct route or a more zigzag one, depending on your preference.

The peak has a relatively flat summit, about a kilometre across at its longest axis. Of all that you see around you only Somerset-Sneeukop is higher. For me though, Victoria Peak's central position and isolation make it the preferable destination – especially when a luxuriant coating of snow lies all across these mountains.

The northeastern side of the peak falls vertically away into the trident-shaped

Paradise Gorge, which itself leads into Assegaaiboskloof. Unfortunately, there is no easy way down into this gorge and its forest from Victoria Peak. This Afro-montane forest is the same habitat as the Knysna forests, but is poorer in terms of species. The common large trees are much the same though, with yellowwoods (*Podocarpus latifolius*), wild peach (*Kiggelaria africana*), rooiels (*Cunonia capensis*), Cape holly (*Ilex mitis*), ironwood (*Olea capensis*) and Cape beech (*Rapanea melanophloeos*) being the most common species.

▶ To return, either retrace your steps to your car, or take a short cut down the Kurktrekker pass: from the base of Victoria Peak, head west to the top of Zoetenhoopkloof, through a boggy area, while making for the saddle straight ahead. You should pick up a path here, which joins up with the panorama walk path two and a half kilometres from Victoria Peak's base. Turn left and follow this path down a grassy ridge for one and a half kilometres to the saddle between the Kurktrekker pass and Boegoekloof. Turn sharp right to descend the Kurktrekker pass, and head back to the car park area.

Helderberg   Hike B11

Route: *Basil Maskew-Miller Herbarium to southwestern summit*
Distance: *12 kilometres*
Duration: *2-3 hours (there); 2 hours (back)*
Grade: *Severe*
Booking Authority: *Helderberg Nature Reserve (Tel. (024) 51 7256) (permit needed)*

General Information: *The Helderberg protrudes at right angles from the Hottentots-Holland range, pointing towards Somerset West. It really consists of numerous connected peaks, the highest of which is the inner or northeastern one at 1 237 metres. This route description explains the route to the southeasternmost of the three main summits, from which excellent views across the Cape Flats and False Bay to the Cape Peninsula and along the full length of the Hottentots-Holland range are gained.*

▶ The route begins at the picnic area in the Helderberg Nature Reserve (an entrance fee of a few rand is asked). From between the kiosk and the Basil Maskew-Miller Herbarium, follow the path uphill towards a ridge. Red, yellow and blue walking routes are signposted: you should keep to the right-handmost loop of these circular walks, making your way upward towards Disa Gorge, the large and very obvious gorge running up the ridge.

For the first two kilometres you walk through lush riverine vegetation and open fynbos, alternately, where you will see large wild almond (*Brabejum stellatifolium*) and keurboom (*Virgilia oroboides*) trees up the river courses. The open slopes are a delight, with proteas *coronata* (apple green bracts), *cynaroides* (king protea), *neriifolia* (blue sugarbush), a few bushes of *nana* (the exquisite mountain rose), *lepidocarpodendron* with its purple-black beard on pinky-white bracts, the yellowy-white-and-red-tipped *repens* (sugarbush), and many large *nitida* (waboom), fields of *eximia*, as well as the ground proteas, *cordata* (with rounded, heart-shaped leaves) and the longer-leafed *scabra* and *scolopendriifolia*.

There are also many tall blue aristeas, watsonias, the soft, golden featherhead (*Phylica pubescens*) and other flowering geophytes, conebushes such as *Leucadendron xanthoconus*, *L. sessile*, *L. salicifolium* and *L. salignum*, as well as a host of other flowering plants along the steep, clayey paths that can become waterlogged in places and very slippery in wet conditions.

▶ As you approach Disa Gorge, you are likely to see orange-breasted sunbirds, Cape sugarbirds, Cape robins and rockjumpers flitting about in the rank vegetation. The path moves only a few metres up the steep gorge – where some large Cape holly (*Ilex mitis*) and witels (*Platylophus trifoliatus*) trees grow – climbs steeply out again, and contours for a short distance on the shoulder above the gorge before beginning a series of steep zigzags up to Porcupine Buttress.

▶ On reaching the buttress's rock band, the path continues around the corner to the right and then heads upwards by way of some neatly constructed steps. On reaching the top of the buttress, you will find some nicely level rocks, encrusted with deep-red, pale-yellow, green and white lichens, where you can stop for a breather.

▶ From this level, the path makes its way up more constructed steps, to another similar level area. Here the path moves back from the vertical cliff-line, into the nek between the two outermost summit peaks. At this point you think you are almost there. You are wrong, there is more to come.

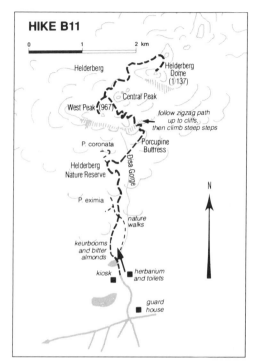

HIKE B11

▶ The walk up to the nek proper goes along a narrow ledge, where the rocks are deeply pocked and covered with more bright lichens, mainly buttercup yellow. The last leg up to the nek is a steep bush-covered slope but the path is easy.

▶ Just before reaching the nek's watershed, a side path to the left takes you to the top of Disa Gorge, which is flanked by a large pillar of rock. Carry on past this to a junction at the watershed.

▶ Turn right at the junction if you want to climb the highest of the Helderberg's three peaks, moving right around the ascent from the 'inside', passing the middle peak, Helderberg Dome, until you can see where this range hinges onto the Suurberg. The Helderberg juts out between the Suurberg peak (1 092 m) to the west and Haelkop (1 384 m) to the east, but it is only when you have reached this point that you fully appreciate its bulk.

▶ Your path goes off to the left from the nek junction, 'behind' the mountain and then it begins its ascent up the large, natural rocky steps. Shortly thereafter, you reach a lone, prominent candlewood tree (*Pterocelastrus rostratus*) on one of these 'steps'. From here you have to more or less scramble up the rock-fall chute to the left, which is overgrown with climber's friend (*Cliffortia* sp.) and other prickly nasties. This easy rock scramble leads to the summit.

The views from around the trig beacon are every bit as magnificent as you imagined they would be. Once you turn around to look across the rest of the Helderberg ridge, with the fluted sides of the Hottentots-Holland rising up to Pic-Sans-Nom and the Somerset-Sneeukop, and the Kogelberg above Gordon's Bay, you may be tempted to tackle the higher summit. The route to this summit goes from the saddle, skirting the base of the middle peak and then heading around 270° to the right, and takes about one hour to negotiate the rocky slopes, boulder-hopping much of the way... well, maybe next time.

▶ For now, just retrace your steps along the route you have come.

LANGEBERG

Before the arrival of the European colonists, the Langeberg area would have been settled, or perhaps used as seasonal range land, by semi-nomadic Khoi (Hottentot) groups. However, little is known of the history of these people before the beginning of the 18th century, by which time most of them had sold off their livestock to the white settlers and forced themselves (with a little coercion from the colonists) into indentured labour.

In 1743, Governor-general Baron Gustav Wilhelm van Imhoff decreed that a new sub-drostdy should be established far east of Stellenbosch, to control the trekboers who were moving further and further eastward to search for grazing lands and escape the tyrannical rule of the Dutch East India Company. In 1745, the territory was declared separate from the Stellenbosch district of which it had been part, and Johannes Rhenius was made landdrost of the region. The new territory was named Swellendam, after Governor Hendrick Swellengrebel and his wife, Helena ten Damme, and permission was given for the building of a drostdy at the foot of the Langeberg mountains. A small village soon sprung up around the drostdy, and began to flourish.

As the town grew, however, so too did the dissatisfaction of its citizens with the mismanagement of the Dutch East India Company, with the result that, in June 1795, the people of Swellendam rebelled against the Company. They dismissed the magistrate, declared an independent republic and elected Hermanus Steyn 'national land-drost'. In August 1795, however, the British attacked the Cape. Swellendam sent a detachment of burghers to assist in the defence of the colony, but by mid-September the Dutch were defeated, and Swellendam's four-and-a-half-month moment of glory as a capital came to an end.

The town nevertheless continued to grow – a village management board being set up in 1862 – but in 1865 much of it was destroyed in the 'great fire'. This fire started near George and swept across the southern Cape, destroying farmlands and fynbos, and – perhaps the greatest loss – decimating the temperate evergreen forests of the area. Some of the largest surviving patches of indigenous forest in the western Cape are to be found in sheltered gorges of the Langeberg mountains. Few of these, however, are accessible to the average hiker.

The Langeberg range certainly offers some magnificent mountain scenery, and spectacular floral displays. I have hiked the Swellendam Trail three times: once doing the five-day variation in snow and sleet; once the alternative five-day route in freezing, pelting rain; and once the full route in dripping heat and summer squalls. Each time it has been a fantastic experience, and each time the mountains were alive with a vibrant floral display. The mountains may not be as spectacularly endowed with botanical rarities as their counterparts in the Boland, but what they lack in rare species, they more than make up for with their overwhelming display of form and colour. I have certainly seen a greater variety of ground orchids here than anywhere else in the western Cape.

Hiking in the Langeberg

Swellendam is the same distance east of Cape Town as Clanwilliam is north, and is, in fact, the easternmost extent of the region covered in this book. Although this chapter is called 'Langeberg', it also includes a walk in the less-visited Riviersonderendberge to the south (the Boesmanskloof Traverse – Hike L8).

There is no real 'best time' to hike in this area, since, being part of the western Cape mountain chain, it experiences much the same weather as the rest of this region – hiking here, whether in winter or midsummer has its special attractions. Since you always have to book in advance for the Swellendam Trail, the weather will be an unknown factor when doing a multi-day hike. Generally, though, March and April or October and November are the kindest times, weather-wise, for hiking.

The numerous towns in this region – Swellendam, Robertson, Montagu, Greyton, McGregor – offer a range of accommodation. Most of the hikes described here include places to overnight: hikers arriving early for the Swellendam Trail can party at Koloniesbos hut, and the Boskloof, Goedgeloof, Proteavallei, Nooitgedacht and Wolfkloof huts provide accommodation on the trail; hikers on the Dassieshoek Trail can use the Silverstrand holiday resort, near the starting point just outside Robertson; in Greyton, should you be stuck there for a night, there is a municipal campsite with no facilities, or you can take advantage of the 'hikers' deal' at the Central Hotel.

On the subject of more refined recreation, Robertson is an excellent, under-utilized area for wine-buying. The Rooiberg Co-op has fine reds, whites and dessert wines at even finer prices.

The main hiking attraction in the Langeberg is undoubtedly the Swellendam NHW Trail, although a number of other excellent walks can be found. Newest of these is the Dassieshoek Trail just outside Robertson, and others are the Bloupunt and Cogmanskloof trails near Montagu. Between Mcgregor and Greyton, lies the Boesmanskloof Trail (in the Riviersonderend mountains). The Dassieshoek, Bloupunt, Cogmanskloof and Boesmanskloof trails are

one- or two-day outings and are therefore perfectly suited to weekend ventures away from the urban hum or rural drum.

The Swellendam Trail is situated almost entirely within the Marloth Nature Reserve, and was the first major NHW trail conceived as a circular hike. This layout proved so favourable that the original idea of developing one continuous trail around the country was amended to consist rather of numerous circular trials. The trail was 'hacked out' in 1979/80 by the intrepid Jaynee Levy during her fruitful stint with the local forestry directorate. She walked the six-day route in three days – but then that's Jaynee for you. I certainly agree with her that this is the

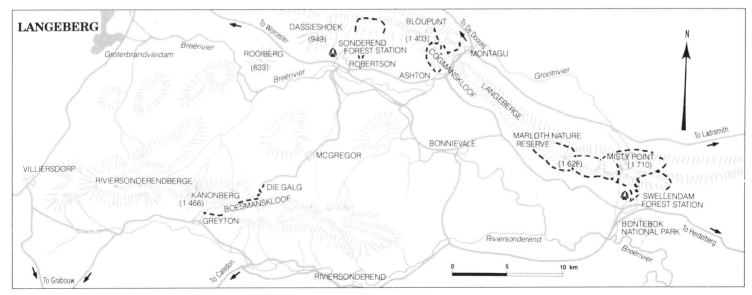

finest NHW route in the western Cape, though this is partly because it is the only one exceeding three-days' duration.

The trail has four variations: a two-day hike, two five-day (or four-day if you're energetic) options, and the full six-day trail. All the options start at Koloniesbos; you can either walk the four kilometres there from the forest station, or drive there to unload your gear – you must, however, then drive back and park at the forest station. If you overnight here, you can braai, but most hikers just pass by this '*jol plek*'.

For awfully eager amateur botanists like myself, the NHW map is a wealth of information, with numbers and a key marking quite accurately the major species and communities found along the paths.

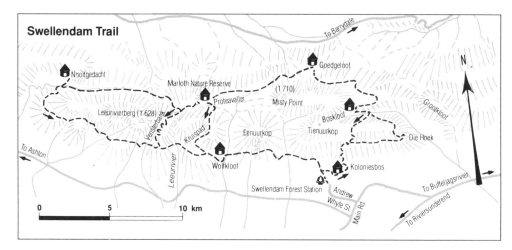

Swellendam Trail

Tienuurkop NHW   *Hike L1*

Route: *Koloniesbos, Boskloof and back via Tienuurkop*
Distance: *24 kilometres*
Duration: *2 days*
Grade: *Severe*
Booking Authority: *NHWB office (Tel. (021) 402 3093) (permit needed)*
General Information: *This route was opened only in 1989, to give townies the chance of fitting in a bit of the Swellendam Trail between squash and boozy lunches. As two-day hikes go, this one is quite short, though you may be glad of this when tackling some of the steeper sections. The walk to the start of the trail is messy, using logging tracks and tentative paths through plantations to get to*

Koloniesbos, but the rest is excellent. Just remember to take it slowly and enjoy the climbs instead of fighting them. To get to Koloniesbos, proceed from Swellendam Forest Station down the road for a few hundred metres, and then turn off to the right along the marked path. The path enters a pine plantation, veers left, and then descends along a logging track to a stream near some deserted buildings. Keep right here, through the bush, and after about two and a half kilometres, you will reach the hut.

Day 1: Koloniesbos to Boskloof – 16 kilometres (6 hours)
▶ From Koloniesbos, follow the gravel road uphill towards the pine plantation. At the top of the hill, footprints show the path going off to the right, downhill into the indigenous Wamakersbos. The path crosses two

streams – one at each end of the forest. This one-kilometre section is an easy-going, pleasant stroll in the verdant embrace of the wood. After crossing the second stream, the path suddenly turns uphill to negotiate a very steep, eroded bank, which becomes slippery in wet weather.
▶ After climbing about 100 metres, the path levels off somewhat onto the mountain-fynbos zone. Where moisture and shade are available, the path is often flanked with tall *Leucadendron eucalyptifolium*, or the smaller but more widespread yellow conebush (*L. salignum*). It is the latter species that gives these mountains their yellow glaze in spring. You should be able to identify four species of erica heath along this section, and the Caledon bluebell (*Gladiolus rogersii*).
▶ The path makes its way along the range's southern slope, climbing up between

terraces – with the climbs getting longer each time. As the path approaches Die Hoek, *Mimetes cucullatus* plants add a bright splash of colour to the surrounding vegetation, their red brushes glowing like torches from spring to midsummer.

▶ From the solitary red candlewood tree (*Pterocelastrus rostratus*) at Die Hoek, the path zigzags tightly up the hardest part of the route, and then climbs diagonally up the still steep mountainside to Hoekrus. Sticking out above the level of the heaths, the small, tight balls of brunia flower heads attract the scarab beetles and various butterflies which are so essential to pollination.

▶ Finally, rounding the corner after Old Kraal, the path drops over the final ridge to descend for four stony, ankle-twisting kilometres, crossing the narrow gorge at Tierkloof. Standing out from the general botanical brilliance along this section are

the everlastings: brilliant white *Helichrysum vestitum*, with dark centres; tall stalks of *H. foetidum*, with red balls opening into typical large, white, papery flowers; and red *Phaenocoma prolifera* on bunched heath-type stems.

▶ At the 10-kilometre mark, the hanging bridge is taken over Tierkloof. From here, follow the sign to Boskloof. Funnily enough, I have always reached this point at last light. The last two kilometres to the hut have therefore always been something of a blur – compounded at various times by sweat and rain running over my face. In mid- to late summer you might look for the 15-20-centimetre-high stalks of *Disa cornuta* sporting blue outer and white inner petals with a dark spot in the middle.

▶ Once at Boskloof you will be able to appreciate the formation of this range, which consists of a number of parallel ridges within

the folded rock massif. Hiking here is a matter of climbing up over the main ridges and then going down, up and over the intervening knife edges. Just upstream of the hut there is a marvellous swimming pool with slippery sides, and ice-cold water at all times. The temperature of the water, though, has never stopped me from taking the plunge.

Day 2: Boskloof to Koloniesbos – 8 kilometres (3 hours)

▶ Originally the short-cut route back to Koloniesbos went over Twaalfuurkop, but this has since been rerouted to pass over the main ridge close to the summit of Tienuurkop. From Boskloof hut, make your way back down the NHW path to the suspension bridge over Tierkloof. Just after crossing the bridge, about two kilometres downhill from the hut, take the path up to the right as indicated by the signpost.

▶ From the bridge, the path climbs diagonally up towards Tienuurkop, keeping some 60 to 80 metres above the stream, for just over two kilometres. At about 1 140 metres the path crosses over a saddle, with Tienuurkop (1 195) to the right.

From here, if you are not surrounded by swirling cloud, you can look out south over Swellendam and the Bontebok National Park, or north over mountains flowing out in all directions.

▶ From the saddle, the path executes several wide and steep zigzags down the Langeberg's south-facing slope to about the 700-metre contour, and then cuts diagonally down above Wamakersbos. Where the path

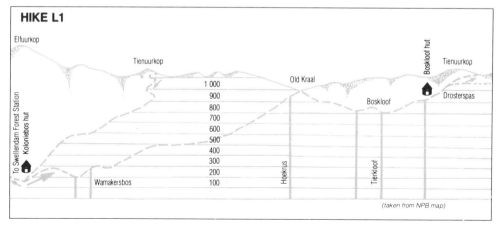

HIKE L1

(taken from NPB map)

arrives above, and midway between, Duiwelsbos and Wamakersbos, it turns left to take a spur towards the plantation abutting the Wamakersbos forest. For your sake, and that of the mountain, keep at all times to the zigzags and never take short cuts. If erosion is caused by hikers taking short cuts, the forester in charge will merely close this route and then there will be no week-end hike available.

▶ For the last kilometre, the path follows the edge of the plantation, to approach Koloniesbos hut from behind. From here, though, it is still about four kilometres back to the forest station.

Kruispad NHW   *Hike L2*

Route: *From Koloniesbos, via Proteavallei and Wolfkloof, to the Swellendam Forest Station*
Distance: *48,2 kilometres*
Duration: *5 days*
Grade: *Severe*
Booking Authority: *NHWB (Tel. (021) 402 3093) (permit needed)*
General Information: *Although given as a five-day walk, you can complete this hike in four days. If you wish to do this, I would recommend hiking either from Boskloof to Proteavallei (20 kilometres) – stopping at Goedgeloof for lunch – or from Proteavallei to the end (18 kilometres). The choice is yours. If you wish, you can take a longer variation on day four, hiking from Proteavallei to Wolfkloof via Vensterbank. This will lengthen the total distance of your hike to 56,6 kilometres.*

The Vensterbank route is, as I remember it, very dramatic and steep, and can become treacherous in wet and icy conditions – such as those I encountered on my descent. If you are concerned about poor weather, take the easier Kruispad route instead.

Day 1: Koloniesbos to Boskloof – 16 kilometres (6 hours)
▶ From Koloniesbos, follow the gravel road uphill towards the pine plantation. At the top of the hill, footprints show the path going off to the right, downhill into Wamakersbos. The path crosses two streams – one at each end of the forest. After crossing the second stream, the path suddenly turns uphill to negotiate a very steep, eroded bank.
▶ After climbing about 100 metres, the path levels off somewhat onto the mountain fynbos zone. It then makes its way along the range's southern slope, climbing up between terraces – with the climbs getting longer each time. Finally, rounding the corner after Old Kraal, the path drops over the final ridge to descend for four kilometres, crossing the narrow gorge at Tierkloof.
▶ At the 10-kilometre mark, a hanging bridge is taken over Tierkloof. From here, follow the sign to Boskloof (for a more detailed description, see Hike L1).

Day 2: Boskloof to Goedgeloof – 10 kilometres (3-4 hours)
▶ From Boskloof, climb up the ridge behind (north of) the hut – the range's central ridge. After climbing steeply for 100 metres, you reach the easy-going Drosterpas, which, for me, has always been one of the most

outstanding sections of this walk. Rainbows, masses of splendid mimetes, bunches of king proteas (*Protea cynaroides*) and the sun-smoothed mist spreading golden streams into the kloof below, these are the images I remember.
▶ Follow the Drosterpas until you reach the high, rocky ridge at Vulture Rock, where you can look along the entire mountain spine down the Grootkloof to Buffelsjag and beyond to the east, and towards Ashton to the west. Up here you will find a small species of the *Mimetes* genus growing as dense, low shrubs. This is *Mimetes cucullatus*, which flowers throughout the year, with clusters of bright-red 'cowls' standing above each of the white tufts surrounding the styles. Thus it is the cowls that give the flowers their specific name.
▶ From Vulture Rock, the path executes two zigzags to turn you around facing westward, still climbing steadily up the ridge. It then crosses a stream and takes a long curve around to the left, towards Knuckle Rock. This, finally, is the proverbial turning point – this is the top. Among the numerous heaths growing on the cobbled ridge are Riversdale heath (*Erica blenna*) and beautiful heath (*Erica pulchella*).
▶ The path now descends into the Zuurplaats valley. There has always been a sense of magic about this place for me, and I make it a compulsory tea spot. In late summer, check the river banks and pool edges for the yellow variety of *Disa tripetaloides*, and the mauve, five-petalled *Chironia jasminoides*. In spring to early summer, the valley floor is covered with pink and red heaths.

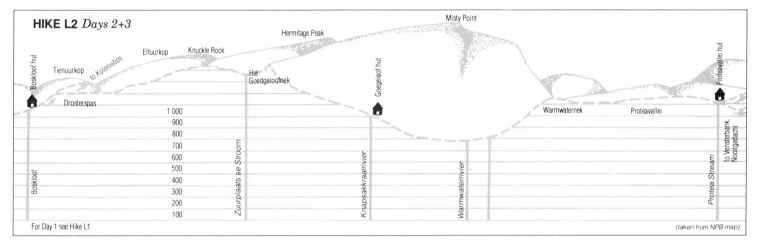

HIKE L2 *Days 2+3*

Misty Point

Hermitage Peak

Elfuurkop   Knuckle Rock

Boskloof hut

Tienuurkop   to Koloniebos

Het
Goedgeloofnek

Goegeloof hut

Proteavallei hut

Drosterspas

1 000
900
800
700
600
500
400
300
200
100

Boskloof

Zuurplaats se Stroom

Knapsakkraalrivier

Warmwaterrivier

Warmwaternek   Proteavallei

Protea Stream

to Vensterbank,
Nooitgedacht

For Day 1 see Hike L1

(taken from NPB map)

After climbing back out of the valley, the path breeches the Het Goedgeloofnek, to begin the arduous descent to Goedgeloof hut. The northern slope that you are now on becomes drier and stonier as you descend into the Klein Karoo. Above you loom Hermitage Peak (1 554 m) and Misty Point (1 710 m). After the wonderful solitude, it can be something of a let down to re-enter the realm of mankind here. The small huts are cosy, and a sheltered area provides for outdoor living.

Day 3: Goedgeloof to Proteavallei – 10 kilometres (3-4 hours)
From Goedgeloof continue along the path, which drops down to follow a jeep track to the Warmwaterrivier, where the penetrating call of ground woodpeckers is often heard. Tall leucadendrons and low blombos

are found here – as well as a few proteas such as the blue sugarbush (*Protea neriifolia*).
After another kilometre, you cross a second stream, and approach the demanding Warmwaternek. For two kilometres, you will climb this long ramp, with no physical respite.

Some magnificent specimens of bearded protea (*Protea magnifica*) grow next to lichen-encrusted boulders, but you are more likely to see the pretty heads of *Leucospermum calligerum*, bobbing on top of their slender stems, delicate creamy-white flower heads with thin protruding styles making the pins. These plants flower from July to January, the flower heads turning to pink and carmine as they age.
Then, just as your legs start rebelling and your eyes tire of false horizons, you suddenly peer over into that most beautiful of all

mountain glades, the aptly named Proteavallei. The hut is four kilometres from here, at the far end of the valley, along a more-or-less level path. You should plan to spend some time exploring this valley, weather permitting, because you are unlikely to see such a variety of flowering plants in such a confined area anywhere else. Why the hut was built to face the drain and not up the valley is a mystery to me.

Day 4: Proteavallei to Wolfkloof – 7,5 kilometres (2 hours)
From the Proteavallei hut, continue on the path down the valley for a short way before turning southwards (to the right) along the Kruispad. The path descends slightly, and then goes over a bump to leave the valley and follow the high road above the upper reaches of Wolfkloof. As soon as you leave

Proteavallei's floral profusion, the vegetation becomes surprisingly bleak, dominated by prickly cliffortias and scraggly everlastings. I can barely recall this route as I did it, in a blinding storm. I do remember some erosion, nice views of the rock bands across a wide valley on the Keurboomrug, a long but easy descent, and an orange-breasted sunbird. And stinging rain.

▸ The Kruispad joins the main path from Nooitgedacht just over six kilometres from the Proteavallei hut. From here it is two kilometres down what becomes a very steep descent into Wolfkloof. This is a place where you can plan to spend some time – perhaps even a whole extra day to explore the kloof. You can bundu-bash your way for a considerable way up the kloof, particularly if you are prepared to get your feet wet. Another advantage to staying at the

Wolfkloof hut is that it is one of the very few places in the western Cape mountains where you can make fires.

For the alternative route to Wolfkloof via Vensterbank, walk back from the Proteavallei hut to the main path and turn left. It is a gentle two-kilometre walk through the dense protea and erica veld to a fork at Dwariganek. *Protea exemia* is the dominant flower species here, though some fine specimens of *P. longiflora* and the more attractive *P. grandiceps* can be seen as well. Sugarbirds and sunbirds are often seen darting from flower to flower, and, if you are stealthy, you should be able to get quite close to them. Just remember to move slowly and smoothly with your camera poised (and set at the highest possible shutter speed), and freeze whenever your jittery target shows signs of alarm.

At Dwariganek you peer down the Twistnietvallei; be thankful that you are not going that way this time. Instead take the path up to the left from here, to the dramatic viewpoint overlooking the deep cleft called Vensterbank. The kloof within the vertical rock walls is Leeukloof, where the Leeurivier rises. You will meet this river again.

The path skirts around the top of Vensterbank, and climbs up over a spur leading down from Leeurivierberg (1 628 m), the second highest peak in the Marloth Nature Reserve, after Misty Point. Once that spur is surmounted, you enter a narrow chute, and it's just a matter of slip-sliding down the tightly zigzagging path that is the Vensterbankpad.

The trail then veers slowly away from the Vensterbank gorge, tracking towards the lesser Bakovenkloof to the west. This is a very wet route, so the large Cape bamboo (*Elegia capensis*) sprouts almost everywhere, as do other hydrophyllic restios.

As you make your way from deep, shaded kloof to open fynbos slope, the vegetation changes quite markedly: you should be able to make out six types of heath here, as well as at least two proteas, trees such as the mountain cedar (*Widdringtonia nodiflora*), rooiels (*Cunonia capensis*) and blue berry bush (*Diospyros glabra*). Lower down, where the restios start taking over, the fountain bush (*Psoralea* sp.), a shrub with needle-like leaves and blue-and-white flowers, grows. Nearing the bottom of Vensterbankpad, king proteas (*Protea cynaroides*) and splendid flamebushes will make their flamboyant appearance.

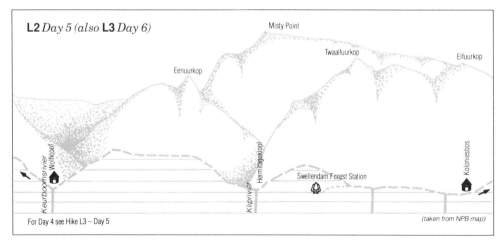

L2 *Day 5 (also* L3 *Day 6)*

Misty Point

Twaalfuurkop

Elfuurkop

Eenuurkop

Keurboomsrivier / Wolfkloof

Kliprivier

Hermitageskloof

Swellendam Forest Station

Koloniesbos

For Day 4 see Hike L3 – Day 5

(taken from NPB map)

Where this route joins the main – for want of a better word – contour path, turn left. You will immediately begin the descent into Kleinhoutboskloof. This is a very pleasant area: the river emerges from its narrow gorge here, before disappearing down into a dark, mysterious cleft.

Once in the Kleinhoutboskloof, the path negotiates a short tricky section where a wire railing has been provided for the faint-hearted. The massive tree growing in the gorge is a witels (*Platylophus trifoliatus*). The specific name (*trifoliatus*) is the key to identifying this grand forest species: the foliage comprises clusters of three narrow, serrated leaves, each between five and seven centimetres long.

The path leaves the gorge up narrow steps and climbs easily for another 100 metres, before dropping into Leeukloof. Along this route, the fynbos is dominated by the ever-lasting *Helichrysum sesamoides* and the fountain bush, interspersed with the odd king protea and *P. grandiceps*. Thereafter, the path undulates for about 100 metres before passing Aalwynkoppie, and then taking a short but steep final descent to Wolfkloof hut.

Day 5: Wolfkloof to Swellendam Forest Station – 10,7 kilometres (4 hours)
The last section of this hike is, unfortunately, nowhere near as exciting as the rest of the walk, and is particularly strenuous. This can be somewhat irritating, as all the effort needed to negotiate the ascents and descents on the path doesn't really seem to get you anywhere much.

▶ So my description is as follows... from Wolfkloof the path goes steeply up, then down, then up, then steeply down to Hermitagekloof – nice but for the ugly picnic area.
▶ Then the path goes steeply up again, and then down, before following a long route through the pine plantation to Swellendam Forest Station. The trail should end at Hermitagekloof – but it doesn't.

Nooitgedacht NHW *Hike L3*

Route: Circumnavigation of Marloth Nature Reserve
Distance: 81 kilometres
Duration: 6 days
Grade: Extreme
Booking Authority: NHWB (Tel. (021) 402 3093) (permit needed)
General Information: This walk can be shortened to five days, though I would not recommend that you do this unless you are feeling particularly strong. The section between Nooitgedacht and Wolfkloof looks acceptable on the map cross section, but be warned that the map hides the path's true devious nature. There is the odd two- or three-hundred-metre climb and descent omitted, for instance; something that might upset you after a long day's hike. Nevertheless, the full Swellendam Trail is a five-star hike and one of the finest trails in the country.

Day 1: Koloniesbos to Boskloof – 16 kilometres (6 hours)
▶ From Koloniesbos, follow the gravel road uphill towards the pine plantation. At the top of the hill, footprints show the path going off to the right, downhill into Wamakersbos. The path crosses two streams – one at each end of the forest. After crossing the second stream, the path suddenly turns uphill to negotiate a very steep, eroded bank, which becomes slippery in wet weather.
▶ After climbing about 100 metres, the path levels off somewhat onto the mountain fynbos zone. It then makes its way along the range's southern slope, climbing up between terraces – with the climbs getting longer each time. Finally, rounding the corner after Old Kraal, the path drops over the final ridge to descend for four stony, ankle twisting kilometres, crossing the narrow gorge at Tierkloof.
▶ At the 10-kilometre mark, a hanging bridge is taken over Tierkloof. From here, follow the sign to Boskloof (for a more detailed description, see Hike L1).

Day 2: Boskloof to Goedgeloof – 10 kilometres (3-4 hours)
▶ From Boskloof, climb up the ridge behind (north of) the hut – the range's central ridge. After climbing steeply for 100 metres, you reach the easy-going Drosterpas, which you must follow until you reach the high, rocky ridge at Vulture Rock.
▶ From Vulture Rock, the path executes two zigzags to turn you around facing westward, still climbing steadily up the ridge. It then crosses a stream and takes a long curve around to the left towards Knuckle Rock – this, finally, is the top.
▶ The path now climbs in and out of the Zuurplaats valley, and then breaches the

Hike L3 *Day 4*

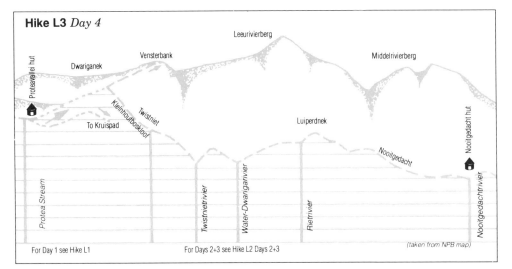

Leeurivierberg
Vensterbank
Dwariganek
Middelrivierberg
Proteavallei hut
Kleinhoutboskloof
Twistniet
To Kruispad
Luiperdnek
Nooitgedacht hut
Protea Stream
Twistnietrivier
Water-Dwarigarivier
Rietrivier
Nooitgedacht
Nooitgedachtrivier

For Day 1 see Hike L1   For Days 2+3 see Hike L2 Days 2+3   *(taken from NPB map)*

Het Goedgeloofnek, to begin the arduous descent to Goedgeloof hut (for a more detailed description, see Hike L2).

Day 3: Goedgeloof to Proteavallei – 10 kilometres (3-4 hours)
▶ From Goedgeloof continue along the path, which drops down to follow a jeep track to the Warmwaterrivier, where ground woodpeckers can be heard. After another kilometre, you cross a second stream, and approach Warmwaternek.
▶ After a two-kilometre climb to the top of Warmwaternek, you will see Proteavallei below you. The hut is four kilometres from here, at the far end of the valley, along a more-or-less level path (for a more detailed description, see Hike L2).

Day 4: Proteavallei to Nooitgedacht – 13 kilometres (6 hours)
▶ Before leaving the Proteavallei hut, make sure that you are carrying water, as there is none for the first six kilometres of this leg. From the hut, head back the way you came until you reach the junction. At the junction, turn left. After making your way for two kilometres through the dense protea-veld to Dwariganek, stop a while just to take in the view down the daunting Twistnietvallei and along the gnarled northern aspect of the Langeberg.
▶ Follow the path steeply down to a stream nearly three kilometres from the nek, then up again to a ridge and down to the Water-Dwarigarivier. Although the map shows plenty of water along the way, I didn't see

any for the first six kilometres, and the going was tough.
▶ From the river, it is a slow, plodding, two-kilometre climb to Luiperdnek, along which some interesting plants may be seen. The proteas in this region are different species to those encountered earlier on the walk – more suited to the drier conditions here. The most common species are *Protea laurifolia* (hard to distinguish visually from *P. neriifolia*) and the sugarbush (*P. repens*).

Another species of Proteaceae here is *Paranomus candicans,* which occurs between the Langeberg and Worcester. It is not the most glamorous plant of the genus, but next time you are grinding your way up to Luiperdnek and you see a one- to two-metre-high shrub, with soft, reddish branches, feathery leaves, and flowers (in spring) like reddish-grey cigarette filters that have been ripped open, you can say: 'Oh look, *Paranomus candicans*!'
▶ On reaching Luiperdnek, sigh with relief, then find one of the comfortable boulders lying among the restios on which to plonk down. Make some tea and savour the views down into the Nooitgedachtrivier valley. On the left, the knuckled ridge of the main Langeberg range marches on, while on the right pleated green folds of mountain fall down into the valley.
▶ The path now heads essentially downward, though there are a few irritating bumps along the way. As you near the hut, the vegetation on the valley floor becomes greener and more dense, while on the slopes above you wabooms (*Protea nitida*) tell of much drier conditions.

On reaching the bottom of the valley, you will see a signpost for the Nooitgedacht hut pointing up a path to the right. The hut is tucked away around a corner, a few hundred metres off the main path. And what a pleasant surprise it is: the stone building, an old foresters' lodge, stands in an opening cut out of the thick bush. Find your way to the large pool just upstream of the crossing close to the hut, and immerse yourself in water. Above this pool there is a series of smaller pools and rock slides.

If you are here in mid- to late summer, like I was, look for the bright-green shoots and long, scarlet petals of the flamboyant *Disa cardinalis*. An inconspicuous but curious protea found near here is *Protea humiflora*. It is a purplish-green ground species which is pollinated by mice, and emits a yeasty odour for this purpose. While reading about termites in the dying light outside the hut, my heart was shaken by a grunt and a brief crashing through the bush – it was a leopard. The greatest charm of Nooitgedacht is, I believe, the fact that so few hikers care to visit it.

Day 5: Nooitgedacht to Wolfkloof – 21,3 kilometres (9 hours)

From Nooitgedacht hut, return to the main path, turning right onto it and following it up an easy climb through waboom-veld. Although the river valley looks lush, you are still in the mountains' rain shadow, and the plant species here reflect the relatively dry conditions. Gird your loins here, because the road ahead is a long series of ascents and descents.

Rounding Harmesheuwel (863 m), the view opens out towards the southwest where Bonnievale hides among the wrinkled hills. The veld here is dominated by cliffortia shrubs and the common sugarbush (*Protea repens*).

After about four kilometres, the path reaches the wetter southern slopes of the Langeberg, and a change in climate is evident from the subtle changes in the vegetation. Flamebushes (*Mimetes cucullatus*) and 'kol-bols' (genuses *Brunia* and *Berzelia*) make the surrounding bush both higher and more lush than before.

For some time, the path follows an old jeep track, the surface of which is stony in places – although it is generally easy to negotiate.

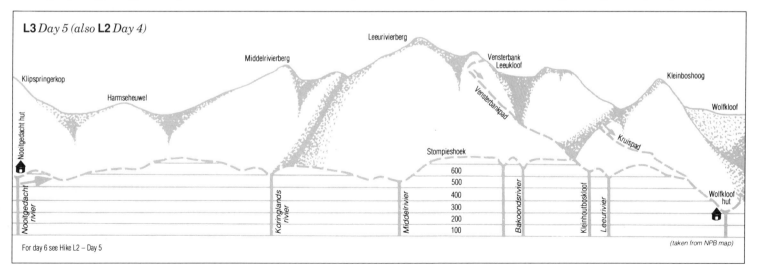

L3 *Day 5 (also* L2 *Day 4)*

For day 6 see Hike L2 – Day 5

(taken from NPB map)

An unusual creamy-yellow form of the king protea (*Protea cynaroides*) grows along this section of the trail, flowering from mid- to late summer.

Apart from the vegetation, the seemingly constant presence of cloud around the mountain peaks, and an increase in the number and size of the streams encountered give ample indication of your entry into a wetter climate zone. Along the stream banks, the common small trees seen are the water pea (*Podalyria calyptrata*) which erupts with sweet-smelling pink blooms during springtime, the water witels (*Brachylaena neriifolia*) and the lance-leaf myrtle (*Metrosideros angustifolia*).

▸ Stop at Middelrivier – the half-way mark – where a hut is proposed, though I doubt that it will ever be built. You can sit and stare at the waterfall cascading over a prominent band of rock higher up the Middelrivier gorge. For those who prefer looking down, keep a lookout for a pretty blue disa (*Herschelianthe graminifolia*) hiding among the restio stems.

▸ From Middelrivier, you must climb steeply up to Stompieshoek (or Flamebush Corner), where the flamebush (*Mimetes cucullatus*) is conspicuous, although the dominant shrubs here are the conebushes *Leucadendron salignum* and *L. salicifolium*.

▸ The next section involves some horribly steep, zigzagging ascents around gorges, with an equal number of descents just to bring you down to earth – what with all the enraptured botanizing. The small gorges are, however, quite pleasant and full of gurgling water, trees and shade.

▸ You have to negotiate three of the aforementioned ascents and descents before meeting the Vensterbankpad coming sharply down from the left. Thereafter, you head down into Kleinhoutbos, on past the Leeukloof, and then up again for another 150-odd metres, before finally beginning the long descent to the Wolfkloof hut.

Day 6: Wolfkloof to Swellendam Forest Station – 10,7 kilometres (3-4 hours)
▸ From here to the end of the trail, follow the path from Wolfkloof as it heads steeply up, then down, then up, then steeply down to Hermitagekloof – nice but for the ugly picnic area. It then goes steeply up again, and then down, before following a long route through the pine plantation to Swellendam Forest Station. If you want to, you can arrange for someone to collect you at Hermitagekloof. But let me not put you off.

Dassieshoek Trail *Hike L4*

Route: From Robertson to the Dassieshoek hut and back
Distance: 36,2 kilometres
Duration: 2 days
Grade: Severe
Booking Authority: Robertson Municipality (Tel. (02351) 3112) (permit needed)
General Information: Make an early start to this walk if the weather is hot, otherwise you will suffer some. This is a long trail, along the first 11 kilometres of which no respite is offered from the steady climb. To add further stress to the first day, there is no water for the first 15 kilometres. After that, water is abundant. Once the crest of the Langeberg is reached, the views south to the Riviersonderendberge and over the Klein Karoo to the distant, hazy Swartberg are very fine indeed. This is an ideal weekend hike. Collect your permit at Silverstrand caravan park on the western outskirts of Robertson.

Day 1: Silverstrand to Dassieshoek hut – 21,6 kilometres (8 hours)
▸ The trail starts at the farm stall opposite the Silverstrand resort, and the first kilometre is through farmlands. There are many paths which will confuse you, but, from the right-hand side (facing it) of the farm stall, head for the fence up ahead and cross it via the stile. Now head for the wooden bridge, cross it and head for a second bridge further on. Once over the second bridge, you leave the confusing network of paths behind and can concentrate on things more mountainous.
▸ For the next one and a half kilometres, the path remains level. When you reach a fork, take the left-hand path towards the enticing mountains. From the fork, the path begins a steady climb up the Langeberg. Pace yourself and get into a steady, rhythm, for remember, you have a long way to go.
▸ Continue along the footpath until you reach a jeep track, where you will see a sign declaring 'permit holders only' – pat your permit. Now you must follow the footprints, a fairly important bit of advice if you want to reach the hut by way of the shortest route.
▸ Continue along the jeep track for just under a kilometre, up to a fence. Cross the

fence and carry on along the footpath on the other side. Although you continue the general gradual climb, much of the hike is actually along level stretches which allow you to rest your legs.

▶ With magnificent views of Robertson and the surrounding countryside opening up, the path winds around one pleated spur after another, keeping to a general contour. After quite a bit of inning and outing, upping and alonging, you will reach a large boulder, indicating that you still have another 15 kilometres to go.

▶ After another few kilometres you come to Dries se Bos, which provides the first shady stretch of the hike – and the thirsty part is nearly over.

▶ From the 'bos' it is easy to lose the faint path in the rank grass, so keep a lookout for those footprints. Also keep an eye out for dangerous animals, such as the odd cow, that you might encounter here.

▶ Soon the footpath joins with a jeep track. Take heart here, for the first water is close at hand – it may be reduced to just a trickle in summer, but it is water.

▶ The jeep track takes you to the summit ridge of the range, into the mountains that you peered at from below. Now the vistas in both directions are sublime.

▶ With eight kilometres to go, you pass a shack, where the trail leaves the jeep track and follows a narrow but well-defined footpath. The name of the game is now kloof and not spur, as the path climbs in and out of one kloof after the other, each one washed by a clear mountain stream. There are some delightful swimming spots within these shady

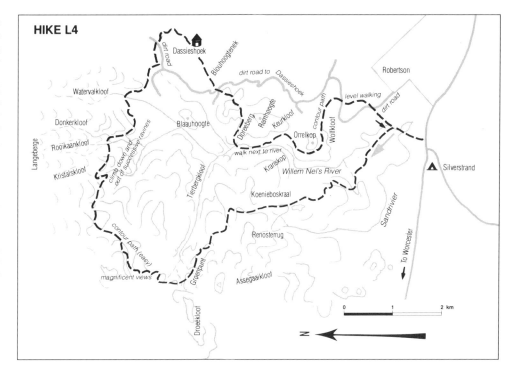

HIKE L4

kloofs, and the intervening path traverses a narrow ridge with steep drops to one side or another.

▶ After negotiating the umpteenth kloof, the path makes a steep descent to regain the jeep track, though after only a few hundred metres you must swing off to the left along a footpath to follow those painted footprints. Soon you will reach a gravel road, and the Dassieshoek hut – a converted stone farmhouse – will be reached after a further

kilometre through prickly climber's friend (*Cliffortia* sp.) and renosterbos (*Elytroppapus rhinocerotus*) bushes. The hut is situated at the end of a tortuous pass, in the gentle but dramatic surroundings of a secluded valley.

Day 2: Dassieshoek hut to Silverstrand – 14,6 kilometres (5 hours)
The return journey to the farm stall is short and easy. It is a lovely walk through riverine

bush and rich mountain fynbos, with numerous swimming spots available.

▶ Your route begins to the left of the hut, and follows the road for about one and a half kilometres, until the faithful footprints show you where to turn off onto a footpath to the right (marked on the iron grille at the top of a rise). The footpath is well defined and climbs gradually but continuously for some way with impressive views of the Dassieshoek valley. The vegetation here is mainly fynbos, with proteas and blombos (*Metalassia* sp.) bushes, but succulent Karoo elements are in evidence, suggesting the climatic edge of Klein Karoo conditions around Robertson.

▶ On reaching the top of the ridge, the path levels off for a few hundred metres before taking a short and steep descent. At the bottom of this descent you reach the first water point on the return leg.

▶ Depending on what time you depart the hut, this makes an ideal breakfast, tea or lunch spot. Next to the river, there is a wide rock platform that can be used for your comfort. If you are walking in the summer heat, it is recommended that you make an early start to climb the ridge and descend into the river valley, which will be followed for some way from here, before the sun gets high and oppressive.

▶ The path makes its way along the river, crossing over and back again – four times in all. Some boulder-hopping is involved along this stretch, and at the third crossing you will come to a false dead end, a rock face with the river below. You have to make your way across this face, trying not to fall into the water on your left (this sounds far more dangerous than it actually is). You will then see that the path continues on the other side.

▶ After the previous day's walk, it is a real pleasure to walk in the cool shade, still following the course of the river and the yellow footprints.

The fourth river crossing is your last, so take full advantage of the water.

▶ After the fourth crossing, the path climbs out of the river valley, and as it climbs, the vegetation changes from forest to fynbos, and very soon to a drier habitat characterized by aloes and euphorbias.

▶ The path crosses a gravel road and then winds its way around private farmland. On nearing the realm of civilization, you are once again confronted by a maze of paths, but by closely following the yellow footprints you should manage to find your way through it. A little further on, you come to an area of renosterveld, a floral community associated with the more fertile, lowland areas of the fynbos biome, and dominated by the renosterbos (rhinoceros bush). Renosterveld is, like much of the biome, an endangered habitat, which itself is thought to be a degraded veld type, having first been overgrazed – initially by Khoi herders and later by white settlers – and then forced to make way for the various cereals, vineyards and other crops that were planted in the fertile, clayey, shale-derived soils.

▶ Soon, you should recognize the fork, now a convergence of paths, where, the day before, you took the left-bearing option up the mountain. Continue left until you reach the farm stall.

Bloupunt   Hike L5

Route: *Circular walk from the Klipspringer huts to Bloupunt*
Distance: *15,6 kilometres*
Duration: *7 hours*
Grade: *Severe*
Booking Authority: *Montagu Municipality (Publicity Association) (Tel. (0234) 4 1112/4 2678) (permit needed)*
General Information: *The local council has done a splendid job in the building and siting of the stone huts in Donkerkloof, and have been spirited in making this trail generally available to us towny hikers. The two huts sleep six people each, and have a donkey boiler, hot showers, braai facilities, a range stove and a flush toilet. You do not have to make use of the trail huts to do any of the walks here, nor do you have to do any of the walks if you make use of the huts – but it would be foolish to do one without the other. If you have booked one of the huts, get the key from the publicity officer. He will direct you to the huts, which are found across the Keisierivier from town, up the kloof past the old mill. Sections of the trail are very exposed, so take protection against both sun and possible rain and cloudy weather. You are likely to meet several townsfolk strolling in the kloof or up the mountain, or early-morning joggers out for a nature amble. It is obvious that the townsfolk hold this reserve dear, and it is a privilege to make use of their generosity.*

▶ The walk starts from the huts, and heads up the kloof through fairly dense riverine bush, where the tall trees are – believe it or not – rooikrans (*Acacia cyclops*). Follow the small markings painted on rocks along the way. As with all mountain outings, the path up the kloof gets steeper and steeper on its four-kilometre wander. Once the path climbs above the kloof, you will not see water again until well on your way down the other side of the mountain – and that's still a long way from here.

▶ For the next four kilometres to the summit of Bloupunt, the path moves up through familiar restios, ericas and proteas, and fields littered with cheerful, papery everlasting blooms where sugarbirds dart from flower to flower, never letting you get too close to them.

▶ From the summit, you command magnificent views over a vast stretch of mountain ranges and intervening lowlands: to Montagu at the foot of the mountain, McGregor, Robertson, Ashton and Bonnievale to the west and south, and the parched stretches of the Karoo to the north.

▶ The path now heads back down the mountain. After just under four kilometres, you pass a waterfall, and here the gradient starts to ease off. Seven hundred metres further on, you pass a second waterfall, and, after another 300 metres, a third. By late summer, the first and third falls have dwindled to mere trickles, while the second is little more than that. The pool into which the second waterfall plunges is unfortunately too small and muddy in summer for a much-needed swim.

▶ About 500 metres from the last falls, you meet up with the jeep track that runs up the kloof from the huts. From here it is an easy two-kilometre stroll in the shady valley back to the huts. In summer, this hike can be extremely hot, and this will make it much harder than it is in winter, especially when no water is found in the streams and no cooling winds stir the reeds. So, if the weather is very hot, perhaps you'd like to try one of the following two walks instead.

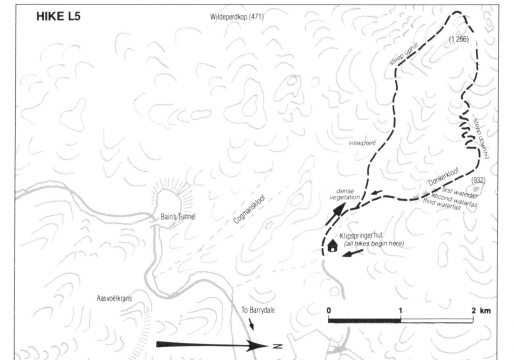

Cogmanskloof   *Hike L6*

Route: *Circular walk from the huts around Cogmanskloof*
Distance: *12,1 kilometres*
Duration: *4 hours*
Grade: *Moderate*
Booking Authority: *Montagu Municipality (Tel. (0234) 4 1112 / 4 2678) (permit needed)*

General Information: Despite its name, this hike does not so much follow a kloof as make its way around the extremely dry and exposed slopes of the Waboomberge. Throughout the year, you should carry enough water for the entire hike; if it is going to be a hot day, be sure to drink your fill before setting off. The only watering point is reached a short distance from the end of the hike. Nevertheless, the height climbed is only about half that of the Bloupunt hike. If you have booked to stay in the local hiking huts, get the key from the publicity officer in town, or arrange a collecting point with him. He will give you directions for the huts, to which you can drive to off-load your gear. They are found across the Keisierivier from town, up the kloof past the old mill.

Since this walk takes place in the Waboom-berge, this is a better place than most to give some information about this ubiquitous 'wagon tree' (*Protea nitida*). British traveller W.J. Burchell (after whom the plains zebra were named) recorded that the wood of the trees was used to make the felloes of wagon wheels. It seems that most of the larger trees were felled for this purpose, and for general use of the attractive reddish timber. From 1800, it was recorded that the crushed leaves, when mixed with a solution of iron in water, made a passable ink substitute. Many old documents and bibles of these times would have been transcribed with quills dipped in waboom ink. Other practical and medicinal uses were found for the bark.

▶ From the huts, follow the jeep track up the valley for about 300 metres, and then take

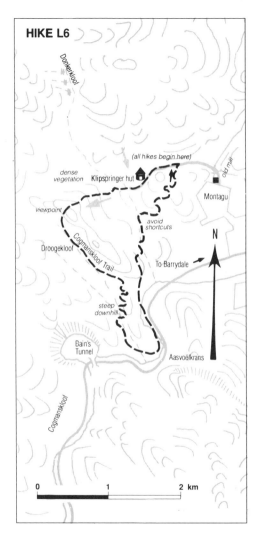

the path going to the left, out of the verdant coolness. The path moves off in a southwesterly direction, snaking its way up the dry slopes until the two-kilometre mark. Here, the trail curves around to the left, and begins a steep 500-metre ascent, before turning again to round the mountain. Having rounded this bulge, you look out across the Aasvoëlkrans (the vultures have long gone) and down towards Montagu, the Keisierivier's pleasant course, and the outlying hills.

▶ From this viewpoint, the path makes its way back down towards and along Cogmans-kloof for about two kilometres, on its way to executing a complete circle. Although there are ups and downs, they are not strenuous.

▶ As the path keeps curving around to the left, it finds itself making its way up a valley. The path crosses the river, follows it for some way, recrosses it and then zigzags for about two and a half kilometres to make its way over a ridge and back into the Cogmanskloof. From here you can see the mill house where the kloof reaches the outskirts of Montagu, as well as the huts further up the kloof.

▶ The trail meets the road up Cogmanskloof just below the mill, where it crosses the Keisierivier. From here it is a gentle and shaded walk back to the huts.

Lovers' Walk   *Hike L7*

Route: The Klipspringer huts to the Montagu spa resort and back
Distance: 5 kilometres
Duration: 40 minutes (there); 40 minutes (back)

Grade: Easy
Booking Authority: Montagu Municipality
(Tel. (0234) 4 1112 / 4 2678)
General Information: This pretty walk is
really an excuse to visit the famous spa with
its hot mineral baths. Along the stream, however, some pleasant pools occur, swimming in
which is a most enticing prospect. The resort
is very easy to find – merely follow the path
up Badkloof; the name refers to the natural
springs which you will encounter along the
way. You have to pay an entrance fee at the
spa, but if you are spending some time in the
Montagu area, it is worth it. Since this is
such a simple walk, a full route description
is hardly necessary, but here goes...

▶ Walk down the jeep track from the huts, to
the mill house. Pass the mill and turn left
(eastwards) up the left-hand bank of the
Badkloof river. Continue up the bank for just
over a kilometre, then cross the shallow
stream, as the bank becomes overgrown at
this point.
▶ After you have crossed the stream, either
follow the right-hand bank all the way, or
cross back to the other side wherever you
wish. The path moves in a basic north-
easterly direction, away from the town. The
valley is gentle and fertile, engulfed by
mountains. There are no trees to speak of
along the walk, but the civic authority has
kindly provided benches along the way if you
do need a rest. This is a well-used but also
well-maintained path, so it is very pleasing.
When you've had enough of the hot mineral
water at the spa, head back to the huts and
solitude.

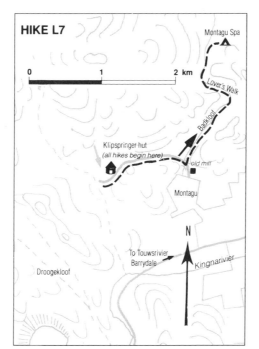

HIKE L7

0   1   2 km

Montagu Spa

Lover's Walk

Badkloof

Klipspringer hut
(all hikes begin here)

old mill

Montagu

N

To Touwsrivier
Barrydale

Kingnarivier

Droogekloof

Boesmanskloof
Traverse
Hike L8

Route: From Die Galg above McGregor to
Greyton
Distance: 36 kilometres
Duration: 2 days
Grade: Severe
Booking Authority: Sonderend Forest Sta-
tion (Tel. (02351) 3079) (permit needed)

General Information: This is a very popular weekend hike, going, as it does, between
two of the region's most attractive historic
villages. The path follows the Boesmanskloof, for much of the duration way above the
river. Water is plentiful, even when you are
far above the main kloof. This is the only
easily accessible hike through the Riviersonderendberge, which mountaineers know as
the 'waterless mountains'. Some hardy (fool-
hardy) hiking types have been known to attempt complete traverses of the rugged range,
but a lack of water and paths has defeated
most good intentions to date. There are three
popular hotels in Greyton, ranging from expensive and up-market, to reasonable with a
special deal for hikers. Since this quaint village became the yuppie hangout for Capetonians in the '80s, some hotels' prices have shot
up. The Post House – restored in the town's
historic idiom – and the Greyton Lodge are
expensive, but the less pretentious Central
Hotel offers reasonable food and shared accommodation. The hotel has a bar, pool table
and swimming pool. My companions and I
certainly enjoyed all its facilities at a very
reasonable cost (under R150-00 dinner, bed
and breakfast for four).

*Day 1: Die Galg to Greyton – 18 kilometres
(6 hours)*
After collecting your permit from the forester in Robertson (past the graveyard), drive
through McGregor and on for another 15
kilometres up the northern slope of the Riviersonderend range to Die Galg (the
gallows) near the head of Boesmanskloof.
You can park safely here at the forestry

education centre, next to a field of orange pincushions (*Leucospermum oleifolium*).

▶ You begin at a copse of blue-gum trees and follow the track along which Italian prisoners of war started constructing a mountain pass to Greyton – the pass was never completed. When you reach the sign pointing into the kloof, turn left down the steep path (alternatively, you can continue to where the old road peters out and there take the steep descent to the valley floor). The descent involves zigzagging down wooden steps, often with cable hand rails. In early 1987, a fire swept across the gorge, and much of the spectacular vegetation was destroyed. Along the first part of the hike, however, as one descends into the gorge, the path cuts down through rank protea bush growing up to three metres high. At the height of the flowering season (winter), these proteas make a fine sight. In summer, pelargoniums, ericas, watsonias and disas (*Disa tripetaloides*, to be more precise) are most common. In wet areas, look out for the pretty, leafless, orange root parasite, *Harveya bolusii*, and the white inkflower, *H. capensis*, which turns dark purple when bruised or damaged. Unfortunately, many small pines are beginning to invade the natural vegetation in this area. As you go, try to pull out the smaller pines without disturbing the surrounding soil too much.

▶ The kloof is very secluded, yet the path crosses mostly open ground, making the going very hot in summer. On a tributary of the Boesmanskloof river, you will meet Oom Piet se Waterval. Here the main path crosses over the river to the left-hand bank, going downstream. From here on, for most of the route, the path lacks the typical kloof vegetation that one would expect, being covered instead with grass and low fynbos.

▶ After crossing the second tributary, the path begins to climb none too steeply (but for one short stretch) up the left-hand bank of the river. Some aloes cling to the eroding cliffs here, like torches, in winter, with their brilliant-red flowers.

▶ Hereafter you don't get near the main river until just before entering Greyton at the end of the hike. However, you are granted some spectacular views of the rugged mountains, and down the Boesmanskloof river gorge where the green flanks of interlocking spurs recede far back along the range. Lording over the gorge to the west is Jonaskop, which, at 1 646 metres, is the second highest peak in the Riviersonderend range.

▶ At the halfway mark, you come to a large pool on a tributary coming down from the left. This perfectly round pool seems to hang suspended against the side of the mountain; it is certainly one of the finest mountain pools that I have seen. It is also the only decent swimming spot on the hike. People walk here from Greyton for a day's outing, so the main pool may be occupied – but there are other pools. Our party spent a long time exploring further upstream, watching lizard behaviour and spotting disas. Whatever the rest of the trail lacks in water spots, this side-gorge makes up for.

▶ From the pool you round a spur and head toward a saddle, the path getting progressively steeper. After crossing a small tributary, the path executes several long zigzags up to the saddle. The views from here across the Overberg towards Hermanus and Gansbaai, and back into the green embrace of Boesmanskloof are, you will admit, worth the return journey tomorrow.

▶ But the hike is still far from over, and to even see Greyton you have to head around the next long spur. The path becomes a jeep track, and this you must follow for another five kilometres, along a ridge that undulates for some way. This is most tiring when you think you are so near your destination.

▶ Finally, the track slips down a steep slope to your left, and into a small side valley, before emerging on the pebble-cluttered bed of the main river.

▶ From here, you just follow your nose to the main street, turn left and head for the hotel in the 'middle' of town. From the outskirts it is about a kilometre to the Central Hotel (if you have decided to stay there). The pretty town huddles beneath avenues of trees; it is laid out in the gridiron style of an English town, but incorporates a few features that are typically Dutch – such as water furrows.

Day 2: Greyton to Die Galg – 18 kilometres (6 hours)

▶ The return trip is simply a reversal of the first day's walk, beginning with the long, steep road back up to the saddle... The final climb from the kloof to Die Galg is steep, and is best avoided in the heat of summer, when shade and water are in short supply. Don't follow the kloof right to the end, instead break out up the constructed steps on your left near the end of the kloof, and follow the track at the top to Die Galg.

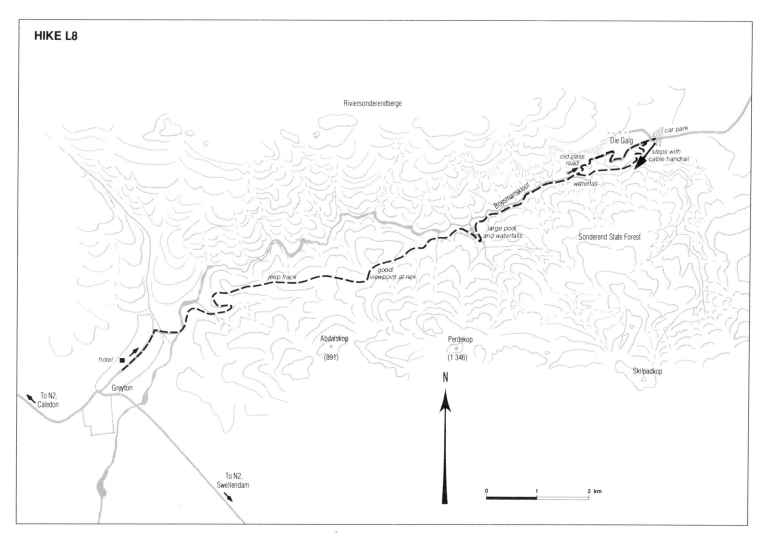

HIKE L8

Riviersonderendberge

Die Galg

car park

old pass road

steps with cable handrail

waterfall

Boesmanskloof

Sonderend State Forest

large pool and waterfalls

good viewpoint at nek

jeep track

hotel

Greyton

To N2, Caledon

To N2, Swellendam

Abdalskop (891)

Perdekop (1 346)

Skilpadkop

N

0   1   2 km

OVERBERG

The Overberg is a large area, consisting mainly of a wide coastal plain with random mountain outcrops. The seductive name was coined by the early Dutch settlers who considered the 'Mountains of Africa' – Hottentots-Holland to we space-agers – to be the end of the known world. Once they found a way over this coastal range up the Gantouw Pass, they were said to be 'overberg'. If only they knew what still lay ahead...

The area lies south of the Langeberg and Riviersonderend mountain ranges, stretching from the Elgin-Grabouw valley in the west, to the Breërivier in the east. The main attraction of the region – also the flagship of the provincial nature conservation authorities – is the De Hoop Nature Reserve, though the smaller reserves in the area are also well worth a visit.

The most impressive of these small nature reserves is the Harold Porter National Botanical Garden in Betty's Bay, which is a satellite garden of Kirstenbosch. Other reserves that will be given brief coverage at the end of this chapter are the Caledon Nature Reserve and Wildflower Garden, the Fernkloof Nature Reserve in the Kleinriviersberge behind Hermanus and the Bredasdorp Mountain Reserve.

With the exception of Potberg, which is the southernmost outcrop of Table Mountain Sandstone, most of the De Hoop reserve falls on a calcrete layer – concrete-hard limestone deposits that represent a raised sea bed. The limestone-derived soil gives rise to a fynbos community unique to the southern Cape coastal region. Although the basic fynbos families are all well represented on these calcrete plains, the species are mostly quite different to those found on the protruding Potberg (which are more closely allied to the mountain fynbos communities).

Of the approximately 8 500 plant species counted in the Cape Floral Kingdom, 1 500 are found in the Bredasdorp/Agulhas area. Of these, 108 species are considered to be rare or endangered, 50 species are endemic and 13 are either newly discovered or undescribed. The reason for so many species' status being precarious is due to the intense wheat cultivation here. However, it is on the rich shale-derived soils that most of this cultivation has occurred, and not on the poorer limestone soils. Remnants of very rare south-coast renosterveld occur west of Potberg, where a small pocket of Bokkeveld Shale falls within the De Hoop reserve.

The main habitats in the reserve are the rocky coastline east of Koppie Alleen, the beaches and sand dunes to the west (the largest such protected habitat in the country), the coastal plain, comprising limestone hills also known as 'hard dunes', the Potberg, and De Hoopvlei – a brackish lake.

De Hoopvlei is, with Barberspan in the Transvaal, one of only two wetlands in the country registered at the Ramsar Convention as being of international importance as a wildfowl habitat – although I could think of many others, such as Verlorenvlei, that should be included on the convention's list. Although the vlei is an inland lake, the presence of marine organisms suggests that it was once a river estuary at least partly open to the sea, before the coastal dunes closed the mouth off two and a half kilometres from the present shoreline.

The northern shore of the lake is lined with limestone hills, behind which stands the elegant Cape-Dutch De Hoop homestead, now serving as park offices. If you are lucky, you may find the fossils of marine shellfish cemented into these cliffs. Above the vlei, gnarled milkwood (*Sideroxylon inerme*) trees, some hundreds of years old, stand on the plain; around the homestead the branches of wild fig (*Ficus capensis*) trees spread huge canopies across the lawns.

The reserve is attractive not so much for its wild herds as for the rare animals – such as mountain zebra, eland and bontebok – that find refuge there. The type and structure of the vegetation mostly determine what animals will be found in specific habitats, as do the smaller invertebrates, which form a food link between the plants and

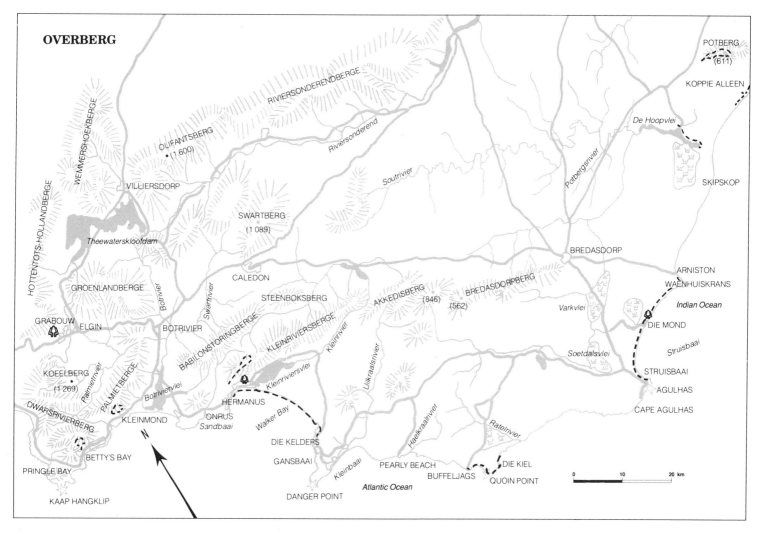

OVERBERG

POTBERG
(611)

KOPPIE ALLEEN

De Hoopvlei

SKIPSKOP

RIVIERSONDERENDBERGE

WEMMERSHOEKBERGE

OLIFANTSBERG
(1 600)

Riviersonderend

Soutrivier

Potbergsrivier

VILLIERSDORP

HOTTENTOTS-HOLLANDBERGE

Theewaterskloofdam

SWARTBERG
(1 089)

BREDASDORP

ARNISTON
WAENHUISKRANS

GROENLANDBERGE

CALEDON

STEENBOKSBERG

AKKEDISBERG
(846)

BREDASDORPBERG
(562)

Varkvlei

Indian Ocean

DIE MOND

Botrivier

Swartrivier

GRABOUW

ELGIN

BOTRIVIER

BABILONSTORINGBERGE

KLEINRIVIERSBERGE

Kleinrivier

Uilkraalsrivier

Soetdalsvlei

Struisbaai

STRUISBAAI

KOEELBERG
(1 269)

Palmietrivier

PALMIETBERGE

Botriviervlei

Kleinriviersvlei

AGULHAS

DWARSRIVIERBERG

KLEINMOND

HERMANUS

ONRUS

Sandbaai

Walker Bay

Haelkraalrivier

Ratelrivier

CAPE AGULHAS

N

DIE KELDERS

BETTY'S BAY

GANSBAAI

PEARLY BEACH

DIE KIEL

PRINGLE BAY

Kleinbaai

BUFFELJAGS

QUOIN POINT

0   10   20 km

KAAP HANGKLIP

DANGER POINT

Atlantic Ocean

many of the larger animals. Most visible of the animals are bontebok, eland, grey rhebok, duiker and steenbok. Small predators like caracal and mongooses are fairly common, while the remains of larger carnivores have been found in the dune sands.

Many caves on Potberg shelter important colonies of bats, of which there are five insectivorous and four fruitarian species, totalling a maximum summer population of 150 000. The largest cave is used as a breeding colony by at least three species, most important of which is Scheiber's longfingered bat. Other species include the Cape and Geoffrey's horseshoe bats, the Cape hairy bat and the Egyptian slitfaced bat. It has been estimated that the insectivorous species consume 410 kilograms of insects every night, which is a very effective form of biological insecticide for neighbouring farmers. The guano-thick cave floors host an independent ecosystem of fungi (52 species) and invertebrates (47 species).

Reptiles are well represented by tortoises, terrapins and snakes, including potentially harmful ones like puffadders, boomslangs, and mysteriously beautiful Cape cobras, and, to a lesser extent, molesnakes.

It is the large population of breeding and migrant birds, however (at the last count, there were 234 species of bird known to occur in the reserve), that generates the most interest. Along the coast, you might see shy black oystercatchers, small sanderlings and grey plovers scuttling after the retreating surf, whitebreasted cormorants, kelp gulls, giant kingfishers, egrets and herons near the vlei, rock kestrels, redwing starlings,

and doves on the limestone cliffs. The dunes between the reserve and Arniston are home to a breeding colony of 25 per cent of the world population of 3 000 Damara terns. This is the rarest coastal bird of southern Africa, being extremely sensitive to disturbance and – like the oystercatcher – having a very low breeding success rate.

The sandy coastal plains are inhabited by, of course, ostriches, but also by black korhaans and Stanley bustards, capped wheatears, Namaqua sandgrouse, secretary birds, steppe and jackal buzzards, sunbirds, starlings and plovers.

On the vlei live 16 species of water fowl; large waders like flamingoes and spoonbills; smaller waders such as plovers, sandpipers, stilts and avocets (and this does not include migrants such as curlew sandpipers); reed skulkers such as crakes, flufftails, moorhens and gallinules; the pelicans and seabirds that visit the lake; or even the two resident pairs of fish eagles whose high-pitched call is the song of the wild African waterways.

The most important inland birds, from a conservation perspective, are the vultures that nest on the southeastern cliffs of the Potberg. This is, ironically enough, the only remaining breeding colony of Cape vulture in the winter rainfall area. Recently, this species, endemic to southern Africa, has been scratched from the endangered list due to the current success of breeding colonies in the Transvaal.

Hiking in the Overberg

Many of the hikes in this area are coastal walks, though there are also numerous

nature reserves where short rambles are in order. In these cases it is quite unnecessary to include a full route description, as the walks are mostly short and obvious; people are expected to ramble around the reserves by whichever route they choose.

De Hoop has a great diversity of natural habitats and offers three basic types of walk: along the coast, up the Potberg, and around the edge of the vlei. The reserve has two focuses: the historic De Hoop homestead where the main rest camp has been built, and the equally appealing Potberg farmstead which has been converted into an education and information centre.

Accommodation in the Overberg area is as varied as the area, ranging from luxury coastal hotels to low-rent caravan parks patronized by fishermen and their disgruntled families. Overnight facilities have recently been made available at De Hoop.

Potberg Klipspringer Walk
Hike O1

Route: From the Potberg Education Centre to Potberg summit and back
Distance: 11 kilometres
Duration: 2 hours (there); $1\frac{1}{2}$ hours (back)
Grade: Fair
Booking Authority: De Hoop, CPA (permit needed to enter the reserve)
General Information: This short hike is ideal for an easy morning or afternoon outing, and the mountain's summit allows grand views over the reserve and

surrounding areas. It is a lovely walk on a gradually climbing path through rich fynbos and riverine bush, with plenty of water along the way. Because of its isolated nature, the Potberg has its very own ecosystem with numerous endemic plants, some even named after the mountain.

▶ Just left (southwest), facing the mountain, of the Potberg Education Centre's display room, a sign with painted feet directs you to the start of the walk, which begins with a short descent to a shady stream. The route is well defined, with regular erosion gabions across the path. The path climbs out of the gully, and, after about five minutes, reaches a sign at the point where the Klipspringer and Potberg trails diverge. The path continues around a spur, where the bush is brightened by bunches of helichrysum everlastings. The protea family is also well represented in this area: look out for ground species like *Protea denticulata*. The small deep-red, brown-tipped flowers are pollinated by rodents that feed on the seeds.

As you go, look for a cave in the cliffs high above; this is one of the major bat caves on Potberg.

▶ You continue climbing easily until you reach a sign saying 'The Cave'. It is a steep, 10-minute climb to the cave entrance, and the views from here over the distant dune fields and the ocean are excellent, but it can be bypassed on your way to the summit.

▶ From here, return to the Klipspringer path and continue through protea-dominated fields with equally impressive views to the south. The path continues its ascent to the

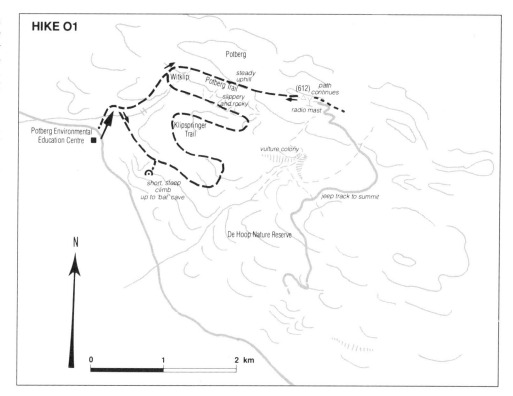

HIKE O1

crest of a ridge, and then levels off and heads for the summit. To the north lies the Breërivier valley, while the ocean can be seen way off to the south.

▶ After a customary halt at any spot along this ridge for refreshments and to enjoy the panoramic vistas, continue along the path to a fork, where either option will lead you down again. The left-bearing path is, however, the more attractive of the two. (The other path climbs easily up to the radio mast, where the views make the effort required worthwhile. Take the same path back and then turn right where you reach a junction to go back down to civilization on the Potberg Trail.)

▶ After a short level course, this path descends steeply into a kloof. Take care on the descent, as the path is loose and eroded in places. In the bed of the kloof is a large rock pool that, on hot days, is most inviting. A short but steep climb takes you out of the kloof to another fork in the path, where a sign marks the Klipspringer and Potberg trails. The right-hand option takes you back down into the kloof where it rejoins the path that was bypassed near the summit. There is usually plenty of water in the kloof, making it a good place for a lunch stop, if you haven't had lunch already.

▶ The left-hand option will take you more or less straight down to the education centre. The path is fairly rough and rocky, but, if you move at a good pace, it will take only 45 minutes to reach the bottom – just be careful not to twist an ankle, or stand on the puffadder that nearly accounted for my companion.

On the drier northern slopes you will see more crassulas and aloes than on the moist, southern slopes, where thick fynbos predominates by virtue of the sea mists.

De Hoopvlei   Hike O2

Route: *From De Hoop homestead to the end of the vlei*
Distance: *24 kilometres*
Duration: *3-4 hours (there); 3-4 hours (back)*
Grade: *Easy*
Booking Authority: *De Hoop, CPA (permit needed to enter the reserve)*
General Information: *From 1739, this area was known as 'loan place' as it was leased for grazing by the Dutch East India Company. One Pieter Lourens Cloete built the original H-plan homestead now used as administration offices, as well as other buildings such as the sheep-shearing shed. The homestead complex is a national monument. In 1956, De Hoop farm was purchased by the CPA, with other farms being added over a period of time to form the existing nature reserve. The ecological status of the vlei has been covered to some extent in the introduction above, but one other interesting point is that it fluctuates from virtually dry to flood level, depending on conditions in the catchment area.*

▶ Starting on the calcrete cliffs behind the homestead, follow the edge of the vlei as best you can. You will see bitou bushes (*Chrysanthemum monolifera*) with their pretty yellow flowers, gnarled milkwoods (*Sideroxylon inerme*) where weavers nest and boomslangs lurk, bastard wild olive (*Olea exasperata*), Cape sumach (*Colpoon compressum*) and sea guarri (*Euclea racemosa*) among the many plants on the banks. With luck you may catch a glimpse of the sandy-coloured Cape fox that lives in the vicinity.

The reserve was created for the breeding of rare mammals, and in the open grassy areas around the vlei – where the best grazing is found – you are likely to see Cape mountain zebra, bontebok, eland and ostrich, as well as tortoises and baboons. The vlei margin is a sensitive ecosystem and hikers should take care to stick to the path where it is clearly established. The cliffs are the best place from which to observe the water birds.

▶ This hike follows the eastern shore of the vlei from opposite the De Hoop homestead, to where coastal dunes block its access to the sea. First it makes its way along the calcrete cliff line, where you have to pick your way through the milkwood and thorn bush. Then, where the cliffs peter out, you have to follow a narrow path (try to stick to one main path) slightly above the vlei's high-water mark so as to avoid degrading the area unnecessarily. The grassy verge is much favoured by grazers, so don't trample it – rather let them trample it if they choose. The route is really straightforward once you follow the vlei edge. As you near the wide terminal lagoon, veer away from the water and keep quiet (if you want to see waders and water fowl, that is). Then, slowly and crouched, approach the vlei.

Where the cliffs give way to a sandy shoreline towards the south, you can take a closer look at the lake ecosystem. Although it is a permanently brackish lake, the salinity level depends on the inflow of fresh water from the main feeder, Soutrivier, and various springs such as Tierhoek fountain – as well as evaporation. During a drought, when salinity is high, the freshwater organisms in the lake survive by collecting in pools around freshwater springs in the vlei. The battle not to be eaten must be extremely stressful under such conditions.

The vlei is a rich source of primary foods (those at the beginning of the food chain), where phragmites (whistle) reeds, bulrushes and sedges line the shores, along with the water onions and various water grasses that provide food for the many water

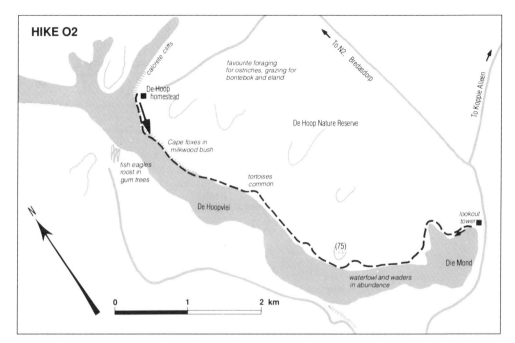

De Hoop Nature Reserve

favourite foraging
for ostriches, grazing for
bontebok and eland

calcrete cliffs

De Hoop
homestead

Cape foxes in
milkwood bush

fish eagles
roost in
gum trees

tortoises
common

De Hoopvlei

To N2, Bredasdorp

To Koppie Alleen

lookout
tower

Die Mond

(75)

waterfowl and waders
in abundance

N

0   1   2 km

---

fowl. The only indigenous fish in the vlei is the Cape kurper (bream) while introduced tilapia from Malawi have also established themselves.

In the bush along the vlei edge, the observant hiker will be rewarded with sightings of tchagras, woodpeckers (olive, cardinal and Knysna), fork-tailed drongos, Cape and sombre bulbuls, rameron pigeons and fiery-necked nightjars whose call of 'whip-poor-will' is the sombre refrain of bright moonlit nights. Along the hike, you might also see some of the reserve's large animals that

congregate near the vlei in dry times, while mongooses and elusive otters are known more by their spoor in the mud than by sightings.

De Hoop Coast   *Hike O3*

Route: *From the Koppie Alleen car park, along the coast*
Distance: *Unlimited*
Duration: *Depends on distance walked*
Grade: *Easy*

Booking Authority: *De Hoop, CPA (permit needed to enter reserve)*
General Information: *From the starting point you can walk in either direction: westward past the dune fields towards Arniston, or east along the rocky shore towards Kaap Infante. The latter walk would be about 30 kilometres long, falling almost entirely within the reserve boundary. The western walk would be about 35 kilometres long if done in full. These would both be long day outings, where you could plan to be collected at the end points. I will describe shorter walks, better suited to day visitors to the reserve. (At the time of writing there was no overnight accommodation in the park, but a rest camp is planned. Also, the originally conceived hiking trail at De Hoop has been shelved in favour of the three shorter walks described in this book.)*

▶ From the car park at Koppie Alleen, boardwalks carry you over the dune section until the path reaches either the limestone cliffs above the sea or the dunefield area (depending on which boardwalk you take). You should take the long boardwalk directly toward the sea, bearing left at the end.
▶ Along the first 200 metres of coastline are some magnificent rock pools, scoured into the sandstone intertidal sea bed below the cliffs. The cliffs and sea bed have been eroded by wave and chemical action into fantastic shapes: sea stacks, arches and caves, gullies and reefs. If you take goggles and a snorkel, you can explore the colourful circus of the intertidal rock pools: hermit crabs vying for bigger and better shells,

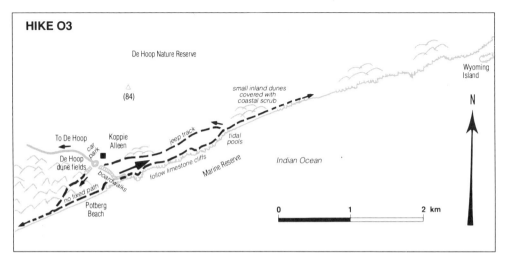

HIKE 03

De Hoop Nature Reserve

Wyoming Island

(84)

small inland dunes covered with coastal scrub

N

To De Hoop

Koppie Alleen

jeep track

tidal pools

car park

De Hoop dune fields

boardwalks

follow limestone cliffs

Marine Reserve

Indian Ocean

no fixed path

Potberg Beach

0   1   2 km

---

anemones with stinging tentacles, spiky urchins sliding across the algae-encrusted rocks, predatory starfish cornering small molluscs, tiny rock fish, red bait and alikreukels, and even the occasional octopus.

At the upper limit of the intertidal area are shellfish living in a stressful habitat that alternates pounding waves with searing winds and burning sun. But the brown mussels, various limpets, barnacles and oysters seem quite content to stay here.

Between June and December, the southern right whales that breed in South African waters do so between Arniston and Infanta – watch the swells just behind the breaker line and you are bound to see them.

Although most of the 4 800 black oystercatchers endemic to this country's coastal strip prefer to breed on the sandy beaches,

the De Hoop population of about 50 birds prefers the rocky coast east of Koppie Alleen. They are shy birds, but, because they confine themselves to the narrow shore margin, their black plumage, bright-red legs, stout bills and startling, high-pitched call make them highly conspicuous and unmistakable. Gulls, cormorants and kingfishers are conspicuous piscivores along this stretch, while sanderlings, and whitefronted and grey plovers are the little birds that race after the retreating surf line, darting after the tiny crustaceans and molluscs that tumble around in the churning water.

▶ It is possible to follow an imprecise path along the cliffs and across the sandy coves and, depending on the tide, on the rocky intertidal ledges. Coming back, it is easier to follow the equally imprecise paths through

the low prickly scrub on the dune sands behind the coastal cliffs. Doves and redwing starlings are common residents in the cliff apartments, and the occasional rock kestrel may be seen here. I also spotted a huge beehive with 10 dripping combs hanging from the roof of an overhang, not 10 metres from the shore.

▶ From the car park, another shorter boardwalk leads one over the dune lip and into a land of shifting sands and curvilinear dune crests. When the southeaster is blowing, these dune fields are not a pleasant place to be caught in – being particularly unhealthy for cameras and binoculars, which should be protected from the flying sand and salt. These dunes are part of a mobile belt of sea sand that circulates around our coast, and from which the country's famous beaches are fed after winter storm waves have eaten their fill. Coastal development, especially that of holiday townships, has stabilized much of these dune fields thus cutting off the natural supply of sand around our coast.

Few plants are able to survive the tenuous conditions here, but where moisture gathers in depressions, various hardy grasses and small shrubs such as the bitou, blombos, cancer bush and waxberry bushes do provide a splash of softening vegetation. In early days, these dune fields (especially those of the Cape Flats) were considered to be a danger to farmers, so they were planted with alien Australian acacia bushes (mainly *Acacia saligna* and *A. cyclops*). These plants proved to be virtually unstoppable invaders once they took root in their new environment, and now the country spends great energy and money trying to contain their spread into our natural vegetation.

The birds of the dune fields have been discussed above, and the animals that you might see here are baboons that pass through in search of anything edible, tortoises, some lizards, mice, moles, and even steenbok or the occasional duiker. The dunes may, at first glance, seem to be sterile, but an ecological eye will discern the delicate dance of nature here, no less fascinating than elsewhere.

▶ It is up to you how far along the coast you wish to go. I would recommend a round trip that circumnavigates the rocky coast and western dunes, turning back to the Koppie Alleen car park after an approximately two-kilometre (45-minute) walk. Because it is a reserve, there is no chance of having to dodge destructive beach buggies, or see fishermen stripping the rocks for bait – a most pleasing experience in a nation of fanatical fishermen, few of whom seem to care much for the conservation of the very resources upon which their sport relies.

Struisbaai
Hike O4

Route: *Struisbaai to Waenhuiskrans*
Distance: *32 kilometres*
Duration: *10 hours*
Grade: *Moderate*
Booking Authority: *CPA, Die Mond (permit needed to enter the reserve)*
General Information: *It is best to book in advance and have your permit waiting for you, if you wish to do this walk, or you might*

not find the conservation officer available. The route is a long one, but you can make it half the length (16,5 kilometres) by starting at Die Mond, where you must collect a permit during normal office hours. If you choose to start at Struisbaai, you must still collect a permit on your way through Die Mond. For most of the way, the walk is an easy one along firm beach sand. However, for about four hours around high tide, you are forced to walk on the softer, often sloping beach above the high-tide mark. This can cause your ankles to take strain and your calf muscles to ache a little, but with the wind in your hair and the world open before you, what should you care. On reaching Arniston, the well-laid-out caravan park and campsite is a reasonable and comfortable place to stay. There is also a luxury hotel here, as well as cottages that can be hired, but since this is a popular holiday resort you must book in advance for these. Take a windcheater with you as protection against the cold winds that blow in this area. This walk is linear, so make sure you have transport to and from either end.

▶ The route from the Struisbaai resort follows a path across a wide arc of open beach. This is a beautiful, unspoiled stretch of coast, where the members of your group are likely to be the only people you will see for the duration of the hike. The solitude and starkness of this hike make it perfect for appreciating the overwhelming sound of the surf and sea birds, the delicate interplay of hues between water, sand and sky, the dynamic artistry of waves, and the static yet transient form of flotsam on the beach.

▶ At about the halfway mark of your hike, you reach the estuary at Die Mond, probably the most interesting place on your hike. From the barely vegetated dunes, you move up the western bank of the Heuningnesrivier estuary – where the shores are laced with milkwood trees (*Sideroxylon inerme*), bietou (*Chrysanthemoides monilifera*) and other bushes – to the nature conservation office, where you collect your permit.

▶ From the office, you can either cross the estuary by way of the wooden foot bridge, or retrace your steps back to the beach and carry on there.

The shoreline from Cape Agulhas to Struispunt near Arniston is dominated by reefs, which are well known to spearfishermen, and much feared by sailors. Some 35 ships have been wrecked along this stretch of coast, of which the *Oriental Pioneer* (1974) at Northumberland Point is the most conspicuous landmark.

▶ As you near Struispunt, just before Arniston, you may see the distinctive black oystercatchers with their scarlet beaks and legs. Like the Damara terns, they are rare endemic birds which breed here, and are highly susceptible to any disturbances. Kelp gull are the most conspicuous of the shore birds, but you are likely also to spot the smaller greyheaded and Hartlaub's gulls (the latter species at the southeastern extreme of its range), possibly an odd representative of the three skua species that visit shores and inland waters, and, if you are very lucky and observant, a blackbrowed or yellownosed albatross gliding offshore or bobbing on the water.

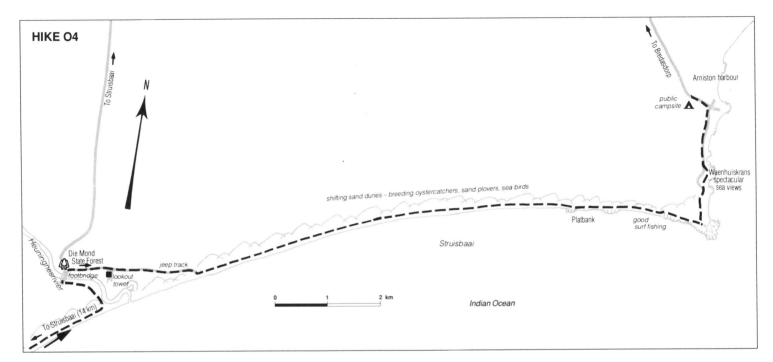

When southern right whales are wallowing in the shallows of Struisbaai or Arniston, you might see grey petrels and shearwaters, or the swallow-like, zigzagging flight of storm petrels. On first sight, many people mistake the large forms of Cape gannets for albatrosses, an acceptable mistake on first appearances. The difference will become obvious when the gannets tuck in their wings and drop like arrows into the water to catch the pilchards, mackerel or anchovies which make up the main part of their diet.

▶ Your arrival at Arniston will be heralded by the appearance of coastal limestone cliffs, creating ledges and rock pools that should be observed when the tide is out. The most famous feature of the intertidal zone here is the Waenhuiskrans. This enormous sea-cave is a protected place, where, according to legend, a group of trekboers hid from British soldiers (for their sake I hope the tide didn't come in while they were in hiding). The cave's name means 'wagon house', not, as many people believe, because it was once used to house wagons, but because it is big enough to do so.

▶ As you approach the resort, make sure to dodge the dune buggies that use the beach as a racetrack. Since it is difficult to follow the rocky shoreline all the way to the Arniston resort and caravan park, rather walk the final one- or two-kilometre section along the gravel track. The track goes from the Struisbaai beach to the village and can be picked up anywhere from the first headland at Waenhuiskrans.

Quoin Point

Hike O5

Route: *Buffeljags to Die Dam caravan park and camp site;*
Distance: *10 kilometres*
Duration: *3 hours*
Grade: *Fair*
Booking Authority: *None*
General Information: *This is a diverse hike with sandy beaches, coastal cliffs, vegetated dunes, small settlements, a lighthouse and numerous shipwrecks. It is essentially an easy walk, but the sand along the first and main bays is soft, while, at the adjoining cliffs, the high-water mark is along the base of the cliffs (which you can go behind). The glare from the sea and white beach sand becomes intense with bright sunlight, so sunglasses are recommended, as is a windcheater for the cool southeasterly wind that prevails. This walk has excellent swimming and fishing opportunities, while the many rock pools afford the chance of observing the fascinating intertidal life. Unless you want to turn around and walk back the long way you have come once you have reached the end, remember to arrange for transport to and from the walk.*

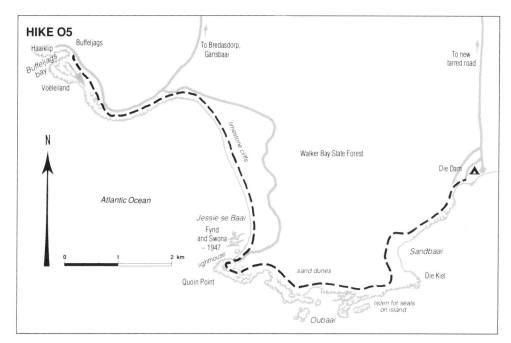

▶ Start at the Buffeljags settlement – part holiday resort, part permanent fishing village – situated on a beautiful piece of coastline where rocky shore is interspersed with small, sandy bays. From here, follow the jeep track that runs parallel to the shore (alternatively, you can indulge in some boulder-hopping along the beach). The track is at first grassy, and then sandy, ending at a lovely stretch of beach called Jessie se Baai.

This bay was named after a ship that was wrecked on the rocks here in a westerly gale, mist and huge swells on the night of 7 October 1829. Many lives were lost, as well as the cargo of wine, corn, spirits and horses.

Along much of the bay, the shore is traced by a line of calcrete cliffs, where limestone from shell deposits has been leached and formed into a concrete-hard formation. This is part of the larger Bredasdorp/Agulhas limestone deposit that characterizes the extreme Cape south coast and inland areas. The physical and chemical wave erosion shapes the soluble calcrete into fantastical shapes that delight the eye and can be used to great effect in photography.

▶ In the distance you will be able to see the lighthouse at Quoin Point, and, in front of that, a deserted fishermen's village. As you approach the ghost village, the wrecks of two ships are clearly outlined in the sea when the water is clear.

These are the wrecks of the *Fynd* and the SS *Swona*. The latter was wrecked in

December 1946 when she lost her propeller and a gale forced her aground. The SS *Swona* was a salvage vessel that, at the time, was ferrying cargo from the *City of Lincoln* that had itself run aground near here a month earlier. The owner of the ship, a Capt. van Delden, was killed when a hatch cover on the *City of Lincoln* blew. The *Fynd*, also owned by Van Delden, was wrecked while trying to pull the SS *Swona* off the rocks. The *City of Lincoln* was later refloated.

▶ Ignore the fence that runs across your path and continue along the shore to a delightful little bay, from where you can follow a track through the settlement (or boulderhop along the shore, from one small bay to the next).

▶ You can follow the jeep track as it winds its way just above the shore, passing the lighthouse at Quoin Point, until it ends once again at a sandy beach. A note on lighthouses here, which landlubbers probably won't know, is that each one has its own signal code which is plotted on a chart. In this way a navigator only has to check on the sequence and duration of light flashes to know his or her position.

▶ As you approach the rocky shore at Die Kiel – directly east of Quoin Point and part of the same peninsula – you may be perplexed by distant grunting sounds. The sound comes from a seal colony on a rocky island about 500 metres offshore. The offshore reefs around Quoin Point and Die Kiel are a major shipping hazard; to date 25 ships are known to have been wrecked in this area.

▶ Continue past Die Kiel, through the windsheared scrub, and then along a narrow beach of extremely soft sand, often covered with bluebottles and plastic bottles, until you come to the campsite at Die Dam, from where most of the litter comes. What a pity that an area so rich in marine life as this should be fouled by fishermen and holidaymakers. (Perhaps the landowners here should be given a gentle reminder to clean up their operation, for not only is it disgusting, but it also poses a danger to the plentiful marine life in the area).

▶ Carry on past the campsites to a gravel road, where your transport should be waiting for you.

Walker Bay   Route O6

Route: *Hermanus to Die Kelders*
Distance: *21 kilometres*
Duration: *6-7 hours*
Grade: *Moderate*
Booking Authority: *CPA, Hermanus*
General Information: *Our hike takes us around Walker Bay, the entire stretch of which is a nature reserve. Although no permit is needed to do this hike, it would be courteous to report at the conservation offices on the main road, on the eastern outskirts of town (opposite the caravan park on Kleinriviersvlei). As there is no fresh water anywhere on this walk, you should fill up water bottles in Hermanus before setting off. You will need transport to get you to the start and from the end of the walk.*

▶ The walk begins in the town of Hermanus, at the historic old harbour. From here a path follows the top of the cliffs along the rocky coastline of Voëlklip, allowing expansive views of the bay. You can follow this if you wish, but the more interesting route is across the rocks just above the surf line (if the tide allows). For some way you have to pass between the edge of the town and the sea, but after a few kilometres you reach the beginning of the endless beach. The rest of the walk is along the beach.

From the end of May to January you should keep a lookout for whales, which use the bay as one of their favourite nursery areas in South African waters. The species you will see here are southern right whales – they were said by whalers to be the 'right' whales to hunt because of the high oil and bone yield, and because they did not sink when harpooned. Since the mid-19th century, however, whale populations have been mercilessly cut and today there are only about 5 000 of this species left, 750 of which breed off our coast.

The whales can usually be seen with their calves about 500 metres offshore, blowing a V-shaped spray into the air. Southern right whales have been protected since 1935, and only now do their numbers seem to be increasing. The whales, which reach a length of 28 metres and weigh up to 55 tons, feed on krill (small shrimp-like crustaceans) in sub-Antarctic waters from late summer to autumn, before moving north to breed.

Walker Bay is also an important fishing area, however, and there is much concern among whale lovers that trawlers and pleasure boats disturb the whales when breeding and nursing. Also, the controversial use

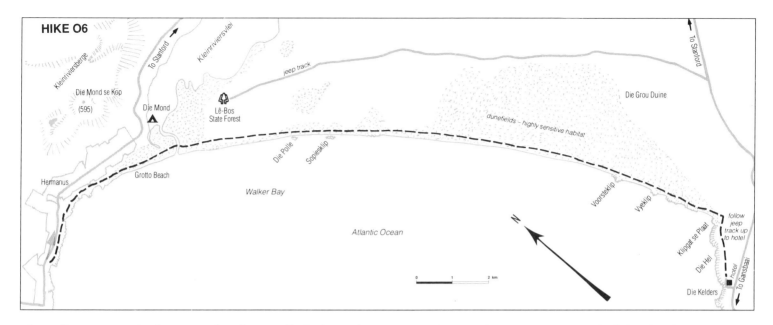

of trawling nets in the bay is said to be harmful to pelagic fish population dynamics, as well as to porpoises, seals and other marine animals that get caught in these nets and drowned.

‣ At the five-kilometre mark, you pass the mouth of Kleinriviersvlei, a popular boating and fishing spot which is usually cut off from the sea. A further five kilometres on you will come to a rock outcrop that has been hollowed out by wind and wave erosion, and turned into a shelter – should you need one. The beach will most likely be heavily invaded by kelp gulls and other sea birds, but they will retreat as you approach. The kelp

gulls feed mainly on organic detritus that has been washed up, as well as on shellfish, insects and other birds' eggs.

A healthy sandy beach has been likened to a vast respiratory and digestive system that circulates water and air through its wedge-shaped filter, processes organic matter on it and returns it to the sea in basic form as food for other creatures. Most of the animal life of a sandy beach ecosystem is less than one millimetre long, living between the sand grains. As the water level, food supply, oxygen and other levels fluctuate, these animals (called meiofuana) can migrate within the beach sand to locate an optimal

environment. And this they have to do with each tide, covering vast distances for such small creatures.

The biomass – the total mass of all the living matter – of a beach like this one is greater than that of a similar-sized area of any natural terrestrial system, and that includes the savanna with its herds of elephants, antelope, insects, birds and so on. The bacteria, tiny insects and other small creatures on a healthy beach can, helped by the birds, recycle just about any amount and manner of organic detritus that lands there – including heavy oil slicks. One of the most harmful things that can befall a beach is for

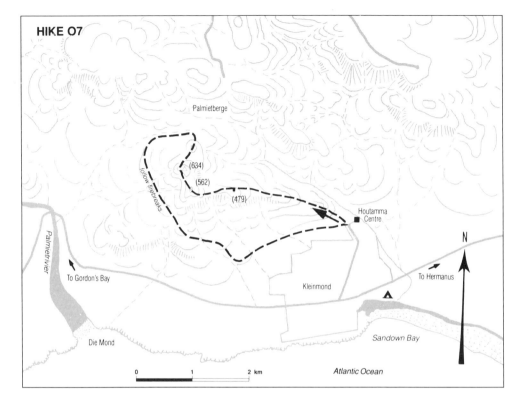

calcrete cliffs that characterize the southern Cape coastline. At the edge of the small town, you come to some wooden bungalows administered by the conservation officer at Hermanus. Carry on along the beach, or follow the gravel road behind these bungalows, to the hotel that stands above the celebrated caves here. You will have to pay to visit the caves (which, in any case can only be visited at specified times), but the pleasant bay just to the left of them is a good place to cool off at the end of the walk.

Kleinmond Triplets *Hike 07*

Route: *Up Triplets ridge and down Palmiet-rivier valley*
Distance: *8 kilometres*
Duration: *3-4 hours*
Grade: *Moderate*
Booking Authority: *Kleinmond Municipality (Tel. (02823) 3030/90) (permit needed)*
General Information: *To do this walk you must obtain your permit from the Kleinmond Municipality, which, on weekends, can be done by calling at the police station. The walk is just one of many that can be undertaken in the Kleinmond Coastal and Mountain Nature Reserve, where a 14-kilometre network of paths has been laid out. The walk is very steep in parts, something obvious at first sight to anyone who looks up the gnarled ridges behind the village. However, the splendid condition of the fynbos here, and the superb views gained from the summit of the ridge make for a lasting impression. The fynbos is extremely lush and dense, owing to*

vehicles to ride on it, for they compact the sand and effectively suffocate the meiofuana – not to mention killing smaller animals and chasing off breeding birds such as the rare black oystercatchers (see route description Hike O3).

Unfortunately the beach and dunes behind Walker Bay are a favourite playground of off-road hogs who spoil the environment here. Conservation officers attempting to apprehend these vandals have frequently been abused by them: in one case, the officer was badly beaten up by a bunch of buggy riders who felt they had a right to destroy nature as they pleased and have 'fun'.

❱ On approaching Die Kelders, the dune area at Die Plaat increases in size. At Klipgat se Plaat you make first contact with the

the inception of sea mists and the formation of clouds from moisture-laden winds coming off the sea. Collectively, the mountains here are known as the Palmietberge, after the Palmietrivier below, which, in turn, is named after the restiod 'palmiet' reed that grows along this and other rivers in the southwestern Cape.

▶ The very steep path ascends the western spur from near the Houtamma Education Centre. Where the spur meets the main mountain spine, it curves around to the left to gain the summit point – a beacon marks 634 metres – after a climb of about 580 metres. Once your breathing has been normalized, the magnificent views will once again take your breath away. To the west, you look out across the Palmietrivier valley to the Hottentots-Holland mountains, dominated by the Kogelberg slightly to the north. Sweeping around to your left, you can make out the Palmietrivier mouth and Kleinmond settlement below; turning to the east you can see across the Botrivier estuary to the Onrusberge and Danger Point jutting out to sea in the far distance.

▶ From the beacon, the path descends northwards, before swinging sharply left down towards the main river valley. The path makes its way down through the protea-rich veld, crossing numerous small tributaries of the Palmietrivier, to an old firebreak, before circling to the left around the mountain, back to the town. A common protea found here is *Protea lacticolor*, which gets its species name from its predominantly milk-white flower, although the flowers may

sometimes be pink. On the way, the path passes two quarries cut carelessly into the mountain's lower slopes.

From the beacon on top of the western and highest triplet, it is possible to continue in a northerly direction, beyond where our path heads down sharply to the left, to join up with the Perdeberg Walk that lies within the Highlands State Forest reserve. You will then circle the Perdeberg whose highest point (575 m) lies three and a half kilometres to the northeast of the Triplets' summit beacon. From there, the path descends along a pleasant stroll towards the forest station.

Harold Porter National Botanic Gardens   *Hike O8*

Route: *Various walks from entrance*
Distance: *Up to 3 kilometres*
Duration: *Up to 1½ hours*
Grade: *Easy to fair*
Booking Authority: *National Botanic Gardens (permit needed for Tierkloof)*
General Information: *There is a striking similarity between Kirstenbosch and this, its little sister among botanical gardens: the lower areas are formally cultivated gardens complete with nursery and herbarium (closed to the public), which blend in with the natural vegetation as one moves up the mountain slopes. Although no permit is needed to enter the gardens, you must get one from the curator for Leopard's Kloof. The Harold Porter Gardens is a truly delightful place to spend a few hours, to stroll in and*

discover the delights of the fynbos and mysteries of the mountain kloofs – it was not without good reason that this site was chosen as a botanical garden.

Near the entrance there are numerous short paths through the formal gardens, where mimetes, proteas, pincushions and other plants burst out in floral celebration. With permit clutched in sweaty hand, you can venture up the rough path into the bowels of Leopard's Kloof, where the booming sound of the far-off waterfall envelopes you. At the base of the impressive falls you will find a large pool so typical of the treasures that one discovers in the large gorges of the folded mountains. In mid- to late summer, you will see flowering red disas here.

Should you be driven to discover what lies above the waterfall, take the Rod Smitheman self-guided trail up the steep slopes of Platberg, where fynbos blooms in splendid profusion, and orangebreasted sunbirds and sugarbirds flit between protea bowls and pincushion heads. In spring, one of the most conspicuous plants here is the wild geranium (*Pelargonium cucullatum*).

The signposted path leads off to the left (looking landward) of the planted gardens, and zigzags up the mountain slope to the left (west) of Tierkloof. After a 200-metre climb, the path levels off, before heading up a lesser gradient to meet the river a way above the waterfall. To get to the top of the falls is a steep and potentially dangerous manoeuvre from the path, but the views over Betty's Bay and the sea are elevating.

Return the way you came.

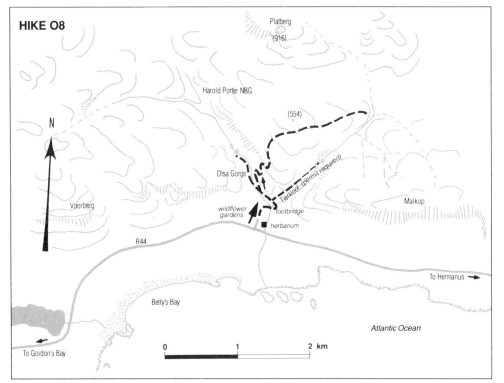

Platberg
(916)

Harold Porter NBG

(554)

N

Disa Gorge

Tierkloof (permit required)

Voorberg

wildflower gardens

footbridge

herbarium

Malkop

R44

To Hermanus →

Betty's Bay

Atlantic Ocean

To Gordon's Bay

0   1   2 km

Fernkloof

Hike O9

Route: *Walks from visitors' centre*
Distance: *Various*
Duration: *Various*
Grade: *Easy to moderate*
Booking Authority: *Hermanus Munici-pality (Tel. (0283) 21122) (permit needed)*

General Information: *There is a 40-kilometre network of paths in the Fernkloof Nature Reserve, which lies in the lower western extreme of the Kleinriviersberge. Your choice of walk ranges from an easy four-and-a-half-kilometre self-guided nature trail to steeper routes within the 1 500-hectare reserve. Limited overnight accommoda-tion is available at Galpin's hut, for which*

you must book in advance. It sleeps two people comfortably – four, on cold winter nights – but no fires are allowed, so you must carry your own stoves. The hut is about six kilometres (two to three hours walk) from the car park past Galpin se Kop.

The Fernkloof Nature Reserve spans a wide gorge-like valley in the Kleinriviers-berge, with Die Mond se Kop and Olifants-berg standing as sentinels to the gorge. The Aasvoëlkop summit forms the northeastern corner of the reserve, to the east of which – abutting the Fernkloof reserve – lies the private Vogelgat Reserve.

The vegetation is typical of this coastal range's rich and dense fynbos, with 98 re-corded species of bird, baboons, klipsprin-gers and other small animals that are seldom seen.

As you walk up the main valley, the most conspicuous plants are the rounded leucos-permum bushes which erupt in yellow-white pincushion heads in early summer. There are also *Protea cynaroides* (king protea) spe-cimens, larger leucadendrons, and the tall sparse stems of *Gnidia oppositifolia* shrubs, which grow up to three metres tall.

A contour path runs along the left slope above the valley floor, winding in and out of the spurs below the narrow tiers of rock.

The visitors' centre is very well set out, with botanical displays and an interpretive centre where slide shows and lectures are held. Literature on the reserve is available here. The herbarium is open to the public on Monday mornings and Friday afternoons; some 2 500 species are represented here.

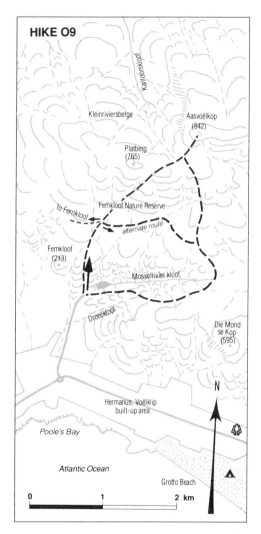

Kanloorskloof

Kleinriviersberge

Aasvoëlkop
(842)

Platberg
(765)

To Fernkloof

Fernkloof Nature Reserve

alternate route

Fernkloof
(213)

Mosselrivier kloof

Droëkloof

Die Mond
se Kop
(595)

N

Hermanus, Voëlklip
built-up area

Poole's Bay

Atlantic Ocean

Grotto Beach

0   1   2 km

Caledon Wildflower Garden
Hike O10

Route: *Circular walk from tearoom to Swartberg ridge*
Distance: *10 kilometres*
Duration: *4 hours*
Grade: *Moderate*
Booking Authority: *Caledon Municipality (Tel. (0281) 21090) (permit needed)*
General Information: *This 214-hectare wildflower and fynbos reserve is famous for its 50-hectare wildflower garden, which has attracted visitors in spring since its opening in 1927. A 10-kilometre circular walk leads up the southern slopes of the Swartberg to the far northeastern corner of this narrow reserve – although the summit (1 089 m) lies well outside the reserve boundary. The tearoom is open only during the spring wildflower season, but the toilets and braai facilities are available all year. There is very little natural water on the trail, so be sure to fill up before you leave the visitors' area.*

The reserve is open only during daylight hours, though camping facilities are available at the nearby Caledon mineral spa. It is found to the north of the national road, behind the provincial hospital; turn left where the road to Caledon branches off the N2 to the right. From the highest point reached on the Swartberg crest ridge (834 m), you gain views over the rolling wheat lands of Caledon and the folded Swartberg range.

Bredasdorp Mountain Reserve
Hike O11

Route: *Unspecified*
Distance: *Varied*
Duration: *Varied*
Grade: *Easy*
Booking Authority: *Bredasdorp Municipality (Tel. (02841) 41135) (permit needed)*
General Information: *As in the case of the Caledon Wildflower and Nature Reserve, this 800-hectare reserve encloses a smaller (86-hectare) formal wildflower reserve within its borders. Although the hill around which the reserve lies can hardly be called a mountain, its mainly shale base is a remnant of those loftier folded mountains to the north. About 20 kilometres of nature trails have been laid out within the reserve, complete with occasional resting shelters.*

The vegetation in the reserve is a patchwork of fynbos and renosterveld, two main components of the Cape flora.

Renosterveld is named after the predominant renosterbos (*Elytropappus rhinocerotis*), but this plant's overwhelming dominance suggests that the renosterveld is a degraded habitat.

Today, the fertile soils on which renosterveld grows have been all but completely taken over for cultivation. There are consequently many rare and endangered plants protected in this ecological island, one of which is the Bredasdorp lily (*Cyrtanthus guthrieae*), otherwise called the *brand lelie*.

APPENDIX 1

USEFUL CONTACT TELEPHONE NUMBERS

Algeria Forest Station – Tel. (02682) ask for 3440.

Bredasdorp Municipality – Tel. (02841) 41135.

Caledon Municipality – Tel. (0281) 21090.

Cape of Good Hope Nature Reserve – Tel. (021) 80 1100.

Ceres Municipality – Tel. (0233) 21177.

CPA, Nature Conservation Office – Tel. (021) 461 7010.

De Mond Nature Reserve – Tel. (02841) 42170.

Franschhoek Municipality – Tel. (02212) 2055.

Greyton Central Hotel – Tel. (02822) 9892.

Greyton Lodge – Tel. (02822) 9876.

Greyton Post House – Tel. (02822) 9995.

Grootwinterhoek Forest Station – Tel. (02623) 2900.

Hawequas Forest Station – Tel. (02211) 62 3172.

Helderberg Nature Reserve – Tel. (024) 51 7256.

Hermanus CPA Nature Conservation – Tel. (0283) 77 0062.

Hermanus Municipality – Tel. (0283) 21122.

Highlands Forest Station – Tel. (02824) 655.

Jan Du Toit's Kloof (Mr van Zyl of 'Somaso') – Tel. (0231) 93746.

Jonkershoek Forest Station – Tel. (02231) 5715.

Kleinmond Municipality – Tel. (02823) 3030/3090.

Kluitjieskraal Forest Station – Tel. (0236) 30 0759.

La Motte State Forest – Tel. (02212) 3079/2061.

Lebanon State Forest – Tel. (0240) 2638.

MCSA – Tel. (021) 45 3412.

Montagu Municipality and Publicity Association – Tel. (0234) 41112/42678.

NHWB Office, Cape Town – Tel. (021) 402 3093.

Nuweberg Forest Station – Tel. (0225) 4301/4785.

Robertson Municipality – Tel. (02351) 3112.

Sonderend Forest Station – Tel. (02351) 3079.

Swellendam Forest Station – Tel. (0291) 41410.

Tweede Tol Campsite – Tel. (02324) 607.

Villiersdorp Municipality – Tel. (0225) 31130.

APPENDIX 2

FURTHER READING

Bristow, D., 1988 *Drakensberg Walks* C. Struik, Cape Town.

Bristow, D. & Ward, C., 1985 *Mountains of Southern Africa* C. Struik, Cape Town.

Burman, J., 1964 *A Peak to Climb* C. Struik, Cape Town.

Burman, L., Burman, J., & Bean A., 1985 *Hottentots-Holland to Hermanus: SA wildflower guide no. 5*. Botanical Society, Cape Town.

Clarke, J., & Coulson, P., 1984 *Mountain Odyssey* Macmillan, Johannesburg.

Levy, J., 1987 *The Complete Guide to Walks and Trails in Southern Africa* C. Struik, Cape Town.

Maclean, G.L., 1985 *Roberts' Birds of Southern Africa* The Trustees of the John Voelcker Bird Book Fund, Cape Town.

MCSA journals, 1897-1989.

Palgrave, K.C., 1988 *Trees of Southern Africa* Struik, Cape Town.

Vogts, M. and Paterson-Jones, C., 1982 *South Africa's Proteaceae, Know them and*

INDEX

Individual birds, mammals, reptiles and plants are not included in the index. Page numbers in *italics* indicate that the subject is illustrated. Entries and page numbers in **bold** refer to individual hikes.